# THE UNCHANGING

# WORD OF GOD

A Signature Collection of
Writings by Dr. David Jeremiah

# Dr. David Jeremiah

Editorial Director: Myrna Davis
Editorial and Design Services: Mark Gilroy Creative, LLC with ThinkPen Design.

# CONTENTS

*To Donna*

*My wife, my best friend,*
*my number one cheerleader.*
*There is a part of our story*
*in each one of these chapters.*

# INTRODUCTION

Maybe you're old enough to remember 1982—or maybe not. It's a year I'll never forget. The headlines were dramatic. That's the year a jetliner crashed into a bridge in Washington, D.C. and plunged into the frozen waters of the Potomac. War broke out in 1982 between Great Britain and Argentina over the Falkland Islands. In America, the Equal Rights Amendment failed. In England, an intruder at Buckingham Palace surprised Queen Elizabeth II in her bedroom.

In Florida, EPCOT opened. On Wall Street, the Dow closed at a record 1,051. In 1982, Johnny Carson hosted the Academy Awards, with the Best Picture going to *Chariots of Fire,* the story of Scottish Olympian Eric Liddell, a Christian athlete and a missionary of incredible courage.

Michael Jackson released his megahit, "Thriller" in 1982, and Cal Ripken, Jr. played the first of 2,632 consecutive Major League Baseball games.

*Time* Magazine surprised everyone in 1982 by naming a non-human as its Man of the Year. It was the *computer.* The digital age had dawned.

Yes, I remember it well. But I remember something else too. That's the year Donna and I, after much prayer and consideration, launched Turning Point. The previous year, I'd become the senior pastor of Shadow Mountain Community Church in El Cajon, California, a ministry for which I was and am infinitely grateful. But we longed to reach people for Christ beyond the borders of our city or the boundaries of our state and nation. After earnestly seeking the Lord's guidance and blessings and with the counsel and support of our friends and our church, we felt the Lord leading us to begin Turning Point in June of 1982, exactly thirty years ago.

In the decades since, God has given us a great team and an army of supporters who have labored tirelessly to find every possible means to reach every possible person with the unapologetic and undiluted teaching of God's Word through sermons and lessons, rallies and speaking engagements, radio and television, and through books, magazines, and online resources.

At the heart of it all are the simple sermons I've tried to preach at Shadow Mountain. It's not the sermons themselves, mind you. It's the power of God's revealed Word. But from those sermons have come the books and broadcasts that have comprised much of Turning Point's ministry.

The book you're holding in your hand represents the distillation of three decades of preaching and writing. In this volume, we've skimmed the cream off the top. I've gone through years of sermons and books to personally select those chapters that have touched my own heart and, I believe, will touch yours too.

Here you'll find a word of encouragement, a remedy for loneliness, a primer on prayer, and a heads-up about soon-coming events. You'll find a chapter about the ministry of angels, and another about the obligation of obedience. I'll show you how to develop gratitude in a thankless world and confidence on a chaotic planet. The topics vary from chapter to chapter, but there's a common denominator—they are all based on the unfailing and unchanging Word of God.

We have never deviated from a high view of Scripture. Every word I've spoken throughout my ministry is based on an unshakable trust in the inspired and infallible Word of God. Psalm 89:34 says, "My covenant I will not break, nor alter the word that has gone out of My lips." Jesus proclaimed, "Heaven and earth will pass away, but My words will by no means pass away" (Matthew 24:35).

Theologians call this "immutability." When we say God is immutable, it means He is not subject to mutation or change. He can never grow or improve. He can never be more or less than He has always been. The universe had a beginning and will one day collapse. The stars will fade. The world will melt. "They will perish, but You will endure; yes, they will all grow old like a garment; like a cloak You will change them, and they will be changed. But You are the same, and Your years will have no end" (Psalm 102:26-27).

In commenting on this passage, the old Puritan, Stephen Charnock, wrote that even if the foundations of the world were ripped up and the heavens clatter and collapse, we can maintain stability in our lives because our durability doesn't depend on the changeableness of the times but on the unchangeable rock of the truth of God.

If God could change, He wouldn't be perfect, for change implies development or decline, one or the other. God does neither. His power is unyielding. His promises are unfailing. His love is undying. His life is unending. His wisdom is unsearchable. His Word is unbreakable. He is the Father of lights, with whom there is no variation or shadow of turning (James 1:17). The Word incarnate is the same yesterday, today, and forever (Hebrews 13:8). And the Word inscribed is forever settled in heaven (Psalm 119:89).

For the life of me, I cannot understand those who doubt the inspiration of Scripture or question its authority. If there is a God—as there surely is—He must, by the very definition of His reality, know how to communicate. Logically, we would expect Him to communicate in a way that matches His perfections, and in a form that could be read and reread, studied and translated, spread abroad and passed down from generation to generation. If God is unchanging, we would expect a Bible unfailing. This is the Book on which I rest my life and base my work. From its riches have flowed decades of sermons; from the sermons, the books; and from the books we've excerpted the following chapters, all based on *The Unchanging Word of God.*

My deepest affection and appreciation go to my wife and colaborer Donna, and to our precious family, our dear church at Shadow Mountain, our gifted and dedicated team at Turning Point, and to the many who have prayed for us, supported our work, and been touched by our ministry for three decades.

"So now, brethren, I commend you to God and to the word of His grace, which is able to build you up and give you an inheritance among all those who are sanctified" (Acts 20:32).

# 1

## THE ENCOURAGEMENT ZONE

From: The Joy of Encouragement—
Unlock the Power of Building Others Up

Their wedding picture mocked them from the table, these two whose minds no longer touched each other. They lived with such a heavy barricade between them that neither battering ram, nor words, nor artilleries of touch could break it down. Somewhere between the oldest child's first tooth and the youngest daughter's graduation they lost each other. Throughout the years, each slowly unraveled that tangled ball of string called self, and as they tugged at stubborn knots, each hid his searching from the other.

Sometimes she cried at night and begged the whispering darkness to tell her who she was. He lay beside her, snoring like a hibernating bear, unaware of her winter.

Once after they had made love, he wanted to tell her how afraid he was of dying, but fearing to show his naked soul, he spoke only of her beauty.

She took a course in modern art, trying to find herself in colors splashed upon a canvas, complaining to other women about men who are insensitive.

He climbed into a tomb called "The Office," wrapped his mind in a shroud of papers, and buried himself in customers.

And slowly the wall between them rose, cemented by the mortar of indifference. One day, reaching out to touch each other, they found a barrier they could not penetrate. Recoiling from the coldness of the stone, each retreated from the stranger on the other side.

For when love dies, it is not in a moment of angry battle, nor when fiery bodies lose their heat. But it lies panting and exhausted, expiring at the bottom of a carefully built wall it cannot scale.[1]

If you have done any counseling at all, you are nodding your head in understanding. You know the story; it is all too familiar. Some marriages that start out strong, end up gasping for air and dying a slow, painful death.

By the time the couple realizes how bad things are, they have already passed the point of no return.

Part of our predicament today is the media-driven expectations most couples have as they enter into marriage. George Bernard Shaw summed up the problem when he wrote:

> When two people are under the influence of the most violent, most insane, most delusive and most transient of passions, they are required to swear that they will remain in that excited, abnormal, and exhausting condition, continuously until death do them part.[2]

One middle-aged woman described it this way:

> We are led to believe that love is passionate eye-locking gazes, throbbing temples, and rippling muscles. My husband and I can only experience eyelocking gazes if we both happen to be wearing our eyeglasses at the same time. To us, throbbing temples warn of possible high blood pressure and our muscles tend to be more jiggling than rippling.

Don't you just love honest people?

Some years ago, *Christianity Today* published an article titled, "The Ideal Relationship and Other Myths about Marriage." The writer, a Reformed Church pastor from New York, wrote:

> I believe marriage is in trouble today because society and the church have a faulty view of it—a deified myth of this human, delightful, yet flawed institution.
>
> Though fertility gods have been dethroned by the advance of Christianity, today's culture seems to be resurrecting them in a more palatable form…. Most voices today laud a romantic image of marriage as life's ultimate source of true joy.

What is the result? A crash. Thousands of crashes…. Why? Because in reality every marriage faces conflict, misunderstanding, smashed fantasies, and bruised egos. Any real marriage held up against the yardstick of total joy will measure short. And if relationships that are meant to give total joy fail, lives are shattered.[3]

"Conflict, misunderstanding, smashed fantasies, and bruised egos"— not too encouraging, is it? And this is not just a report, this is reality. In 1960, 37 percent of all first-time marriages failed; by 1990, chances of a first-time marriage surviving were only 50 percent. The June 1993 issue of *Psychology Today* reported that 75 percent of all couples in America will be affected by infidelity.[4] In marriage the natural tendency is toward deterioration, not improvement. And the only way marriage partners can offset the process of decay is by taking a proactive approach toward improving their relationship. Both husband and wife need to master the art of encouragement.

## WE REALLY DO NEED EACH OTHER

Perhaps we should begin our discussion by affirming that marriage is from God. It was His idea! It still is! Five times in the creation narrative in Genesis 1, we read that God looked at what He had created and "saw that it was good" (2:9, 12, 18, 21, 25). Then when He had finished with the creation of man, God surveyed His entire work: "Then God saw everything that He had made, and indeed it was very good" (Genesis 1:31). Six times God said that His work in creation was good. No wonder we snap to attention when we read this statement in Genesis 2: "And the LORD God said, 'It is not good that man should be alone; I will make him a helper comparable to him'" (Genesis 2:18).

*"The men who are lifting the world upward and onward are those who encourage more than criticize."*

ELISABETH HARRISON

It was God's assessment that man should not be alone, that He needed someone to relate to him. So God created woman. Contrary to what some have jokingly said, woman is not a cognate of the words "woe to man." The word "woman" in the Hebrew language is the word *isha*. The word for man is *ish*. Man is *ish,* woman is *isha*. In Genesis 2, we discover how *isha* came to be:

> And the LORD God caused a deep sleep to fall on Adam, and he slept; and He took one of his ribs, and closed up the flesh in its place. Then the rib which the LORD God had taken from man He made into a woman, and He brought her to the man. And Adam said: "This is now bone of my bones and flesh of my flesh; she shall be called Woman *[isha],* because she was taken out of Man *[ish]*." Therefore a man shall leave his father and mother and be joined to his wife, and they shall become one flesh. And they were both naked, the man and his wife, and were not ashamed (Genesis 2:21–25).

When God saw that it was not good for the man to be alone, He set out to change things. He caused a great sleep to come upon Adam (the first anesthesia). He took a rib from his side (the first surgery), and out of that rib God fashioned a woman. She was taken from Adam's side, not molded from the ground as was her husband. She was taken from a part of Adam so that Adam was naturally incomplete until they were together. *Ish* could not be complete without *Isha*. St. Augustine put it this way:

> If God had meant woman to rule over man, He would have taken her from his head. Had He designed her to be his slave, He would have taken her from his feet. But God took woman out of man's side, for He made her to be a helpmeet and an equal to him.

When God was finished with the creation of Eve, he brought her to Adam and the first wedding took place. When Adam saw Eve, he said,

"This is now bone of my bones and flesh of my flesh" (Genesis 2:23). *The Living Bible*, which I sometimes read for my own personal enjoyment, says that when Adam first saw Eve, he said, "This is it!" There is great excitement in the heart of the first man when he meets the first woman!

Over thirty years ago, in one of the first books on marriage I ever read, I copied this beautiful comment on these words from Genesis 2:

> The man is restless while he is missing the rib that was taken out of his side, and the woman is restless until she gets under man's arm, from whence she was taken. It is humbling for the woman to know she was created for the man, but it is to her glory to know that she alone can complete him. Likewise, it is humbling to the man to know that he is incomplete without the woman, but it is to his glory to know that the woman was created for him.[5]

The Old Testament carefully describes how man and woman came into being. Marriage originated with God. When God's blueprint for marriage is followed, it is one of the most wonderful, encouraging experiences one can know while on this earth. We can begin now to create a zone of encouragement at home. Genesis 2 includes some enduring principles which even today can mature, strengthen, and breathe new life into marriages.

## A COMMITMENT TO RESPONSIBILITY

For marriages to survive in this decade of divorce, there must be a commitment to responsibility. Unless matrimony is built upon a foundation of mutual dedication, no amount of encouragement will stave off the forces pulling against it. Dr. Robert B. Taylor, author of the book, *Couples: The Art of Staying Together*, wrote, "We're now living in the age of disposability: Use it once, and throw it away. Over the past decade, there has developed a feeling that relationships are equally disposable."[6]

But the Bible knows nothing of throw-away marriages. In the poetic language of the Old Testament, marital responsibility is described in these words: "Therefore, a man shall leave his father and his mother and be joined to his wife, and they shall become one flesh" (Genesis 2:24). There is far more to this statement than first meets the eye:

> "Leave" *(asav,* Hebrew) and "join" *(davaq,* Hebrew) are terms associated with covenant treaties. Here, marriage is interpreted as a new relationship bound by mutual oath. Sexual intimacy is an expression of the union of the two people; however, sexual union by itself is not sufficient to define the biblical concept of marriage.[7]

We have a phrase we use to describe marriage. We call it "tying the knot." I once read a comment from a mountain climber who said that the reason mountain climbers are tied together is to keep the sane ones from going home. Now, there's a thought! One of the reasons God ties the knot in marriage is to keep us from running away when the going gets tough.

Where there is this kind of commitment, the Christian family can truly be an encouragement zone. Ken Canfield thinks this enduring bond between husband and wife affects more than just the two of them:

> The challenge for this generation is to make marriage a prerequisite to fathering. Every day hundreds of children are born without two parents who are committed to building a solid family together. Research confirms that these children are more likely to commit delinquent acts, drop out of school, have children out of wedlock, suffer poverty, receive welfare, and abuse drugs and alcohol. The future is much brighter for children who have two parents in a committed relationship. But the operative word is committed.[8]

For many years Robertson McQuilken was the president of Columbia Bible College. Some years ago he had to resign his position because his wife, Muriel, was suffering the advanced stages of Alzheimer's disease.

In March 1990, Robertson announced his resignation in a letter, with these words:

> My dear wife, Muriel, has been in failing mental health for about eight years. So far, I have been able to carry her ever-growing needs and my leadership responsibilities at CBC. But recently it has become apparent that Muriel is contented most of the time she is with me and almost none of the time I am away from her. It is not just "discontent." She is filled with fear—even terror—that she has lost me and always goes in search of me when I leave home. Then she may be full of anger when she cannot get to me. So it is clear to me that she needs me now full time.
>
> Perhaps it would help you to understand if I shared with you what I shared at the time of the announcement of my resignation in chapel. The decision was made, in a way, 42 years ago when I promised to care for Muriel "in sickness and in health…till death do us part." So, as I told the students and faculty, as a man of my word, integrity has something to do with it. But so does fairness. She has cared for me fully and sacrificially all these years; if I cared for her for the next 40 years I would not be out of debt. Duty, however, can be grim and stoic. But there is more; I love Muriel. She is a delight to me—her childlike dependence and confidence in me, her warm love, occasional flashes of that wit that I used to relish so, her happy spirit and tough resilience in the face of her continually distressing frustration. I do not have to care for her, I get to. It is a high honor to care for so wonderful a person.[9]

When I first read these words I was reminded of the personal example of commitment I have observed in my own family. A few years ago, my mother also died from Alzheimer's disease. I watched my father, who had made a commitment some fifty years earlier, keep his promise to Mom as he stopped everything in his life to minister to her until she was no longer able to live at home.

And then every week he visited her several times, and every time I came to visit, we would go pick up Mom and take her out to dinner. Even when she could not communicate and did not seem to know any of us, Dad went right on loving her and acting as if nothing had changed in their relationship. "Till death do us part" will never be the same to me again!

## A Commitment to Intimacy

A French historian once described marriage as three weeks of curiosity, three months of love, and thirty years of tolerance. Someone else described marriage as a proposition ending in a sentence. One comic said the honeymoon was the interval between the man's "I do" and the wife's "You'd better!" Still another said, "After man came woman, and she's been coming after him ever since."

I remember hearing the story of a man who was asked about the success of his long-term marriage. He responded, "The secret to our marriage is this: We never have any extended arguments. Whenever my wife gets upset, she takes out her frustrations by rearranging the furniture in the house. Whenever I get upset, I go outside and take a long walk. The secret to our marriage is this: I have substantially led an outdoor life."

I don't endorse these portraits of marriage, but I am sure we would not laugh at these quips if there were not at least a hint of truth in them. Sometimes we create humor to lessen the tensions we cannot control. Have you ever noticed that most of the birthday cards for people over fifty are humorous? It's as if laughing at ourselves makes aging less painful. We do the same thing with our marriages!

*"He who knows he is loved can be content with a piece of bread, while all the luxuries of the world cannot satisfy the cravings of the lonely."*

FRANCES J. ROBERTS

But let's be honest; when your marriage is falling apart, it's not a laughing matter. When you look up one day and realize you are living with someone you hardly know, it's not funny. For a marriage to be an encouragement zone, there has to be a closeness, an intimacy.

The words of Genesis 2:24 certainly speak of intimacy: "Therefore a man shall leave his father and mother and be joined to his wife, and they shall become one flesh."

When the New Testament quotes this passage, the word it uses for "joined" can also be translated, "glue." When I first saw this translation, I couldn't help but think, *That's what's missing in so many marriages today—the glue.* Nothing is holding some couples together. They do not have the resources necessary for holding the relationship together for the long run.

And here's another problem. When we use the word "intimacy" today, we almost always think of the physical side of marriage. While that is certainly a part of the program, it is by no means all that the Bible has in mind when it speaks of a couple being "glued together."

Commonly, when speaking of marriage, the term "intimacy" is used in reference to sexual intimacy exclusively. Our day has strangely majored on a minor in the matter of sexual intimacy. This is only one of the many areas of married life where intimacy can be experienced, so that consistently to restrict the meaning of the word to sexual intimacy is to expose a deficiency in the popular concept of what marriage really is. All too often the romantic illusion that intimacy is created and sustained by the sexual union obscures the higher possibility of achieving intimacy throughout the whole range of the personal relationship in marriage.[10]

Intimacy is not just body-to-body, but soul-to-soul and spirit-to-spirit.

The lack of intimacy can be traced, for many couples, back to the dating relationship where the process of bonding was totally reversed. I am convinced that God intends for couples to grow toward intimacy in a set progression. First, there needs to be spirit-to-spirit union. In one of his letters to the Corinthian Church, Paul confronted this responsibility at the most basic level:

Do not be unequally yoked together with unbelievers. For what fellowship has righteousness with lawlessness? And what communion has light with darkness?" (2 Corinthians 6:14).

After pastoring a church for more than twenty-five years, I can give certain testimony to the struggle for intimacy in a marriage between a believer and an unbeliever. Dozens of men and women have described to me the emptiness they feel in their marriages because they have nothing in common spiritually with their spouse. It truly is difficult for two to walk together if they are not in agreement (Amos 3:3).

After spirit-to-spirit union has been established, the next level of intimacy should be soul-to-soul. This is the opportunity a couple has to get to really know each other's personality…to learn his or her disposition and character qualities…to become good friends who truly enjoy being with each other socially.

Then, finally, after the marriage, there is the body-to-body intimacy as the physical union is established.

Disastrously, the world has reversed this procedure. Too often, the process starts with a sexual encounter early in the relationship. Then perhaps a friendship begins to develop and the couple begins to live together. Sometimes, almost as an afterthought, the pair attends church and become aware of their spiritual bankruptcy. If they accept Christ into their lives, they have to go back to the beginning and start all over, this time really getting to know each other as God intended!

Recently I saw a documentary about a man who had four wives in four parts of the country. None of the wives knew about the others. The man would make up excuses about business trips and shuttle back and forth from wife to wife. Finally—and this is not hard to believe—the man had a heart attack and died. All four of his wives found out at the same time about his polygamy. As the film ended, I remember saying to my wife, "How in the world could a woman live with a man and not know he was doing this?"

But if the only "intimacy" in a marriage is "body-to-body," if there is no closeness of soul-to-soul and spirit-to-spirit, then it is truly possible to live with someone and not really know him or her at all!

## A COMMITMENT TO TRANSPARENCY

In the beginning, the first married couple had no self-consciousness. They were totally selfless. No sense of embarrassment plagued them. "They were both naked, the man and his wife, and were not ashamed" (Genesis 2:25).

Then sin entered into the world (Genesis 3) and the great cover-up began. When Adam and Eve sinned, they realized they were naked, "and they sewed fig leaves together and made themselves coverings" (Genesis 3:7).

The nakedness that our first parents felt was emotional, psychological, and most of all, spiritual. Before sin and self took over, they were both naked and were not ashamed. Afterwards, everything changed.

It is not my purpose here to delve into the theology of this passage of Scripture, but I must apply its wisdom to our modern marriages. Most of us would like to reveal who we really are to the ones with whom we live, but we are afraid. We think, *If my spouse knew me as I know me, she wouldn't love me.* So we continue to provide coverings for ourselves to hide behind.

This is doubly tragic, because in most cases, we would be accepted and loved if we would just give ourselves up to one another. In his book, *Mortal Lessons: Notes in the Art of Surgery,* Dr. Richard Selzer tells about a young married couple who refused to let their transparency be destroyed even in the aftermath of disfiguring surgery:

> I stand by the bed where a young woman lies, her face post-
> operative, her mouth twisted in palsy, clownish. A tiny twig
> of the facial nerve, the one to the muscles of her mouth, has
> been severed. She will be thus from now on. The surgeon has
> followed with religious fervor the curve of her flesh; I promise

you that. Nevertheless, to remove the tumor in her cheek, I had cut the little nerve.

Her young husband is in the room. He stands on the opposite side of the bed, and together they seem to dwell in the evening lamplight, isolated from me, private. Who are they, I ask myself, he and this wry-mouth I have made, who gaze at and touch each other so generously, greedily? The young woman speaks.

"Will my mouth always be like this?" she asks.

"Yes," I say, "it will. It is because the nerve was cut."

She nods, and is silent. But the young man smiles.

"I like it," he says. "It is kind of cute."

All at once I know who he is. I understand, and I lower my gaze. Unmindful, he bends to kiss her crooked mouth, and I so close can see how he twists his own lips to accommodate to hers, to show her that their kiss still works.[11]

This blessed couple connected at the point of potential misunderstanding and lifted each other up. Through responsibility, intimacy and transparency, they found the encouragement zone…and so can you!

## LOVE IN ACTION

Standing outside of their Houston home, Jeneanne Sims kissed her husband off to work about 10:00 P.M. on September 5, 1991. As she walked back into the house she heard three gunshots, and running back outside, she collapsed to the ground beside her wounded husband. She held him until he died a few minutes later.

Some months later Jeneanne wrote:

What do I miss most? A thousand things! After thirty-one years together, I miss his warmth and gentleness and the place I had in his arms…I miss holding hands with him in worship services…I miss hearing him say, "My pretty precious one, I love you!"…I miss the pager he gave me so he could say "I love you" while I was busy at work…I miss his playfulness, his willingness to entertain a whim and go for a hamburger at three o'clock in the morning…I miss sitting for hours in the middle of the day talking, laughing, playing, sharing…I miss preparing his favorite meal…I miss his slightly off-key rendition of "Jeanie with the Light Brown Hair."

Whatever it is that we would miss if our spouse were to be taken from us, we ought not to miss in everyday love, affirmation, and encouragement. Jeneanne admonishes couples who still have each other: "Lavish him with praise and gratitude when he does something for you—even if it's nothing special! Believe me, it is special!"[12]

# 2

# A PERSONAL MAP TO BURIED TREASURE

FROM: PRAYER THE GREAT ADVENTURE

No self-respecting treasure hunter would ever set off on an adventure to dig up buried riches without a map. You know the kind of map I'm talking about—yellow with age, frayed at the edges, heavy with the odor of pirates and gun powder and massive oak treasure chests. The kind of map that hails from a wild land where adventurers of long ago used machetes to cut their way through a dense jungle, looking for just the right spot to unpack their shovels and dig into the moist earth to bury their cache of diamonds and rubies and sapphires and gold. The kind of map that features a big, black **X** to mark the exact spot where the treasure lies.

I assume that you'd like to find that kind of map, wouldn't you? I know I would!

Well, guess what? In a very real sense, I already have discovered such a map...*and I think I can help you find one, as well.*

The treasure map I have in mind will lead you as surely to hidden treasure as any that Long John Silver ever fingered—but I guarantee it will do you a lot more good than any map ever did him. He's long since departed this world and left his gleaming baubles behind, but the treasure you uncover through your map will last eternally.

You see, the kind of treasure map I'm thinking of is one you draw yourself, based on the riches you find through answered prayer. I'm talking about a treasure map that has no one but you for its author.

## HELP FOR THE JOURNEY

When we concluded the last chapter, I am sure we all agreed that staying on schedule should be a high priority. But if you're like me, you know how tough that can be! Life gets so hectic; we get caught up in the journey and forget where we are going. Once in awhile we have moments of awareness and realize we are not where we want to be. How do we keep from getting so far off track?

I have made a personal discovery that I think will help, an effective way to measure spiritual progress and hold myself accountable to God's schedule for my life. The secret? Several months ago I began to keep a spiritual journal.

I first encountered journaling about half a century ago when my uncle Clifford came to live with us for awhile. Clifford was a quiet man who had faced a great many challenges in his life. But he was a godly saint and years before he came to live with us, he began keeping a diary. I can still remember him dragging out his seven-year journal after dinner and asking us if we knew what had happened on a particular date in any of the previous seven years. No doubt most of us kids yawned as we humored our uncle by listening to him read his short diary entries.

I remember thinking it seemed strange that someone would take the time to write down what happened each day and then refer to it later. What was the point? My uncle went to be with the Lord this year and I regret that I never had the opportunity to tell him of my new love for journaling.

My personal interest in keeping a journal began several years ago when I first read Gordon MacDonald's book, *Ordering Your Private World*. Gordon began keeping a journal twenty years before he wrote his book and for him it started this way:

> I became impressed by the fact that many, many godly men
> and women down through the centuries had…kept journals,
> and I began to wonder if they had not put their fingers upon
> an aid to spiritual growth. To satisfy my curiosity, I decided to
> experiment, and began keeping one for myself.[1]

While I did not start journaling right away, I did begin to wonder what it would be like to cultivate such a habit. A few years later I read something Bill Hybels wrote that lodged in my heart. He talked about journaling as a way to slow down the RPMs in his life:

> I have a high energy level in the morning. I can't wait to get
> to the office to start the day's work. And once the adrena-
> line starts flowing, the phone starts ringing, the people start
> coming, I can easily stay at ten thousand [RPMs] until I crash

at night. So I decided to start journaling…. The amazing thing is what happens to my RPMs when I write. By the time I've finished a long paragraph recapping yesterday, my mind is off my responsibilities. I'm tuned in to what I'm doing and thinking, and my motor is slowed halfway down.[2]

What Bill described about his life matched my own experience exactly. I often struggled with taking the time at the beginning of the day to focus on and listen to God. All I could think of was the huge list of "to do's" that awaited me. Could Bill be right about the power of journaling to slow one down at the beginning of the day?

Then in 1994, while recovering from surgery, I received a copy of Gordon MacDonald's book, *The Life God Blesses*. Since I was confined to a recliner for a few days, I started to read his book…and could not put it down. As long as I could remember, I had always wanted God to bless my life. My bout with cancer had taken my desire to a whole new level.

Once again, Gordon talked about his personal discipline of journaling. This time he mentioned that he journaled on his computer. For some odd reason, that clicked with me. That very day I began to keep a record of God's dealings with me, using my computer. Since that time I have been keeping a daily journal. When I say "daily," I do not mean that I never miss a day. But I have become so committed to this discipline that whenever I do miss a day, I don't let it rob me of the joy of returning as soon as possible. More than anything else, this practice has reminded me that my walk with God is a daily experience that can be chronicled and measured.

## A GREAT ASSET

Keeping a journal can become a great asset to those who embark upon the adventure of prayer. For me, as well as for most others I know, the quest to know God and to learn how to communicate with Him more effectively has been more of a journey than an event. Journaling not only provides a road map for where I've been, it often reminds me of where I'm heading.

The Christian life was never meant to be static, but dynamic! As Paul wrote, "Even though our outward man is perishing, yet the inward man is being renewed day by day" (2 Corinthians 4:16, NKJV). The apostle saw spiritual growth as a process that requires personal discipline. That's what he meant in 1 Timothy 4:7 when he encouraged Timothy to discipline himself for godliness' sake. In *The Life God Blesses,* Gordon MacDonald defines discipline like this:

> Discipline is that act of inducing pain and stress in one's life in order to grow into greater toughness, capacity, endurance, or strength. So spiritual discipline is that effort pressing the soul into greater effort so that it will enlarge its capacity to hear God speak and, as a result, to generate inner force (spiritual energy) that will guide and empower one's mind and outer life.[3]

In this book I have attempted to place the practice of prayer within the framework of personal discipline. While I have described it as an adventure, I have not tried to make it sound like a lazy adventure or an easy excercise. I have been discovering over these past months that many of the spiritual disciplines are interdependent. In my case, the spiritual discipline of journaling has helped me in the spiritual discipline of prayer.

## WHAT IS A JOURNAL?

Journals have existed throughout all ages of history. In a sense, large sections of the Bible itself could qualify as journals. The Book of Job is written in the style of a journal, telling the story of one man's suffering and his encounter with his "comforting" friends. Ecclesiastes is another kind of journal which records Solomon's attempt to find meaning in life apart from God. The four Gospels are written accounts of oral stories which circulated for years about the life of Christ. In a way they are the journals of the early church. The Book of Acts is a journal that records how the church grew under the leadership of Peter and Paul and the early disciples.

More recent church history would have huge gaps were it not for the journals of men like St. Augustine, David Livingstone, David Brainerd, Blaise Pascal, Soren Kierkegaard, John Wesley, Jim Elliot, and many others. By one writer's count, there are more than *nine thousand* published journals! And we are immeasurably richer because they exist.

A journal is a diary, but it's much more than that. It is a daily account of your walk with God. It often includes a list of prayers that God has answered. Sometimes it involves interaction with Scripture. It can become one of the best methods for charting your spiritual growth. Someone has defined a journal like this:

> A journal is a book in which you keep a personal record of events in your life, of your different relationships, of your responses to things, of your feelings about things—of your search to find out who you are and what the meaning of your life might be. It is a book in which you carry out the greatest of life's adventures—the discovery of yourself.[4]

As helpful as this is, I like Donald Whitney's definition better because he sees journaling from a distinctly Christian perspective:

> A journal…is a book in which a person writes down various things. As a Christian, your journal is a place to record the works and ways of God in your life. Your journal also can include an account of daily events, a diary of personal relationships, a notebook of insights into Scripture, and a list of prayer requests. It is where spontaneous devotional thoughts or lengthy theological musings can be preserved. A journal is one of the best places for charting your progress in the other Spiritual Disciplines and for holding yourself accountable to your goals.[5]

# WHY KEEP A JOURNAL?

There are benefits in keeping a personal journal. Let me suggest just five:

## 1. To help you remember what God is doing in your life

The Bible is filled with instructions to make "remembering" a high priority. Consider these:

> *Remember His marvelous works which He has done, His wonders, and the judgments of His mouth* (1 Chronicles 16:12, NKJV).
>
> *Remember now your Creator in the days of your youth, before the difficult days come, and the years draw near when you say, "I have no pleasure in them"* (Ecclesiastes 12:1, NKJV).
>
> *But recall the former days in which, after you were illuminated, you endured a great struggle with sufferings* (Hebrews 10:32, NKJV).
>
> *Remember therefore from where you have fallen; repent and do the first works, or else I will come to you quickly and remove your lampstand from its place—unless you repent* (Revelation 2:5, NKJV).

*The most awesome answer to prayer came on the day that the test results from the second surgery were announced. I will never forget that moment of exhilaration in our living room. We knew and know now that this was not a final answer to our prayer for complete healing, but it was a wonderful milestone along the way. I knew that day that You had done that for us ... for me in answer to not only our prayers, but the prayers of so many others as well.*

We all have occasions when we cannot see what God is doing in our lives. Our faith may be weak, our eyes dimmed by sickness or discouragement. But there is no missing what God has done in the past. If a record is kept of God's dealings with us, we will be encouraged to keep trusting Him in difficult times. I think Asaph had this in mind when he penned the words of this Psalm: "I will remember the works of the Lord; Surely I will remember Your wonders of old. I will also meditate on all Your work, and talk of Your deeds" (Psalm 77:11–12, NKJV).

Writing down what you ask God to do, and then recording His answers, will spur you on to greater faith and trust in Him. Use it as your own map to hidden spiritual treasure!

### 2. To help you respond to life honestly

We often have a rosier appraisal of our walk with God than it may warrant. We tend to color our record in bright shades when a more subdued hue is called for. Yet we can't grow until we get brutally honest about where we truly are. If we believe we are growing when we are not, we will never get started with God. Keeping a journal forces us to respond to life honestly. Ronald Klug, who has written one of the few books on spiritual journaling, notes:

> Writing in a journal can…help us to be more honest with ourselves. One friend told me, "Writing in my journal helps me be truthful. If I write something false about my life, I can't get by with it. My rationalizing stands out when I see it in black and white."[6]

Gordon MacDonald also discovered that writing in his journal made it easier for him to face the truth about himself:

> Slowly I began to realize that the journal was helping me come to grips with an enormous part of my inner person that I had never been fully honest about. No longer could fears and struggles remain inside without definition. They were surfaced and confronted. And I became aware, little by little, that God's Holy Spirit was directing many of the thoughts and insights as I wrote. On paper, the Lord and I were carrying on

a personal communion. He was helping me, in the words of David, to "search my heart."[7]

When we read the Book of Psalms, we see how honestly David dealt with life. Sometimes we are shocked by the bluntness of his words. How do you respond when he cries out, "How long, O Lord? Will You forget me forever? How long will You hide Your face from me? How long shall I take counsel in my soul, having sorrow in my heart daily. How long will my enemy be exalted over me?" (Psalm 13:1–2, NKJV)

Two months before missionary Jim Elliot was killed by the Auca Indians, he made this honest entry into his journal:

> In studying Spanish, I left off English Bible reading and my devotional reading pattern was broken. I have never restored it. Translation and preparation for daily Bible lessons is not sufficient to empower my soul. Prayer as a single man was difficult, I remember, because my mind always reverted to Betty. Now it's too hard to get out of bed in the morning. I've made resolutions on this score before now but not followed them up. Tomorrow it is to be—dressed by 6:00 A.M. and study in the Epistles before breakfast. So help me God.[8]

Journaling can help you to be honest in your growth in faith. And honesty is the required first step in anyone's spiritual walk.

### 3. To help you reflect on the meaning of your experiences

When I checked out of the Mayo Clinic a couple of years ago, my Christian doctor sat me down and gave me a little speech. It went something like this: "David, I've never had cancer, but I've dealt with so many people who had it that I almost feel as if I've had it myself. I want to tell you something that I think you will find to be true in the days ahead. You will never, *ever* again drive by the ocean and see just the ocean."

Call the man a prophet! All of a sudden, my perception of life was enhanced from grainy black and white to high resolution Technicolor. I began to see and notice things that I had never before stopped to notice. Everyday experiences were no longer lost in the shuffle of schedules and appointments. I began to observe a pattern in what God was doing in my life.

And when did my more acute observations begin? When I started to write down what was happening to me and when I took the time to reflect on them afterwards. I think this is what Arthur Gordon had in mind when he wrote the following words in *A Touch of Wonder*:

> How do we keep in the forefront of our minds the simple fact that we live in an indescribably wonderful world? It's not easy. Routine dulls the eye and the ear. Repetition and familiarity fog the capacity for astonishment. Even so, moments come to all of us when everything suddenly seems fresh and new and marvelous. The gift of awareness makes possible some of our happiest hours. We need to be receptive to it and grateful for it.[9]

Journaling enables us to better appreciate the world around us, as well as God's hand on our life. It's hard to miss a big, black **X** marking the treasure when you're staring straight at it!

### 4. *To help you record the progress of your spiritual journey*

In his book *First Things First*, Steven Covey makes this interesting statement about journals:

Keeping a personal journal empowers you to see and improve, on a day-by-day basis, the way you're developing and using your endowments. Because writing truly imprints the brain, it also helps you remember and apply the things you're trying to do. In addition…as you take occasion… to read over your experiences of past weeks, months, or years, you gain invaluable insight into repeating patterns and themes in your life.[10]

While Covey was looking at this process from a management or business perspective, his comments are transferable to the spiritual realm. It's really true that "the unexamined life is not worth living." When we don't keep track of our progress, we will never be motivated to grow as we might. This is especially true of prayer. When we begin to take the time (as I am learning to do) to write out some of our prayers, we discover areas of weakness that need to be strengthened and patterns of sin or foolishness that need to be corrected. We can also discover good patterns that are worth strengthening and encouraging.

*I love the promise that though I eat the bread of adversity and drink the water of affliction, the Lord will not hide His teachers from me. They will be there to say to me, "this is the way, walk in it." Truly there seems to be a greater sense of the importance of Your leading in my life because of the affliction and adversity. I also sense, Lord, that in quietness and in confidence I will find new strength. I am sensing a quiet and deep working in my life during this time!*

One of the hidden benefits of computer journaling is the exact way my word processor records dates and times. In the program I use, the date and time of each entry is entered into the text of the journal at the top of the page. I also click in the time at the end of each day's entry. It is amazing what this little routine has done for my consistency. When I look over my journal at the end of the month or at the end of the year, I can see the missing dates. I have discovered from this review that certain situations make me especially vulnerable to missing my time with the Lord. Knowing what those situations are, I can prepare counter strategies to help me overcome my lapses. Without journaling, I'd still be in the dark. But my map to hidden spiritual treasure has shown me the glint of gold!

### 5. To help you regain lost momentum

One of the women in our church made an appointment to see me some time ago. As we began our time together she said, "Pastor, I love the Lord with all my heart; I know I'm a Christian. I've walked with God for as long as I can remember. But something is wrong and I do not know what it is! I've got the spiritual blahs. I don't know how to explain it. There are days when I don't want to read the Bible and I don't want to pray. Sometimes I don't even want to come to church."

With tears in her eyes and anguish in her voice she pleaded, "Pastor Jeremiah, what is wrong with me?"

After encouraging her and praying with her, I gave her an assignment. "I want you to go to the stationery store and buy a notebook," I said. "Each day I want you to write in that notebook. Begin by putting the date at the top of the page. After you have read your Bible, ask God to give you something from your reading that you will want to write down. Write down the things you are praying for and the way you feel about your walk with God. Do that every day for the next thirty days. Then each day go back and read what you wrote the day before. Follow that pattern for the next thirty days, then come back and tell me what God has done in your life."

When she returned one month later, I didn't have to ask if things were better. As soon as she stepped into my office I could tell something had changed. Her face beamed with the joy of the Lord. She told me that about two weeks into the process, she began to see what had happened. God met her in a fresh, new way and the relationship was restored.

Gordon MacDonald made this same discovery. He found journaling to be a valuable resource in regaining lost spiritual momentum:

> On those days when coldness has been more than a matter of outer New England temperatures, I have found myself unable to produce hardly a coherent word from soul-level. The journal has helped at such times…. I have learned to write and describe to the Father in journal form my hardness of soul and spirit. Usually after three or more paragraphs of frank talk, I find the inner stone begins to break up.[11]

Every Christian will experience dry times. If there is no mechanism in place to bring about restoration and renewal, the devil will use those dry times to torment us. Journaling is a good way to prevent it.

# WHAT SHOULD I WRITE IN MY JOURNAL?

There is no right or wrong way to do a journal, but there are several areas you might want to concentrate on. First, write about your *experiences*. Write about the people you meet, the things you accomplish, the problems you encounter, your impressions about the way your life is going. I have discovered that by writing out the things that are making my heart heavy, my load seems lighter and I am able to progress to the more productive parts of my spiritual journey.

Second, I recommend that you write out your *prayers*. Some may find this difficult to do; I admit that when I first started it, I felt as if I were praying to my computer. But I soon got past that and began to realize the benefit of being precise in my conversation with the Lord. This may not be for everyone, but for those who have a difficult time staying on track as they pray, this can be a great help. Once again, Bill Hybels gave me some insight. He wrote, "A good way to learn to pray specifically is to write out your prayers and then read them to God. Many people find they are better able to concentrate if they put pen to paper and arrange their assorted thoughts into an organized format. I've been doing this for several years, and I find that it helps me in several ways. It forces me to be specific; broad generalities don't look good on paper. It keeps my mind from wandering. And it helps me see when God answers prayers."[12]

*Oh God, let me not forget You. Let this record that I am keeping be a reminder to me each day that You are the Rock of my Stronghold and without You I am a 0 (zero). I have so often tried to prove myself and have gone at it all alone leaving You out. I have learned and am learning that there is no real victory or joy in the Christian life unless there is total dependence upon God. I pray, dear Lord, that You will never let me become a heap of ruins. Oh God, spare me from the day of grief and desperate sorrow. I want to finish strong and make a greater impact for You than I have ever dreamed of. Please hear this prayer from Your servant, David Jeremiah!*

Third, it's extremely helpful to write down the *insights you get from God's Word*. Since I began to journal, I have been reading five chapters from Scripture each day and asking God to cause His truth to intersect with my life in such a way that I am impacted that very day. For many of us who spend long hours studying the Bible so that we can teach it to others, finding a way to let the Word of God touch us personally and devotionally can be a real challenge. I have found that this simple plan of reading and responding to the Bible has helped me greatly. After I finish my reading, I enter into my journal the verses God has used to encourage or confront me. Often I write down the thoughts those verses have produced in my heart.

Fourth, I find it useful to write down *quotes from books I am reading*. Several years ago I began the practice of reading a chapter from a book on prayer each day. I usually did this just before I prayed and I found it to be a source of great motivation and encouragement. It became a positive part of my daily discipline. In fact, many of the quotes on prayer scattered throughout this book were taken from my journals. These thoughts have greatly enriched my walk with God. I sometimes feel so blessed to be surrounded by some of the greatest men and women of God who have ever lived. Through their books they have become like personal friends.

Fifth, I would encourage you to write about your *doubts and fears*. Morton Kelsey in *The Other Side of Silence* describes how he expresses emotion in his journal:

> I...write about my angers and fears and hurts, depressions and disappointments and anxieties, my joys and thanksgivings.... In short, I set down the feelings and events that have mattered to me, high moments and low.... The journal is like a little island of solid rock on which we can stand and see the waves and storms for what they really are.[13]

Gordon MacDonald also sees the benefits of recording our emotions:

A key contribution of the journal became its record of not only the good moments, but the bad times as well. When there came times of discouragement, even of despair, I was able to describe my feelings and tell how God's spirit ultimately ministered to me to strengthen my resolve. These became special passages to look back upon; they helped me celebrate the power of God in the midst of my own weakness.[14]

When I examine the entries in my journal during the days of my illness, I see many fearful prayers. Here is an entry I made on the day before I was to have surgery:

> Lord, we are being stretched in our faith, and I know that is for a good purpose. Please help us to continue to trust You with each day and with each bit of news that we receive. As I have already prayed, dear Lord protect Donna's heart on Monday. Keep her in the center of Your will…in Your hands and wrap Your arms around her in a very special way. May those who come to stay with her be an encouragement to her and a blessing! Lord I know that my times are in Your hands…. You are able to do above and beyond all that I can even ask or think. I trust You even when I am afraid!

When we record our fears and anxious moments, later we can see how great a God we have, a Warrior who can conquer our fears and slay those anxieties! But there is also great benefit in the moment of writing. Somehow, in getting those fears out into the open, their power over us diminishes. This has been not only my experience, but that of many others as well. Why not make it your own?

## LEARNING FROM YOUR JOURNAL

While there is great benefit in journal writing, the greatest advantage comes from harvesting its contents. I had never connected the term "harvesting" with the practice of journaling until I read Ronald Klug's book, *How To Keep A Spiritual Journal.* In the closing chapter of his book he talks about the value of going back at certain intervals and rereading larger sections of our journals. This can be done at the end of a month or at the midpoint of the year or even at the end of each year.

Before I read about harvesting I had never completely read through my journals. At the end of this past year, I decided to read my journals through as a way of preparing myself for the new year. I decided to index them by names, subjects, and Scripture references. I was not far into the process before I realized I had waited far too long to undertake this process. (As I write this chapter, I still am not finished with my indexing project. My experience suggests that it's best not to wait longer than six months before you begin to harvest your journal.)

As I reread my journals, I began to be impressed with some significant thoughts:

- There were certain periods in my life when journaling was very difficult for me. These were so predictable (as I looked back on them) that I could have entered the dates in my calendar before they occurred.

- I was consistently asking God for some things that I needed to take responsibility for myself. I was surprised how often I asked Him for the same thing. There was nothing wrong with my persistence, but I could almost hear God saying to me as I read these entries, "David, why don't you just get control of your life and deal with these issues?"

- I was brought to tears on more than one occasion as I read my prayers in an early entry, then the record of God's answer in a later entry. God really heard me! He really did answer my prayer!

- I saw that I had a lot of growing to do in the art of intercession. I've made a good start, but I have a long way to go.

I could list many other insights I gained from harvesting my journal, but these illustrate the point. Luci Shaw sums up the benefits of journal harvesting with these words:

> Rereading a journal is like viewing a forest from a helicopter. From that fluid height you can see the larger contours of the land, the way the trees clump and break, the vivid color contrasts between evergreens and maples, the cliffs and streams and rocks that interrupt the flow of the landscape. When you are lost in the forests of daily crisis, caught in the underbrush, you cannot know where you are. Only from the height of passing months and years can you see your life in proportion and with true perspective.[15]

## MAKE YOUR OWN MAP!

I cannot begin to describe how enormously the practice of journaling has strengthened my spiritual walk and deepened my prayer life. Often it has served as a lifeline in very stormy seas. It does not surprise me that someone as brilliant as Jonathan Edwards would pen these words in his journal shortly after his conversion: "I seemed often to see so much light exhibited by every sentence, and such a refreshing food communicated, that I could not get along in reading, often dwelling long on one sentence to see the wonders contained in it, and yet almost every sentence seemed to be full of wonders."[16]

And Edwards's testimony is far from unique! Earlier I quoted Luci Shaw, widow of the late Christian publisher, Harold Shaw. While these days she is a faithful guide to journaling, it was not always so:

> All my life long I've thought I should keep a journal. But I never did until a few years ago, when the discovery that my husband, Harold, had cancer suddenly plunged us into the middle of an intense learning experience, facing things we'd never faced before. Confronted with agonizing decisions, we

would cry out to the Lord, "Where are you in the middle of this?" It suddenly occurred to me that unless I made a record of what was going on, I would forget. The events, details, and people of those painful days could easily become a blur. So I started to write it all down.[17]

Even C. H. Spurgeon, celebrated as the "prince of preachers" in the last half of the 1800s, said, "I have sometimes said when I have become the prey of doubting thoughts, 'Well now, I dare not doubt whether there be a God, for I can look back in my Diary, and say, On such a day, in the depths of trouble, I bent my knee to God, and ever I had risen from my knees, the answer was given me.'"[18]

Is it any wonder that so many of the people we consider spiritual giants were devoted to the practice of journaling? I don't think so. I think we would do well to consider the question posed by one astute observer of great Christian saints. He asks, "How did men like Edwards and Whitefield become so unusually conformed to the image of Christ?" He answers, "Part of their secret was their use of the Spiritual Discipline of journaling to maintain self-accountability for their spiritual goals and priorities. Before we give all the reasons why we cannot be the kind of disciples they were, let us try doing what they did."[19]

I think that's outstanding advice. We could use a few more like Edwards and Whitefield. If journaling could help nurture men and women like them, then by all means, let's start journaling. I'm convinced that believers like them could create some pretty spectacular spiritual treasure maps. And you know what? I believe God just might be calling you to be one of those map makers.

# 3

## THE BEST EVIDENCE OF THE SPIRIT

## AN ATTITUDE OF GRATITUDE

FROM: GOD IN YOU—RELEASING THE POWER
OF THE HOLY SPIRIT IN YOUR LIFE

*It is good to give thanks to the LORD, and to sing praises to*
*Your name, O Most High; to declare Your lovingkindness in the*
*morning, and Your faithfulness every night.*

PSALM 92:1–2

D r. W. A. Criswell pastored his first church in Chickasha, Oklahoma. One day in the course of calling on residents of that town, he went to see a woman who lived by herself in a dilapidated house. He knocked at the door, and as Dr. Criswell described it, "There came to the door a woman who looked more like wretchedness than any countenance or figure I have ever seen."

The young pastor introduced himself and said, "I have come to see you."

"Well," she replied, "what do you want?"

"I am a pastor," he told her, "and I have come to visit with you."

"There's no need for anybody like you around here," she replied.

"But," Dr. Criswell said, "I have come to visit you and I want to come in."

Seeing that he wouldn't be dissuaded, she reluctantly invited him in and he sat down. "Where do you preach?" she asked, and he told her. "You say you believe in God?" she asked gruffly.

"Yes," Dr. Criswell replied, "I believe in the Lord."

"Well, I do not believe in God," she said, and she cursed Him.

As he visited with her, the terrible story of her life came out. Ever since she and her husband had moved to Oklahoma it had been, as Criswell put it, one wretchedness after another. Her husband had died and her children had scattered, leaving her alone. She lived in poverty, and her eyesight was almost gone. She was bitter and angry at everyone.

Then the woman startled the young pastor by suddenly saying, "I write poetry. Would you like to hear some of my poetry?"

Criswell politely replied that he would. The poem she recited made such an impression on him that he went out to the car after the visit and wrote it out so that he wouldn't forget it. This is what the woman had composed:

I hate Oklahoma!
Not the land of my native birth
But a land by all the gods that be
A scourge on the face of the earth.
I hate Oklahoma!

I hate Oklahoma!
Where the centipede crawls in your bed at night,
And the rattlesnake lifts its fangs to bite,
Where the lizard and the scorpion play on the sly,
And the lonesome vultures sail high in the sky.
Where water and food are an eternal lack,
And a man's best friend sticks a dagger in your back.
I hate Oklahoma![1]

Dr. Criswell said that all of her poetry was like that. She was an unthankful, bitter old woman who saw only the difficult things in life and dwelled on them.

Just a few weeks after the pastor's visit, he was called and told that the old woman had died and had requested before her death that he hold the funeral service. Dr. Criswell said it was the only service he could remember where *no one* came. There was just one somebody there besides the pastor, and it was the woman in the plain pine box.

Ingratitude, said Dr. Criswell, has no friends.

Think for a moment of your own friends and circle of acquaintances. What if I were to ask you this question: What is the greatest evidence of someone being filled with the Holy Spirit? How would you recognize a truly Spirit-controlled individual if you ran into him or her this afternoon and had an opportunity to chat for a while?

What would tip you off?

You might say, "Well, I know that man has a powerful witness for Jesus Christ, and that proves that he's Spirit-filled." Or "I've heard that she speaks in tongues frequently, so that must mean she's filled with the Spirit of God."

But what does the Word of God say? How can we really determine if a person has been filled, or is controlled, by the Holy Spirit? You may find what I'm going to say in this chapter rather strange, and yet as I began to chase this concept, it showed up again and again in the principle texts of the New Testament. For me, it was one of those "Aha!" principles of Scripture where you sit back in your chair and say, "Yes, it makes sense—but I'd never considered that before."

I believe the strongest evidence for a Spirit-filled life is *gratitude*.

## "THANK GOD!"

I don't know whether it has been a good thing for God's people that we have one day a year when we celebrate "Thanksgiving." Does that mean that we can be as ungrateful as we want to be through the other 364 days? In this chapter you will discover that the attitude of gratitude is the very beating heart of a Spirit-controlled life.

It was December of 1914 when Thomas Edison's great laboratories in West Orange, New Jersey, were almost entirely destroyed by fire. In one night Edison lost 2 million dollars' worth of equipment and the record of much of his life-work. Edison's son Charles ran frantically about trying to find his father and finally came upon him standing near the fire, his face ruddy in the glow, and his white hair blown by the winter winds.

"My heart ached for him," Charles Edison said. "He was no longer young, and everything was being destroyed. Then he spotted me. And he said to me, 'Where is your mother? Find her. Bring her here. She will never see anything like this again as long as she lives!'"

The next morning, walking about the charred embers of so many of his hopes and dreams, the sixty-seven-year-old Edison mused, "There is great value in disaster. All our mistakes are burned up. Thank God! We can start all over again."[2]

What a perspective on life! The Bible speaks very strongly to the Christian about the importance of a grateful spirit. In fact, it very carefully links the spirit of gratitude with victory in the Christian life. I don't know if you have ever connected these two thoughts, but in 2 Corinthians

2:14 we read these words: "Now thanks be to God who always leads us in triumph in Christ."

Did you see it? Gratitude and triumph in the same verse. There is something about the attitude of gratitude that seems at home in the scenario of triumph.

That same concept blazes across the biblical sky again in 1 Corinthians 15:57. "But thanks be to God, who gives us the victory through our Lord Jesus Christ." There it is again! Victory and triumph in the same context with gratitude. You show me somebody who is experiencing spiritual victory, who just exudes a sense of triumph, and I can promise you, as you get to know that individual, you will find a man or woman who is permeated with a spirit of gratitude.

Gratitude, you see, is one of the evidences that God is in us and that He is working in our lives. Why do I say that? Because in the world in which we live today, there are so many reasons to be ungrateful. So many reasons to complain. But if the Spirit of God is in us, He will triumph over that. He will give us victory over those negative, self-pitying thoughts, and genuine, heartfelt gratitude will spill through the cracks of our soul like sunlight through venetian blinds as we explain to people what God is doing in our life.

Unfortunately, the doctrine of gratitude, which is paramount in the New Testament, has been relegated by some to an optional and seasonal spirit. Gratitude, as I have watched it, is sometimes looked upon as that which good Christians sometimes do, instead of that which should mark the life of *every* believer. The spirit of gratitude should be true of all of us if we know Jesus Christ and if God's Holy Spirit is in control of our lives.

Walk with me for a few minutes through some biblical thoughts about gratitude. It may prove as revolutionary to your life as it did to mine.

## THE CONTROL OF THE SPIRIT RESULTS IN GRATITUDE

The following passage in Ephesians began this revolution in my thinking. Please take special note of the highlighted words.

> Do not be drunk with wine, in which is dissipation; but be filled with the Spirit, **speaking** to one another in psalms and hymns and spiritual songs, **singing** and making melody in your heart to the Lord, **giving thanks** always for all things to God the Father in the name of our Lord Jesus Christ, **submitting** to one another in the fear of God. (Ephesians 5:18–21)

The words that end in -*ing* are called participles. In this passage, these are words that describe what goes on in the life of a man or woman who is being filled with the Holy Spirit. Zero in with me for a closer look.

### Speaking and singing

When we're filled or controlled by the Spirit, we will be *speaking* to one another in psalms and hymns and spiritual songs, and we will be *singing* and *making melody* unto the Lord.

That sounds like worship to me!

One of the things that happens when you are a Spirit-filled Christian is that you are filled to overflowing with worship to our Lord. Our churches ought to be singing churches. A Spirit-filled congregation will really *sing* when they sing. It won't be a mechanical mouthing of words while we check out so-and-so in the next row or let our minds drift. We will be entering into those words, climbing into that melody, and the music will be coming up from our toes. It will be immediately evident to the visitors and seekers in our midst. They will think to themselves, *My goodness, these people really* BELIEVE *what they're singing!*

I have been in some churches where they say "stand up and sing," but all they do is stand up! Have you ever been in a church like that? I feel like looking around and saying, "Hey, doesn't anybody *sing* in this place?"

The experts on preaching will tell you that pastors are supposed to save their voices; they aren't supposed to sing along during worship time. Sorry, I choose not to comply. I choose to *worship,* and then I preach with what's left over. I sing my preaching voice right out of tune. Sometimes I have trouble finishing the message, but I'll tell you what…I get worship done! It isn't an option with me. I can't help myself because I love the Lord, and the Spirit of God is in my heart. I can't sit on the sidelines when God's people are worshipping before God's throne—I want to be right in the middle of it!

Whenever I read Psalm 42, I am reminded how the psalmist was sustained in moments of loneliness and deep discouragement by memories of joyful praise among God's people.

> These things I remember as I pour out my soul:
> how I used to go with the multitude,
> leading the procession to the house of God,
> with shouts of joy and thanksgiving
> among the festive throng.
> (Psalm 42:4, NIV)

How he missed that "festive throng" of worshippers, singing and shouting praise to the Lord! And so would I, if I had to be away from joyous worship with brothers and sisters in Christ. One of the evidences that you are a Spirit-filled Christian is that you will find yourself singing and speaking to one another in psalms and hymns and spiritual songs, making melody in your heart to the Lord. Not just on Sunday, but all week long.

### Submitting

Submitting (Ephesians 5:21) is as much an evidence of God's Spirit in a life as singing and rejoicing. A man or woman who is controlled by the Holy Spirit will have a submissive attitude. Do you know why I know that is of the Spirit? *Because I am absolutely certain it isn't of the flesh.* It isn't "normal" to submit to one another, whether in the family or in the church or in the business world. But you show me a person who is filled with the Spirit of God, and I will show you a man or woman who has a submissive spirit.

### Giving thanks

One of the evidences of a Spirit-filled Christian is the gratitude in his heart—so very evident to those who are around him—gratitude to God for all that He has done. Literally, the text says, *"Be being filled with the Spirit, giving thanks always for all things to God the Father in the name of our Lord Jesus Christ."* God says that when we are controlled by His Spirit, we will be grateful people, thankful for what we have, anxious to share it with others, always overwhelmed with gratitude for God's goodness to us.

Do you realize what God has done for you? Has it gripped you lately? Has it pushed you to your knees? He gave His Son for you, He put His Spirit in you, and He has given you life everlasting. When you come to grips with those things (who can understand them?), you can't help but be thankful.

William Law, writing centuries ago, made a very good point when he said, "Would you like to know who is the greatest saint in the world? It isn't he who prays most or fasts most. It isn't he who gives most. But it is he who is always thankful to God, who receives everything as an instrument of God's goodness, and has a heart always ready to praise God for it."

The greatest saint is the one who is always thankful.

To be candid with you, I have drifted in and out of this attitude of gratitude in years past. But it's all different now in my life. Every day is a gift. Every moment is a precious treasure. If you haven't been through something like cancer, you can't know what I'm talking about. Sometimes I think God has to beat us up a little bit so we can learn about this grace of gratitude. And then, when He tenderizes us, when He allows circumstances to knock away that ugly cocoon of ingratitude, the Holy Spirit can begin to do His work in us and enable us to take flight in our gratitude and praise.

Somebody said to me recently, "You walk around all the time with a smile on your face."

Amen! I'm grateful to be alive. Grateful to have my family around me. Grateful to have the opportunity to minister to a wonderful church.

Grateful for the California sunshine that spills through my bedroom window every morning.

People say, "I'm glad to see you." And I smile and say, "I'm glad to be seen!"

I'm alive! My Lord has saved me, healed me, and filled me with His Holy Spirit. How could I keep from smiling? It is a wonderful thing. I'm even grateful for my gratitude because I know it is a gift of the Holy Spirit and not something that naturally dwells in the heart of David Jeremiah.

Don't you like to be around grateful people? Isn't it wonderful to be around folks who exude this spirit of gratitude? Sometimes you find yourself thinking, *Is he for real? Is she really genuine about this?* And then when you discover that it is real, you find yourself just wanting to hang around that person.

Ephesians 5 says that when you are filled with the Spirit, gratitude is the result. But there is something else I want you to see too.

## A COMMITMENT TO GOD'S WORD RESULTS IN GRATITUDE

Colossians 3:16–17 is yet another passage rich in gratitude…but I want you to notice something special about it.

> Let the word of Christ dwell in you richly in all wisdom, teaching and admonishing one another in psalms and hymns and spiritual songs, singing with grace in your hearts to the Lord. And whatever you do in word or deed, do all in the name of the Lord Jesus, giving thanks to God the Father through Him.

You say, "That sounds similar to what I just read in Ephesians." It is very similar. And why not? It had the same human author (Paul) and the same divine author (the Holy Spirit). But did you notice the change? In Ephesians it is being filled with the Spirit that creates gratitude in us. In Colossians, it is because we are filled or indwelled with the Word of God.

Did you ever notice that a Spirit-filled Christian is a *Scripture* filled Christian? If you meet somebody who claims to be filled with the Spirit and yet never has time to read or study or meditate on God's Word, something's out of sync. If a brother or sister in the Lord is full of the *Los Angeles Times* or *Newsweek* or even *Christianity Today,* but never mentions the Word of God, something isn't right. You can't be filled with the Spirit of God without also being filled with the Word of God. The Bible is the Holy Spirit's toolbox! It is the instrument He uses to change us and conform us into the image of our Lord.

Paul is saying that when you spend time as a Spirit-filled Christian reading the Book, you will come out a grateful person. It is the natural result of being filled with the Word of God.

But there is a third evidence you may not have considered.

## A PEACEFUL HEART RESULTS IN GRATITUDE

Did you know that? I couldn't believe it when I saw this in Colossians 3:15. Let's go back and read it.

> *And let the peace of God rule in your hearts, to which also you were called in one body; and be thankful.*

A Christian is the only one who has peace with God, because Christ has solved the issue of enmity with God. A believer is the only one who *can* have the peace of God, the peace that passes understanding, according to Philippians. Therefore, when a person is characterized by peace, the result is exactly the same as a person who is controlled by the Spirit and a person who is committed to the Word of God. He will be filled with gratitude.

Do you ever experience gratitude that you are not at war with God anymore? Maybe you were at war with God for a long time but God saved you out of it. I think sometimes people who are saved out of a tough life, saved out of ugly circumstances, and saved when they didn't know anything about God possess a deeper sense of gratitude than others who grew up in the church.

But it takes the same amount of grace to save all of us, doesn't it? No matter what has happened in our lives, when we fully understand what it's like to be at peace with God, our hearts will overflow with a spirit of gratitude.

I have to laugh when I think back to my early years as a pastor and some of my frustration with the apostle Paul. I would be studying my way through one of his epistles, just caught up in what a clear, orderly, logical teacher he is. Then, all of a sudden, he would seem to launch himself into the ionosphere. And I would say to myself, "Paul, I know a rabbit trail when I see one, and that is a rabbit trail! That's not on the subject at all!"

Yes, I know that some preachers are famous for rabbit trails. But *Paul*? The great apostle? In the very text of God's infallible Word? How could it be?

I finally realized something about those "rabbit trails"…and it made me feel a little ashamed.

Whenever Paul did those quick turns in the text and seemed to head down a different track, it was always because he was overcome with a sense of gratitude to God for what He had done for him. He would come to a place in his teaching and his reasoning where the reality of what the Spirit of God was leading him to say would suddenly overwhelm him. He couldn't go on to the next point until he had a little praise party, giving thanks to the Lord for His wisdom and longsuffering and mercy.

Logic, I learned, isn't everything. It has to leave room for praise.

When you are filled and controlled with the Spirit of God, you will be a grateful man. A grateful woman. A grateful boy or girl. The same thing happens when you are controlled with the Word of God. You are grateful. And when you have peace… Remember, now, peace is a fruit of the Spirit—one of the ninefold evidences of being Spirit-filled. And as you enjoy the peace that wells up in your heart and floods the landscape of your life, you will be filled with gratitude…just as I am right now. Praise God for His peace!

# A PRAYERFUL LIFE RESULTS IN GRATITUDE

Are you seeing how the wagons are circling here?

That's the very thought I had while I was studying this. It is almost as though God is saying, "I'm not going to let you escape this. Because everywhere you turn in My Word, I'm going to place this concept right in front of you."

You want to talk about being filled with the Spirit? Then you had better be talking about gratitude at the same time. Do you sense a spirit of ingratitude and complaining in your life? Then you had better search your heart and find out if you have been grieving or quenching the Holy Spirit of God.

Where the Spirit is, there is gratitude. Think of it as the cologne of heaven. When a Spirit-filled man or woman walks through a room, you catch a whiff of a heavenly fragrance…the aroma of a thankful heart.

Notice yet another piece of evidence in a very familiar passage.

> *Be anxious for nothing, but in everything by prayer and supplication, with thanksgiving, let your requests be made known to God.* (Philippians 4:6)

Many people read the verse like this: "Be anxious for nothing, but in everything by prayer, and supplication, and thanksgiving…"

But the word before *thanksgiving* isn't *and,* is it?

The word is *with.*

Don't overlook that distinction! It's so important. The *with* in this verse means that whether it is prayer or supplication or any other kind of praying to God, it is always to be mixed with thanksgiving. Thanksgiving belongs to all of the properties of prayer.

> When you are asking God for something, it is always with thanksgiving.
>
> When you are praising God for something, it is always with thanksgiving.

When you are interceding for someone, it is always with thanksgiving.

When you are a "watchman on the wall" for your church, or for your family, or for your nation, don't forget that with all those requests, all of them should be mixed and blended generously with thanksgiving to God for all He has done.

In Philippians 4:6, Paul seems to be mentioning several kinds of prayer, but he focuses in on one kind of response. And that is the response of gratitude. It is to be present in all of our prayers, no matter what the content might be.

Have you seen one of those automatic bread makers, that sits on a countertop in your kitchen and turns out beautiful loaves of freshly baked bread? I've heard it's a fun gadget to have around. It comes with a little recipe book for all different kinds of bread. You can add raisins and cinnamon. You can add garlic and parmesan. You can add sugar and spice and everything nice. But you'd better not forget the flour! Flour is a basic ingredient in any kind of bread you make. In the same way, gratitude is the indispensable ingredient in every prayer we offer before the throne of God.

## A CONCERN FOR GOD'S WILL RESULTS IN GRATITUDE

You may find yourself saying, "Jeremiah, I don't know if I'm with you yet on this. I've never heard anything quite like this before. How do I know if this gratitude thing is really God's will for my life, or just one of your personal hobby horses?"

Let me bring you back to another familiar verse, a powerful little prescription for life.

> In everything give thanks; for this is the will of God in Christ Jesus for you. (1 Thessalonians 5:18)

How could God make it any plainer? Would it be more obvious if He sent a couple of angels to hold a banner over the side of an overpass for you to see on the way to work? How obvious does He have to be? A Spirit-filled Christian who is concerned about the will of God must be concerned about gratitude! The text says, "THIS IS THE WILL OF GOD." Wouldn't you like a statement as clear as that when you're trying to figure out whether you should move, or take a new job, or marry someone? Can't you just see stumbling across that in Scripture?

*This is the will of God…that you move to Cleveland.*

*This is the will of God…that you marry Bill (or Betty) Jones.*

People come to me all the time wishing they could find that kind of specific direction in Scripture. They want God to jot them out a neat little prescription: "Do this on Tuesday morning at the corner of Seventh and Main Streets."

Do you want a prescription? Do you want specific direction? Do you want to know the will of God? Here it is! *Be thankful.* Gratitude is the will of God for your life. If you are not a grateful person (and in your heart right now, you know very well whether you are or you aren't), you are not walking in the Spirit. You are out of the will of God, no matter how many gifts of the Spirit you might be exhibiting in your life. To be ungrateful is to be out of the will of God.

You say, "Well, I don't like that." I don't like it much either, but I didn't say it. God said it. The Bible isn't only a sword, it is a hammer. Have you ever been hammered by the Word of God? Let's say you find yourself grousing some afternoon. You're singing a sad story about how bad things are, how your talents are unappreciated, how your kids aren't measuring up, how your job is going south on you, how rotten the weather is, how the government did you wrong… and you work yourself into a really bleak, foul mood.

Friend, according to 1 Thessalonians 5:18, you are out of the will of God.

Let me show you how powerfully this is taught in God's Word. In Romans chapter 1, Paul begins describing a culture sliding toward disintegration. We hear a great deal about evolution in the media and in our public school classrooms, but this is *devolution,* a culture sliding backward into darkness. We don't hear much about that, do we? Yet here in Scripture, as the apostle sets the scene, he adds these significant words in Romans 1:21–22 (NIV):

> For although they knew God, they neither glorified him as God *nor gave thanks to him,* but their thinking became futile and their foolish hearts were darkened. Although they claimed to be wise, they became fools.

Paul told the Romans, "Let me tell you what happens to a culture that rejects God and rejects His natural revelation. They will head down, down, down. And one of the evidences of their decadence, of their rebellion against God, will be their lack of gratitude."

That's at the beginning of the process. Now let me tell you what it's going to be like at the end. Paul wrote to his young friend in the ministry and said, "Timothy, let me tell you what it's going to be like just before Jesus Christ comes back. Let me describe to you how decadent the society is going to be in those days just before He returns."

> But mark this: *There will be terrible times in the last days. People will be lovers of themselves, lovers of money, boastful, proud, abusive, disobedient to their parents…*

What are the next two descriptive words?

> *ungrateful, unholy…* (2 Timothy 3:1–2, NIV)

Ingratitude travels in some pretty bad company, doesn't it? Ingratitude is comfortable with all the sins listed in these verses. I think sometimes we try to shrug it off as if it were no big deal. "Well, that's just my temperament." If that's the case, I want to tell you something. You need to get your temperament fixed! You need to let the Holy Spirit take control of your temperament. We excuse ourselves so often, don't we? We say, "Well, that's just the way I am." Or "It's my environment." Or "It's what I experienced when I was growing up."

Listen to me: if I understand the Bible, the Holy Spirit cuts through all that stuff. He slices right down to the center of you and begins to create within you a spirit that isn't your own, because it is God's Spirit, God's own characteristics in you. When you are controlled by the Spirit of God, gratitude will start to exude from your life. It may even catch you by surprise. It will certainly catch others by surprise when they notice your change in attitude. And you will know that what is coming forth from your life is not something that is naturally and normally yours. It is the supernatural evidence of the Spirit of God at work in your life.

This might not be the sort of teaching you were looking for when you purchased this book. Maybe you were looking for something spectacular instead of this nitty-gritty, rubber-meets-the-road sort of attitude exam. But if the Bible is anything, it is an extremely practical book. Yes, it deals with cosmic issues. Its story reaches into eternity past and cracks open the door to eternity future. But in between, there is a great wealth of help and correction and encouragement for day-to-day life in the trenches.

You and I have both met people who say they are believers and yet have all the signs of being ugly, bitter, mean-spirited folks. How could that be? If you are filled with the Spirit of God, your life is going to be marked by a spirit of gratitude that runs to the very core of who you are. And if that isn't true, whatever else you've got, you haven't got the Holy Spirit controlling your life.

One more thought on this matter of God's will and gratitude. Not only is the will of God clear, but the will of God concerning gratitude is comprehensive.

In Ephesians 5:20, Paul says that the Spirit-filled believer gives thanks to God for *all things*.

In Colossians 3:17 he expands "all things." He writes: "And whatever you do in word or deed, do all in the name of the Lord Jesus, giving thanks to God the Father through Him."

> Whatever we do
>> in word
>>> or in deed
>>>> do all
>>>>> …giving thanks.

In other words, in *everything*. And Paul was the kind of man who practiced what he preached. Some of the "all things" in his life would curl your hair! Yet Paul stayed grateful right up to the end. Do you know where Paul wrote most of his words to the Ephesians, to the Colossians, and to his friend Timothy? He wrote them in prison. He wrote them while in chains.

Now, wait a minute! Gratitude belongs in the palace, not in the prison! You get grateful on a cruise ship, maybe. You feel gratitude when you have a soft bed with clean sheets and three square meals a day. But in a Roman prison? In a cell?

Paul got it done. In whatever you do, in whatever you say, he tells us, be grateful. When I read his letters and think over the events of the man's life, I am overwhelmed. Sometimes people in our fellowship say to me, "I know I ought to be grateful, Pastor, but you don't know what's going on in my life. This has been a killer of a year, and I'm not in a grateful mood."

Yet the plain fact is, the man who wrote these letters so permeated with thanksgiving had a killer of a *life*. Listen to this small recitation he gave to the Corinthians from earlier in his career:

> I have worked harder than any of them.
> I have served more prison sentences!
> I have been beaten times without number.
> I have faced death again and again.
> I have been beaten the regulation thirty-nine stripes by the
> Jews five times.
> I have been beaten with rods three times.
> I have been stoned once.
> I have been shipwrecked three times.
> I have been twenty-four hours in the open sea.

> In my travels I have been in constant danger from rivers
> and floods, from bandits, from my own countrymen, and
> from pagans. I have faced danger in city streets, danger in
> the desert, danger on the high seas, danger among false
> Christians. I have known exhaustion, pain, long vigils, hunger
> and thirst, doing without meals, cold and lack of clothing. (2
> Corinthians 11:23–27, Phillips)

To top it all off, he spent his last days in a Roman dungeon and was martyred for his faith. But let me tell you this, Paul was a thankful man. Paul's life trailed the fragrance of gratitude that we can still smell drifting up from these pages two thousand years later.

You see, gratitude isn't something that develops within us because of the good things that happen in our lives. When writing to the Romans, Paul wrote a similar list of "woes" that can happen to a believer. Have you read those words in Romans 8? He writes of tribulation, and distress, and persecution, and famine, and nakedness, and peril, and sword. But then he seems to shout at the end of that long list, "Yet in all these things we are more than conquerors through Him who loved us!"

In all of *what* things, Paul? Distress and persecution, famine and nakedness, sword and peril. He said in all these things we're not just conquerors, we're *more* than conquerors. How can you have a spirit like that? How do you explain it?

The Holy Spirit.

That's the only explanation I have. The Holy Spirit comes to create within you that which is unexplainable in any other terms. When you are filled with the Spirit of God, He gives you a sense of victory and triumph over the issues of life so that you can live in the prison in the same way that you live in the palace.

That's why Paul was able to say, "I can handle it when I abound and I can handle it when I am abased…I can enjoy the good, sweet times, and I can take the dark, difficult times in stride, because my contentment is in the person of Jesus Christ."

Henry Nouwen once wrote, "Where there is a reason for gratitude, there can always be found a reason for bitterness. It is here that we're faced with the freedom to make a decision. We can decide to be grateful or to be bitter."

*When we are filled with the Spirit...*

> We learn how to count our blessings instead of our crosses.
> We learn how to count our gains instead of our losses.
> We learn how to count our joys instead of our woes.
> We learn how to count our friends instead of our foes.
> We learn how to count our smiles instead of our tears.
> And our courage instead of our fears.
> And our full years instead of our lean ones.
> And our kind deeds instead of our mean ones.
> And our health instead of our wealth.
> We count on God instead of ourself.

It's all a matter of perspective. Helen Keller once made an observation when she was growing up. She said, "I have often thought it would be a blessing if each human being were stricken blind and deaf for a few days sometime in early adult life. Darkness would make them more appreciative of sight and silence would teach them the joys of sound."

God has to beat on us sometimes before we wake up to what we have and how grateful we ought to be.

In Africa, I am told, there is a little berry called the "taste berry." It is called by that name because it changes your taste so that everything you eat tastes sweet and pleasant. Someone has said that gratitude is the Christian's taste berry. If you take the attitude of gratitude and devour it in your being, it turns even the difficult, sour things into the sweet.

When you are filled with the Spirit of God, you will be grateful.

Yes, you may live in a shack on a dead end in Chickasha. But oh, those Oklahoma sunrises! God brings a new one every day and delivers it to your window, free of charge.

Pull back those curtains and take a look. Then give Him thanks.

# 4

## The Converting Power of Grace

### I Once Was Lost but Now Am Found

From: Captured by Grace—No One Is Beyond the Reach of a Loving God

A s Jesus sat down to teach, His eyes swept across the hodge-podge of humanity that was eagerly gathering around Him. As usual, it was neither the community's best nor its brightest who sought His wisdom today. Tax profiteers were here. Pleasure seekers were here. It was a representative assortment of the unwashed masses dismissively referred to as "sinners."

The religious leaders took their usual post on the periphery of the crowd—strategic placement for murmuring and whispering caustic commentary, also for avoiding dreaded physical contact with the ceremonially impure.

Then the world seemed to grow silent as the Master began to teach. Or rather to tell stories. The rabbi loved good narratives—long ones, short ones. This time He delivered His tales in a matching set, three variations on a theme. The subject might have been described as "lost and found."

First, there was a quick glimpse of a shepherd combing the rugged hills for a lost sheep, even to the point of neglecting ninety-nine others. Everyone could visualize the shepherd triumphantly bearing the bleating prize across his shoulders as his friends applauded.

Heaven, Jesus said, is something like those applauding shepherds. End of story.

Then He talked about a lost coin. This time the searcher was a frantic housekeeper, shaking every chair and pitcher to find that coin. Finally, with a little shriek of delight, the woman held high her prize. Like the shepherd, she couldn't help but call her friends and throw a party. There was a dash of humor in this story, and the crowd laughed appreciatively.

The angels, Jesus said, have such celebrations when even one sinner has a change of heart.

What must the Pharisees and scribes have made of all this—sheep and coins and clapping? What did misplaced possessions have to do with the Law of Moses? Purity—that was the issue, according to their Law! The only valid question was whether the shepherd or the woman were legally holy.

But Jesus wasn't finished for the day. Now He brought out the main course, to which the preceding dishes were mere appetizers. He told a story for the ages: one that echoes through history, that disarms every hearer, that no one ever tires of retelling. It is a story that loses nothing in any culture or setting, no matter where it is shared. Charles Dickens, the greatest of novelists in the English language, called this the greatest short story of all time.

This story concerned a lost son, but it was more than a quick sketch this time. With the skill of a masterful artist, Jesus painted the picture of the wealthy father of two young men, one of whom disgraces the family on an illicit spending spree. Each of the three main characters—father, elder son, lost son—will respond to the crisis in ways we would never quite have predicted. Yet when the story is complete, the hearer sits quietly and finally says, "Yes. The story is absolutely true. I know it is true because it is *my* story."

This is the power of the Prodigal. No one can help but see himself in the narrative. The painter Rembrandt was transfixed by the picture he found painted in the words of Luke 15. Early in his career, the artist was known to be an arrogant and pleasure-driven young man, and he painted himself into his version as the wandering son from the story, found in the shame of an Amsterdam brothel. Then, at the very end of his life, a wiser man but an ailing one, Rembrandt returned to the story again, this time painting himself into the parable as the loving father, embracing his child. Light emanates from the tender face of the father in a scene of raw emotional power.

The resulting masterpiece, *The Return of the Prodigal*, reached through the centuries to change the life of the Christian writer Henri Nouwen, who spent days silently meditating upon the spiritual resonance of the scene. As a result, Father Nouwen wrote a masterpiece of his own, a book named after the painting: *The Return of the Prodigal.*[1]

Nouwen observes in his book that early in life, Rembrandt had responded, like many people, to the story of the son. As an older and wiser man, he sees the story in a new light. It has become for him a story not of the son who sins but of the father who forgives.

I believe Rembrandt and Nouwen were both on the right track.

## FATHER OF MASTERPIECES

The story told by Jesus is a masterpiece that begets more masterpieces, in every medium. John Newton's "Amazing Grace" is one more in the list, because Newton saw himself as the world-wizened son who stumbled home. How could the words be chosen more simply or poignantly? *I once was lost but now am found.* He was that coin. He was that lamb. Above all, he was that wandering child who had brought shame to his birthright, who had committed acts his conscience would never turn loose. *Once lost; now found.* This is the story of all stories.

That other homeward-bound rebel, the apostle Paul, used the word *lost* only once in all his letters. But he, too, identified with the parable. Every sermon he preached in Acts and every epistle he wrote in our Bible echo with the themes of lost and found—of the helpless child captured by grace. Paul might well have seen himself everywhere in the story and even its setting: in the crowd that surrounded Jesus, among the scoffing Pharisees. He might have seen himself as the elder son, too proud of his own behavior to understand the grace he witnessed. In the end, of course, he had to join each one of us in identifying with the wandering, wasteful son. That identification is the needful step for every lost child in search of salvation.

We tend to focus on the player in this drama who carries the action— he who leaves, sins, and returns. Yet Rembrandt was absolutely right in placing the father at the center of the canvas. The Scriptures do no less, for the forgiving father is mentioned twelve times in twenty verses. He may go nowhere. He may "do" very little, at least visibly. But he is the true hero of this story, the true protagonist. We cannot understand any other character or any other development in this tale unless we see it through the eyes of that radiant father, without whom there is no story, no joy, no hope.

# The Humiliation of the Father

*A certain man had two sons. And the younger of them said*
*to his father, "Father, give me the portion of goods that falls to*
*me." So he divided to them his livelihood.*

—Luke 15:11–12

There is nothing remarkable about the launch point of this parable: another restless young man with the cravings but not the capital. He lacks the maturity to respect the source of all that he has and all that he is. He simply wants what is coming to him.

Any young man would have known exactly where he stood. The Jewish Law made it clear and simple; you can read the fine print in Deuteronomy 21:17. In the case of two brothers, the older got two-thirds; the youngest got the rest. Either portion might be a nice fortune, but the catch was that the father needed to be dead first.

The second son's real message, then, is: "I can't wait for you to die, Dad."

Any normal father in that part of the world (or nearly any other part) would have slapped his son across the face and pushed him out on the doorstep—and he wouldn't have gotten any argument from the Jewish Law. But read between the lines of Luke, and you'll know very soon in the story that this is no common head of household. By the simple act of granting the insulting request, the father showed himself to be a man of grace.

This is a father who could see into the future. He knew the desolation and heartbreak that lay ahead for his son. He knew his own heartbreak. Yet he stood by the door and watched his son turn his back coldly and leave, taking with him one-third of the estate.

And what about that estate? We think in terms of stocks and bonds, the family silver, any real estate. The father in this story is clearly a man of means. We notice that his holdings included cattle and the acreage to keep them, servants and slaves, the ability to throw a great banquet at a moment's notice.

According to strict law, the father's land needn't be sold until his death. Again, a son late for distant parties would ignore such considerations. At the public sale of one-third of the land, every neighbor for miles would see into the family's shame.

In a small country with land at a premium, family inheritance was serious business. For the case of a young man who had lost his birthright among the Gentiles and dared to return home, a special ritual called the *kezazah* ("the cutting off") was established. According to Kenneth E. Bailey, the community would break a pot in front of the boy. They would cry out that the offender was cut off from his people and then turn their backs upon him forever.[2]

This wasn't a matter of sowing a few wild oats with the fallback plan of coming home later to take a place in the family business. This was a forever thing; a matter of drawing a line in the sand, insulting everyone on the other side, and disowning your people before they disown you. It was to say, "I invite you to ostracize me, and I don't care."

We place ourselves in the shoes of the father and wonder how we would respond. What emotions would dictate our actions? For many, the answer would be anger. Yet in this tale, the father's emotion is *disciplined love*. That kind of love has no strings, no conditions. It knowingly leaves every door open to hurt.

God's grace finds an expression infinitely repeated in His willingness to accept our insult. We stand before Him and say, "Give me what is mine," as if responsibility and obedience weren't part of the legacy. Who would want to take leave of His wonderful palace? Yet that's you and me. We go our way, to His heartbreak, until we have injured ourselves to our capacity of being injured.

God could take the stance of many parents and bar the doors, lock us in our rooms, and breed in us hearts of rebellion. Yet He stands and watches us set out on the path of misery, knowing it is the only way we will grow a heart of humble obedience. There is no limit to the mileage He will allow us to wander, no limit to the patience with which He awaits our return.

Paul the apostle and Newton the navigator understood just how far it was possible to travel before sailing off the edge of the world. For Paul, it was possible to take part in the murder of the saints. For Newton, it was possible to assist in the enslavement of the innocent. For Paul, the far country was a few hidden rooms in Jerusalem. For Newton, the far country was the coast of Africa.

This particular distance is measured not in miles but in misery.

## SEPARATION FROM THE FATHER

*And not many days after, the younger son gathered*
*all together, journeyed to a far country, and there*
*wasted his possessions with prodigal living. But when*
*he had spent all, there arose a severe famine in that land, and*
*he began to be in want. Then he went and joined himself to a*
*citizen of that country, and he sent him into his fields to feed*
*swine. And he would gladly have filled his stomach with the*
*pods that the swine ate, and no one gave him anything.*

—LUKE 15:13–16

Cash in hand, the Prodigal sets out for the far country. Jesus gives it no name, because it's a place that is nowhere and everywhere. No matter who you are and where you live, there is a far country. No map is necessary. All you need is a sinful nature and a restless soul, and you are on your way.

For the son, that far country is all about sensuality, dissipation, and sexual adventurism—the cheapest bait Satan has to offer: "Eat, drink, and be merry." The problem with sensuality is that it fails to notice anything but the object of its lust. In this case, the Prodigal hasn't reckoned upon a local famine. Far earlier than he had imagined it (though he most likely never imagined it at all), his wallet runs dry.

Now he must turn from ceaseless partying to ceaseless labor. Poverty leaves him no choice. He finds himself working on the same sort of farm he has only recently liquidated. Every day he cannot help but see the true, enduring value of the land and the cattle.

But it is too late. He cannot bring back the estate he squandered—nor the love of the family he abandoned.

## MANIPULATION OF THE FATHER

> *But when he came to himself, he said, "How many of my*
> *father's hired servants have bread enough and to spare, and I*
> *perish with hunger! I will arise and go to my father and will*
> *say to him, 'Father, I have sinned against heaven and before*
> *you, and I am no longer worthy to be called your son.*
> *Make me like one of your hired servants.'"*
>
> —LUKE 15:17–19

For as many years as I have read and reflected and preached and prayed over this parable, I have been drawn to three words in this passage. Those three words change the whole course of the story.

The three words come when the Prodigal *came to himself.*

What exactly happened when he "came to himself"? I've heard many sermons that fix upon that phrase as the moment of grace. We imagine that the Prodigal feels deep conviction for the sins he has committed, and we imagine him going to his knees to confess and repent.

Frankly, that's a stretch.

Read the passage again and look for any word such as *sorry* or *remorseful.* Is it all about his guilty soul, or is it actually about his empty stomach? Does he sincerely repent, or does he just have good common sense about getting a square meal?

We cannot be certain of the answer—or, more to the point, Jesus keeps it dark. For in a parable we see exactly what the Master desires us to see. And what He wants us to know for now is that the Prodigal knows he needs help. He surrenders. If there is any slim hope of his reinstatement at home, then at the very least he must repay every cent he has squandered. Working as a pig farmer, he knows he will never make it that far. As a matter of fact, he hasn't even been paid for his labor ("No one gave him anything" [verse 16]). He only thought that slopping hogs was reaching the bottom; slopping them for free—even lower.

So now he is desperate enough to consider slinking home. He sees himself at the very bottom of the pecking order, no longer a son but a servant. In time, maybe over a number of years, he could work off his debt.

It is essential that we, Jesus' listeners, understand that the Prodigal is still unprepared for grace. He is still running his own plans, only sadder and wiser in running them. Whether he realizes it or not, he is still securely within the borders of the far country, a self-chosen exile from the rescue of unconditional love.

We might prefer that the Prodigal "redeem himself," but that would be a misunderstanding of this parable and a misunderstanding of grace. No one on this planet has the ability to redeem him- or herself. Every one of us, like the Prodigal, must ultimately throw him- or herself on the mercy of the court.

But wait—are we *certain* the Prodigal isn't penitent? Listen to his speech he is preparing to give: "Father, I have sinned against heaven and before you, and I am no longer worthy to be called your son."

Again, Kenneth Bailey offers us a surprising glimpse behind the details. The Pharisees in Jesus' audience would recognize the son's speech as the words of Pharaoh when he tried to manipulate Moses into lifting the plagues (see Exodus 10:16). The Egyptian ruler certainly had no contrite heart; his words were simply damage control for the natural disasters that were ravaging his land. He would have said whatever Moses wanted him to say.[3]

Many a humble word has been spoken when someone is at the mercy of someone else. Words are cheap and inadmissible as evidence of a repentant heart. The Prodigal was simply seeking access to what he hadn't already consumed of his father's estate.

In other words, he is like you or me trying to save ourselves, completely on our own.

## RECONCILIATION WITH THE FATHER

*And he arose and came to his father. But when he was still a*
*great way off, his father saw him and had compassion, and ran*

*and fell on his neck and kissed him. And the son said to him,*
*"Father, I have sinned against heaven and in your sight, and*
*am no longer worthy to be called your son."*

—LUKE 15:20–21

My mind's eye has always held a vivid image of this scene. I cannot imagine a picture more laden with emotion.

Here is the Prodigal, clad in shredded rags that had once been the high fashion of the moment. He is far thinner than anyone remembers him. His beard is clotted with dust, and his hair falls unkempt over his sagging shoulders. Like vagabonds everywhere, he clutches his meager possessions in a greasy sack, and he bears the odors of desperate alleys. Perhaps during the last few moments he has walked past old acquaintances, boyhood friends, and servants who failed to recognize him.

But the father doesn't even hesitate. He knows his boy immediately, because he has been watching, ever vigilant. His grieving imagination has already worked out how his son would appear on that glorious day of his return.

From the Greek text, we know that the father was not indoors when this storm-beaten scarecrow appeared on the horizon. The patriarch was out keeping watch, as a shepherd would do for a lost sheep, as a woman would do for the lost circle of silver. The father walks down this road each day, as far as he might safely venture from his estate, propelled only by hope for the reunion upon which he has set his heart. We know that he kept watch with all that was in him, for that is the essence of all three stories Jesus tells in Luke 15—a relentless pursuit of the lost treasure.

The father, then, sees the shell of his son from a distance, and he is consumed by compassion. He takes in the labored steps, the bent posture, the very picture of weary surrender, and there is no room in the father's heart for any substance but love. So joyful, so uncontrollable is the emotion within him that he begins to run toward the figure—even to "race," we are told. This would be unseemly for a Middle Eastern man of his estate. Everything was to be done with quiet dignity. To run means taking up his mantle in his hand, so that he won't stumble. It means exposing his bare legs. All of these things are beneath the pride of a patriarch. But true love is a powerful force. It erupts on occasion. It is totally unself-conscious.

If the sincerity of the son is ambiguous, there can be no mistake about the heart of the father. And that touches upon the very essence of this parable. The power comes from the father's grace, not the son's guilt.

There is still, however, the issue of public shame—for the boy and his clan. The father is more than aware of that. Therefore he humbles himself in running. He meets the boy in stride. He enfolds him in the full acceptance of his embrace, and he takes on his child's humiliation by his very body language.[4]

Try to imagine the story otherwise. We might yet have been moved if the son knocked at the door, went down on his knees, and had his apology gruffly accepted by the father. We might call it justice tempered by mercy. But nothing of the kind happens here. Instead, the father commits himself fully before a word can leave the mouth of his son, before the son can come across the property, before the son could even be recognized by anyone other than a parent who brought him into the world. The son's carefully prepared speech will be delivered as planned, but only after he has been showered in joy, grace, and kisses. By this time, the speech is neither rote nor rigid. The Prodigal is a helpless child again, secure in his father's arms with no need to plan or contrive. Only now is repentance genuine, when it floats upon a sea of grace.

There at the very edge of the village, a supernatural event has taken place. On this spot, grace has overwhelmed guilt. The Prodigal has come to that place as a lost person. He has not found himself any more than the sheep or the coin found themselves. In all cases, it took the obsessive love of the searcher for the lost thing to be redeemed.

The primary miracle is the insistence of grace. A secondary miracle is the thawing of a frozen heart. Even the selfish, calculating Prodigal cannot withstand the sight of his running, weeping father surrendering his high position to meet him at the edge of disgrace. In that moment grace takes him captive, and he sees what his rebellious soul has not until now allowed him to see: the beauty of his father's love, the absolute value of his acceptance, the sweet joys of loyalty and obedience. As far as his conscience goes, no one need tell him the depth of the pain he has brought to his home. He knows it now not simply with his mind but in the furthest depths of his heart.

That heart is broken, yet his soul is mended. Such is the supernatural event of grace.

## CELEBRATION OF THE FATHER

> *But the father said to his servants, "Bring out the best robe and*
> *put it on him, and put a ring on his hand and sandals on his*
> *feet. And bring the fatted calf here and kill it, and let us eat and*
> *be merry; for this my son was dead and is alive again; he was*
> *lost and is found." And they began to be merry.*

—LUKE 15:22–24

Joy cares nothing for solitude. Somehow it always wants to invite a few friends.

There are so many things the Prodigal wants to say at this moment, so many things he *must* say to his father. Yet his father seems to be in no hurry to hear the lurid details of history or the fine print of confession. He is whirling in every direction, calling servants and grabbing slaves by the elbow. He sees in his mind a party such as never has been thrown in these parts.

Once it was the son who was so impatient for parties. The roles have reversed. The father wants the most expensive clothing in the house, the finest jewelry, the most elegant shoes. He insists upon the prime cut of the best beef that can be found on the ranch.

Every command is a meaningful expression of love to his son. The best robe would be the father's own, and that would signify the son's complete restoration to the family. The ring was a symbol of business, used to imprint wax and seal a deal. The ring said, "You are part of our daily operations. You may transact business on our behalf." The shoes squelched any possibility of the son returning as a servant. Only the family wore shoes. The fatted calf was simply an expression of deep joy—the best course for the happiest event.

As Jesus has said earlier, "There is joy in the presence of the angels of God over one sinner who repents" (Luke 15:10). Now we have the earthly picture of that joy.

## CONDEMNATION OF THE FATHER

> *Now his older son was in the field. And as he came and drew near to the house, he heard music and dancing. So he called one of the servants and asked what these things meant. And he said to him, "Your brother has come, and because he has received him safe and sound, your father has killed the fatted calf." But he was angry and would not go in. Therefore his father came out and pleaded with him. So he answered and said to his father, "Lo, these many years I have been serving you; I never transgressed your commandment at any time; and yet you never gave me a young goat that I might make merry with my friends. But as soon as this son of yours came, who has devoured your livelihood with harlots, you killed the fatted calf for him." And he said to him, "Son, you are always with me, and all that I have is yours. It was right that we should make merry and be glad, for your brother was dead and is alive again, and was lost and is found."*

—LUKE 15:25–32

So compelling is the interplay between this father and son that we are often taken by surprise when a third character walks onto the stage. As we knew from the beginning, there is an older son. He is the heir who stands to inherit two-thirds of the estate. He has bided his time and paid his dues in the family business.

When little brother came home, the older son was not there. We can only imagine him approaching the homestead after a long day of supervising the activities on a ranch. What is this music drifting across the lawn? What is the laughter and happy shouting coming from a habitually quiet estate?

A servant scurries by on some errand, and the older son takes him aside for questioning. The servant fills him in: "It's your brother—he's back, and your father is throwing the bash to end all bashes!"

The young fellow hurries on, and the brother stands there, trying to process what he has heard. *Can this be? My little brother is not dead after all? And why would our father throw a party for someone who destroyed our name and went through a third of our wealth?*

But for the most part, it's not really about *we*. It's about *me*. The more he thinks about it, the angrier and more self-righteous the older brother becomes. By the time he confronts his father, he is refusing to even call the guest of honor a brother. He is "this son of yours" (verse 30). And the message is, "Is this what you call justice? Rewarding a disgrace and ignoring loyalty?"

I have come to two conclusions about this older brother.

1. *He was a son who was living like a servant.* "Lo, these many years I have been serving you" (verse 29). Has he been doing it for love, or was it just good business? Go back to verse 12, and you might be surprised to discover that the father didn't just give the younger brother his share; he gave *both* sons what they had coming to them. When the father said, "All that I have is yours," he was simply stating what had become fact some time back. The older brother was a wealthy young man—not only in hard cash but in the love of his father. Unfortunately, somewhere along the line, he had *become* his work. He was all about earning, proving. Grace made no sense to him.

2. *The older brother was a sinner who thought he was a saint.* He says, "I never transgressed your commandment" (verse 29). Oh, really? That's a bit hard for us to imagine. There is no such thing as a perfect son. In some sense, every son or daughter among us is a prodigal. The older brother may have never left the estate, but he had still fled to the far country of

pride and self-righteousness—much like Paul, who never left Jerusalem. Remember, prodigal distance is measured not in miles but in misery. The older son appears to be every bit as miserable as his brother. In fact, he refuses to enter the house where the party is in full swing (verse 28).

That's one of the saddest lines in Scripture. One son was so far from obedience, yet he basked in grace. The other was little *but* obedient, and he never received the priceless treasure that was within his reach all along.

How many of us share a frightening resemblance to that older brother? How about you? Could that gift be right there before you even now? Maybe you didn't travel to the Prodigal's den of sensuality. You might have taken the room right next door, where you found the dungeon of grim obedience. In this story, that was the harder one to escape.

These are two sides of the same coin: law and licentiousness. Either one makes slaves, and only in grace is liberation possible.

## LOST AND FOUND

Jesus finishes His trilogy and looks up at the crowd. Before Him are the so-called sinners—prodigals all. Many of them are visibly moved: faces wet or hidden in hands. More than a few are openly weeping. How could they *not* have identified with a character who broke every rule, spat in the face of all that was good and true, and somehow received love rather than condemnation? This is like no story they've ever heard. Could God really be like that father?

Beyond that layer of listeners, Jesus watches for the reaction of the older brothers—the scribes and Pharisees, grimly obedient laborers who pay endless dues on the ranches of Mosaic Law.

What Jesus sees does not surprise Him. Smugness. Smirking. Educated as they are, many of them probably don't identify with the character in the story who so clearly took their part. The self-righteous are like that—amazingly incapable of looking into the mirror of self-inspection.

Jesus has told these stories very deliberately. As He prepared to teach, He couldn't help but hear the mumbled criticisms about how He'd been spending His time—dining with sinners! Socializing with tax collectors! Imagine.

So He has told two stories that answer the question, "What is the value of the lost thing?"

First He has spoken of a sheep, which has reasonable value. The shepherd will go out of his way to find it.

Then He has spoken of a coin, with more buying power than a lamb. Therefore the woman will comb the house with proportionate urgency.

Then, after these sample problems, Jesus has brought the final exam. If a sheep has a value of $x$, and a silver coin has a value of, say, $10x$—then what value is carried by a misplaced soul? Is it $1,000x$? $1,000,000x$? No mathematics can express such a sum. It would crash the theological computer.

That was one they didn't teach in Pharisee school. The value of Law they understood; the value of humanity was simply off topic.

Jesus said, in essence, "Here is the answer to the question. The rescue of one lost soul is worth more than the gold of a billion galaxies; therefore, it is cause for angelic celebration. The rescue of one lost soul brings the Creator of the universe Himself thundering down the path to embrace you. It sets off a celebration that never ends. It restores the lost soul to its family. It affords the soul the right to transact work for the kingdom. It invites the reign of love and grace, so that no sin you've ever committed even enters the equation. That is the value of one lost soul."

And Jesus might well have added, "You Pharisees have more facts about God than anyone. You are walking encyclopedias of holiness. You know what you need to do. As for Me, I'm here to keep watch on that lonely road, at the edge of the village, that highway to the far country. I know the name of every soul who wanders that road. I know the pain of every heartache they feel. And I am here to tell them what you will not tell them. I am here to put a robe of pure white upon their shoulders, to hide their sodden rags forever. And I am here to lay down My life and take on every stroke of punishment they have earned, because I can bear it and they cannot.

"After that, if you will but walk through this open door—we'll throw parties that put the far country to shame."

## Moments of Grace

Which character in the story of the Prodigal Son is most like you? Are you a parent grieved over the sin of another? Are you yourself a backslider and a wayward soul? A responsible citizen yet filled with silent resentment like the older brother? Or is it possible you're a combination of all three?

Whatever your condition, remind yourself that you are worth more to God than the gold of a billion galaxies. He is seeking you, waiting for you, watching over you, and wanting to lead you to new levels of joy, peace, and strength. Today, begin your prayer to the Lord with these words: "Dear Lord, I am just like . . ." and name your character. Tell the Lord all about it, and feel the uplift of His loving grace.

# 5

## INTEGRITY: WHEN THE MIRROR DOESN'T LIE

### (JAMES 1:19–27)

From: WHAT TO DO WHEN
YOU DON'T KNOW WHAT TO DO

*But be doers of the word,*
*and not hearers only, deceiving yourselves.*

A New England teacher quizzed a group of college-bound high school juniors and seniors on the Bible. The quiz preceded a Bible as Literature class he planned to teach at what was generally considered one of the better public schools in the nation. Among the more unusual answers from these students were, "Sodom and Gomorrah were lovers," and "Jezebel was Ahab's donkey."

Other students thought that the four horsemen appeared on the Acropolis; that the New Testament Gospels were written by Matthew, Mark, Luther, and John; that Eve was created from an apple; and that Jesus was baptized by Moses.

The answer that took the misinformation prize was given by a fellow who was academically in the top 5 percent of his class. The question, "What was Golgotha?" The answer, "Golgotha was the name of the giant who slew the apostle David."

In case you think this is an isolated instance of biblical illiteracy, let me quote the findings of a recent Gallup Poll:

> Eighty-two percent of Americans believe that the Bible is either the literal or "inspired" Word of God ... more than half said they read the Bible at least monthly. Yet half couldn't name even one of the four Gospels.... And fewer than half knew who delivered the Sermon on the Mount.[1]

*USA Today* reported a poll showing that only 11 percent of Americans read the Bible every day. More than half read it less than once a month or not at all.[2] The Barna Research Group conducted a survey that focused only on "born-again" Christians and came up with the following statistics: "Only 18 percent—less than two in every ten—read the Bible every day. Worst of all, 23 percent—almost one in four professing Christians—say they never read the Word of God."[3]

The Bible is available in more than 1,800 languages, and yet someone has observed that the worst dust storm in history would happen if all church members who were neglecting their Bibles dusted them off simultaneously.

I read about a very religious father whose son was studying for the ministry. The boy had decided to go to Europe for an advanced degree, and the father worried that his simple faith would be spoiled by sophisticated, unbelieving professors. "Don't let them take Jonah away from you," he admonished, figuring the swallowed-by-a-greatfish story might be the first part of the Bible to go. Two years later when the son returned, the father asked, "Do you still have Jonah in your Bible?"

The son laughed, "Jonah! That story isn't even in your Bible."

The father replied, "It certainly is! What do you mean?"

Again the son laughed and insisted, "It's not in your Bible. Go ahead, show it to me."

The old man fumbled through his Bible, looking for the Book of Jonah, but he couldn't find it. At last he checked the table of contents for the proper page. When he turned there, he discovered the three pages composing Jonah had been carefully cut from his Bible.

"I did it before I went away," said the son. "What's the difference between my losing the Book of Jonah through studying under nonbelievers or your losing it through neglect?"

James has just written to his believing friends that their spiritual birth was the product of God's Word (1:18). Now he is about to challenge them to take this same Word seriously in their daily walk. The reality of outward trials and inward temptations calls for something more than an initial experience with God. His wisdom is needed every day.

In this central passage on the importance and priority of God's Word, James takes us through a six-step process that begins with the necessary preparation for study and ends with a powerful illustration of the difference the Bible can make in one's life.

# STEP ONE—PREPARATION

Here are four clear directives to help you get started in this important endeavor.

### Concentrate Your Attention

James begins his instructions with the encouragement to be "swift to hear." In James' day, this was very important, because most learning was done through listening. Since few believers had copies of the Scriptures in their possession, they depended on hearing it read and preached in public services. If they were not "swift to hear," they were left behind! Paul reminded the Romans that "faith comes by hearing, and hearing by the word of God" (10:17). The members of the church in Thessalonica captured the meaning of James' words in their approach to the Word of God:

> For this reason we also thank God without ceasing, because when you received the word of God which you heard from us, you welcomed it not as the word of men, but as it is in truth, the word of God, which also effectively works in you who believe. (1 Thessalonians 2:13)

In our culture today, many believers are indifferent to the Word of God. We may be living in the period Paul warned Timothy about when he challenged him to be a courageous preacher:

> For the time will come when they will not endure sound doctrine, but according to their own desires, because they have itching ears, they will heap up for themselves teachers; and they will turn their ears away from the truth, and be turned aside to fables. (2 Timothy 4:3–4)

If, as believers, we have no interaction with non-Christians, no vital ministry to growing believers, and no personal struggle for godliness, it will not be long before the Bible will seem irrelevant to us.

A U.S. Army officer told of the contrast in his pupils during two different eras of teaching at the artillery training school at Fort Sill, Oklahoma. In 1958–60 the attitude was so lax that the instructors had a problem getting the men to stay awake to listen. During the 1965–67 classes, however, the men, hearing the same basic lectures, were alert and took copious notes. The reason: They knew that in less than six weeks they would be facing the enemy in Vietnam.

### Control Your Tongue

When James urged his readers to be "slow to speak," he may have had in mind the open interaction that often took place in the unstructured churches to which he was writing. Sometimes, the assembly would be taken over by those who wished to demonstrate their knowledge by their prolonged speaking.

There is nothing wrong with questions and responses, but it does not take an experienced teacher long to determine whether questions are being asked because answers are being sought or because the questioner thinks he has all the answers already! James' reminder is an echo of these words of our Lord:

> But I say to you that for every idle word men may speak, they will give account of it in the day of judgment. For by your words you will be justified, and by your words you will be condemned. (Matthew 12:36–37)

If you have studied the Wisdom Literature of the Old Testament, you have seen this counsel over and over again:

> In the multitude of words sin is not lacking, but he who restrains his lips is wise. (Proverbs 10:19)

> He who has knowledge spares his words, and a man of understanding is of a calm spirit. Even a fool is counted wise when he holds his peace; when he shuts his lips, he is considered perceptive. (Proverbs 17:27–28)
>
> Do not be rash with your mouth, and let not your heart utter anything hastily before God. For God is in heaven, and you on earth; therefore let your words be few. For a dream comes through much activity, and a fool's voice is known by his many words. (Ecclesiastes 5:2–3)

It is said that on one occasion, a young man came to the great philosopher Socrates to be trained as an orator. In his first meeting with his teacher, he began to talk without stopping. When Socrates could get a word in, he said, "Young man, I will have to charge you a double fee."

"A double fee? Why is that?"

"I will have to teach you two sciences. First, how to hold your tongue, and then how to use it."

### Contain Your Anger

Often in the early church assemblies, the anger of the participants would explode as different ones expounded their own personal opinions about various issues. When James commanded them to be "slow to wrath," the term *wrath* meant "an ongoing attitude of bitterness and dislike." Such an attitude was in opposition to the righteousness of God. Look at these warnings:

> He who is impulsive exalts folly. (Proverbs 14:29)
> He who is slow to anger is better than the mighty, and he
> who rules his spirit than he who takes a city. (Proverbs 16:32)
> A fool vents all his feelings, but a wise man holds them
> back. (Proverbs 29:11)
> An angry man stirs up strife, and a furious man abounds
> in transgression. (Proverbs 29:22)

When Paul wrote to the Ephesians, he told them, "Let all bitterness, wrath, anger, clamor, and evil speaking be put away from you, with all malice" (4:31).

### Clean Up Your Life

The fourth guideline is to lay aside all filthiness and overflow of wickedness. If a person's moral life is out of control (which may include the tongue and temper), the result can be devastating to any hearing or understanding of God's Word. James' instruction is clear. There must be a spiritual housecleaning. It is not enough to clean up the outside of the house; the inside must be swept clean of all filth and evil. The use of the word *filthiness* in this regard is most instructive:

> The word ... strictly speaking is used of wax in the ear.... Sin in our lives is like having wax in our ears; it prevents the Word of truth from reaching our hearts; for if it cannot penetrate through the ear, it will not come down to the heart.... We as Christians must take the wax out of our ears, so that the Word may influence our lives. I believe definitely that James here speaks of the born-again Christian whose sin may be like wax in his ear preventing him from hearing and doing the Word of God.[4]

## STEP TWO—EXAMINATION

By concentrating their attention, controlling their tongue, containing their anger, and cleaning up their lives, the believers are now ready to receive the Word that had already been planted in them. This is not the Word of salvation—they have already received that (James 1:18)! This is rather the Word of instruction that is so crucial to growth. Humbly, each believer is to prepare to hear that Word which is able to bring him to maturity in Christ. Simon J. Kistemaker comments:

Once again, the writer resorts to an illustration from nature. A plant needs constant care. If a plant is deprived of water and nurture, it will die. Thus if the readers who have heard the Word fail to pay attention, they will die a spiritual death. The Word needs diligent care and application, so that the readers may grow and increase spiritually.[5]

The word *receive* is translated several times in the New Testament as "welcome" (Matthew 10:40; Galatians 4:14; Hebrews 11:31). We are not to passively examine the Word that is spoken but are to welcome it into our hearts with anticipation and excitement. We are to come to the reading and the preaching of the Word of God with a sense of anticipation! This should be our attitude each time we approach God's truth.

Mortimer J. Adler in his classic *How to Read a Book* makes this intriguing observation:

> The one time people read for all they are worth is when they are in love and are reading a love letter. They read every word three ways. They read between the lines and the margins. They read the whole in terms of the parts, and each part in terms of the whole. They grow sensitive to context and ambiguity, to insinuation and implication. They perceive the color of words, the order of phrases, and the weight of sentences. They may even take the punctuation into account. Then, if never before, or after, they read carefully and in depth.[6]

When Adler's book first came out, it was advertised in the *New York Times* under the slogan "How to Read a Love Letter." A picture showed a puzzled adolescent perusing a letter, with the following copy underneath:

> This young man has just received his first love letter. He may have read it three or four times, but he is just beginning. To read it as accurately as he would like, would require several dictionaries and a good deal of close work with a few experts

of etymology and philology. However, he will do all right without them. He will ponder over the exact shade of meaning of every word, every comma. She has headed the letter, "Dear John."

"What," he asks himself is the exact significance of those words? Did she refrain from saying "Dearest" because she was bashful? Would "My Dear" have sounded too formal? Jeepers, maybe she would have said "Dear So-and-So" to anybody! A worried frown will now appear on his face. But it disappears as soon as he really gets to thinking about the first sentence. She certainly wouldn't have written that to anybody! And so he works his way through the letter, one moment perched blissfully on a cloud, the next moment huddled miserably behind an eight-ball. It has started a hundred questions in his mind. He could quote it by heart. In fact, he will—to himself—for weeks to come....

If people read books with anything like the same concentration, we'd be a race of mental giants.[7]

I cannot help but wonder what "spiritual giants" we might become if we learned to read the Word of God like this!

## STEP THREE—APPLICATION

Jesus concluded the Sermon on the Mount with the story of the wise and foolish builders. When He had finished with the story, He said, "Therefore whoever hears these sayings of Mine, and does them, I will liken him to a wise man who built his house on the rock" (Matt. 7:24). On another occasion the Savior said, "Blessed are those who hear the word of God and keep it" (Luke 11:28).

It is important to become a good listener to the Word of God, but that in itself is of no lasting value. Having heard what the Word says, we must develop the discipline to put it into practice. We must learn to be more than just hearers; we must learn to be doers. The apostle John understood this truth when he wrote, "My little children, let us not love in word or in tongue, but in deed and in truth" (1 John 3:18).

In James' day, the word *hearer* was used as *auditor* is today. In our college, if a person is auditing a course we offer, he does not take tests, does not get grades, is not working for a degree, and is ineligible for any awards. He is just listening in on the teaching. We cannot allow ourselves to become auditors of the Word of God. Our primary purpose in hearing or reading the Bible must be to do what it says.

### The Casual Approach

In order to illustrate his words, James once again reaches into the everyday life of his readers, as he asks them to consider the mirror. The mirrors of the first century were made out of highly polished metal. They were not mounted on walls but rather were placed flat on tables so that the person who wished to see his reflection had to bend over and look down. Even then he would see a very poor reflection of himself.

If we hear the Word of God and fail to do what it says, we are, James says, like a person who casually looks at his "natural" face, the one he was born with, in a mirror, and then quickly walks away, making no changes in his appearance. Phillips translates the verse like this: "He sees himself, it is true, but he goes off without the slightest recollection of what sort of person he saw in the mirror" (1:24). This casual approach to God's Word produces what Howard Hendricks calls *functionally illiterate* Christians:

> Have you ever seen a Bible "parked" in the rear window of someone's car? That's common where I come from. A guy will come out of church, hop into his car, toss his Bible in the back, and leave it there until the next Sunday. That's quite a statement of the value he places on God's Word. In effect, when it comes to Scripture, he's functionally illiterate six out of seven days a week.[8]

There are many Christians today who refuse to look into the perfect law of liberty because they do not want to face the truth about their lives. They would rather live in deception than to know the truth. They are like the African princess that George Sweeting tells about in one of his books:

> She lived in the heart of the uncivilized jungle, and for years this chieftain's daughter had been told by all that she was the most beautiful woman in the entire tribe. Although she had no mirror to view herself, she had been convinced of her unparalleled beauty. One day when an exploring party traveled through that part of Africa, the princess was given a mirror as a gift. For the first time in her life she was able to see her own reflection. Her immediate reaction was to smash the mirror on the nearest rock. Why? Because for the first time in her life she knew the truth. What other people had told her all those years was of little importance. What she had believed about herself made no difference. She saw for the first time that her beauty was not genuine. It was false.[9]

### The Careful Approach

The forgetful hearer simply glances at the Word of God and goes his way, but the true hearer gazes at God's Word. To denote this careful look, James uses a Greek word that means "to look at something that is out of the normal line of vision." It is the same word that was used to denote the way Peter, John, and Mary stooped down to look into the empty tomb on resurrection morning (Luke 24:12; John 20:5, 11). It is also found in 1 Peter 1:12 where we are told that the angels desire "to look into" the glories of salvation that are outside of their personal experience. The careful look intently examines the truth and meaning of the Word because there is a desire to put into practice everything that God is saying.

As James pictures this careful student of the Word, he sees him doing what he hears. The word for "doing," the Greek *poieetai,* is found only six times in the entire New Testament, four of them in the book of James. It conveys far more than routine observance of commands. From *poieetai* we get our word "poet," and it speaks of creative obedience:

> A poet is one who puts words together in order to express a thought or feeling in a beautiful manner. That is what God wants us Christians to be—poets, creators of the beautiful. We are to be creative in life. We are to take all the experiences, pleasant and unpleasant, and present them as attractive poems to the world around us.[10]

## STEP FOUR—MEDITATION

There is yet another step beyond personal application of the Word. "But he who looks into the perfect law of liberty and continues in it."

There is a basic difference between an explorer and a tourist. The tourist travels quickly, stopping only to observe the highly noticeable or publicized points of interest. The explorer, on the other hand, takes his time to search out all that he can find.

Too many of us read the Bible like tourists and then complain that our devotional times are fruitless. Geoffrey Thomas warns us against such an approach to the Scriptures:

> Do not expect to master the Bible in a day, or a month, or a year. Rather expect often to be puzzled by its contents. It is not all equally clear. Great men of God often feel like absolute novices when they read the Word. The apostle Peter said that there were some things hard to understand in the epistles of Paul (2 Peter 3:16). I am glad he wrote those words because I have felt that often. So do not expect always to get an emotional charge or a feeling of quiet peace when you read the Bible. By the grace of God you may expect that to be a frequent experience, but often you will get no emotional response at all. Let the Word break over your heart and mind again and

again as the years go by and imperceptibly there will come great changes in your attitude and outlook and conduct.[11]

It is crucial that we take the time to explore the Bible if we are to grow. Here are some key Scriptures that extol the virtues of meditation:

> This Book of the Law shall not depart from your mouth, but you shall meditate in it day and night, that you may observe to do according to all that is written in it. For then you will make your way prosperous, and then you will have good success. (Joshua 1:8)
>
> Blessed is the man who walks not in the counsel of the ungodly, nor stands in the path of sinners, nor sits in the seat of the scornful; but his delight is in the law of the LORD, and in His law he meditates day and night. (Psalm 1:1–2)
>
> Oh, how I love Your law! It is my meditation all the day. (Psalm 119:97)
>
> Let the words of my mouth and the meditation of my heart be acceptable in Your sight, O LORD, my strength and my Redeemer. (Psalm 19:14)

If you haven't meditated on God's Word in a long time, maybe Donald Whitney's words will set you free to begin anew:

> Because meditation is so prominent in many spiritually counterfeit groups and movements, some Christians are uncomfortable with the whole subject and suspicious of those who engage in it. But we must remember that meditation is both commanded by God and modeled by the godly in Scripture.… The kind of meditation encouraged in the Bible differs from other kinds of meditation in several ways. While some advocate a kind of meditation in which you do your best to empty your mind, Christian meditation involves filling your mind with God and truth. For some, meditation is an attempt to

achieve complete mental passivity, but biblical meditation requires constructive mental activity. Worldly meditation employs visualization techniques intended to "create your own reality." ... We link meditation with prayer to God and responsible, Spirit-filled human action to effect changes.[12]

## STEP FIVE—MEMORIZATION

The casual Bible student is a forgetful student, but the careful Bible student commits to memory the things on which he meditates. Lorne Sanny of the Navigators looked back over his life and evaluated why he took the time to memorize the Bible (NIV). In an abbreviated form, this is what he said:

> *Deliverance from Sin.* The act of memorizing Scripture doesn't keep me from sin. God's Word does: "I have hidden your word in my heart that I might not sin against you" (Psalm 119:11).
> *Victory over Satan.* We are told in Ephesians 6:17 to combat him with "the sword of the Spirit, which is the word of God." (See also Matthew 4:1–11.)
> *Spiritual Prosperity.* Meditating—thinking, chewing, letting the Word of God linger in our minds day and night—brings spiritual prosperity (Psalm 1).
> *Personal Guidance.* Psalm 119:24 says, "Your statutes are my delight; they are my counselors."
> *Helping Others.* "Have I not written thirty sayings for you, sayings of counsel and knowledge, teaching you true and reliable words, so that you can give sound answers to him who sent you?" (Proverbs 22:20–21).[13]

## STEP SIX—DEMONSTRATION

James concludes this section of his letter by giving three concrete examples of behaviors that will flow from the life of the person who has taken God's Word seriously. For the third time in this first chapter, he warns his readers about the danger of deception (1:16, 22, 26). It is possible, according to James, to think you are living the Christian life when, in actuality, you are just fooling yourself. The three tests he offers to his first-century readers are just as important for us today.

### The Test of Self-Control

When James addresses the subject of the tongue later in this letter, he describes it as "a restless evil, full of deadly poison" (3:8 NIV). He says that if a man is able to control his tongue, "he is a perfect [mature] man" (3:2). Now he ties this matter of self-control to the reality of one's religious claims: "If anyone among you thinks he is religious, and does not bridle his tongue but deceives his own heart, this one's religion is useless" (James 1:26).

> The unruly tongue engages in lying, cursing, and swearing, slander, and filthy language. From man's point of view the hasty word, shading of the truth, the subtle innuendo, and the questionable joke are shrugged off as insignificant. Yet from God's perspective they are a violation of the command to love the Lord God and to love one's neighbor as oneself. A breach of this command renders man's religion of no avail.[14]

### The Test of Spiritual Compassion

The second acid test of real religion is one's attitude toward those in distress. Here James mentions two groups of people: the widows and the orphans. The social conditions in the first century were very hard on such people, for there were not agencies to protect or aid them. Their only help was to be found among their brothers and sisters in Christ. Old Testament law demanded that they be cared for by God's people: "… the stranger and the fatherless and the widow who are within your gates, may come and eat and be satisfied, that the LORD your God may bless you in all the work of your hand which you do" (Deuteronomy 14:29).

The Lord Jesus went so far as to equate His followers' treatment of the distressed with their treatment of Him. He said:

> "For I was hungry and you gave Me food; I was thirsty and you gave Me drink; I was a stranger and you took Me in; I was naked and you clothed Me; I was sick and you visited Me; I was in prison and you came to Me." Then the righteous will answer Him, saying, "Lord, when did we see You hungry and feed You, or thirsty and give You drink? When did we see You a stranger and take You in, or naked and clothe You? Or when did we see You sick, or in prison, and come to You?" And the King will answer and say to them, "Assuredly, I say to you, inasmuch as you did it to one of the least of these My brethren, you did it to Me." (Matthew 25:35–40)

I read about a minister who preached a Sunday sermon about heaven. Next morning, as he was going to town, he met one of his wealthy members who stopped him and said, "Pastor, you preached a good sermon on heaven, but you didn't tell me where heaven is." "Ah," said the preacher, "I am glad of the opportunity this morning. I have just returned from the hilltop up yonder. In that cottage there is a member of our church. She is a widow with two little children. She is sick in one bed and her two children are sick in the other bed. She doesn't have anything in the house—no coal, no bread, no meat, and no milk. If you will buy a few groceries, then go up there yourself and say, 'My sister, I have brought these provisions in the name of the Lord Jesus.' Then ask for a Bible and read Psalm 23, and then go down on your knees and pray—and if you don't see heaven before you get through, I'll pay the bill." The next morning the man said, "Pastor, I saw heaven and spent fifteen minutes there as sure as you are listening."[15]

### The Test of Social Corruption

In regard to society, the believer is to walk a fine line. He is to be completely and compassionately involved with the social problems of his day, but he is not to allow the culture that produced those problems to have any impact upon his holy life. In James' words, he is to "keep [himself] unspotted from the world."

When James speaks of the world, he is talking about the system that is under the control of Satan and in opposition to the purpose of God. John Henry Jowett said, "It is life without high callings, life devoid of lofty ideals. Its gaze is always horizontal, never vertical. Its motto is 'forward,' never 'upward.' It has ambition, but no aspiration."[16]

The Christian is to conduct his life in the world in such a way that he will not be ashamed to face His Lord. Peter says that we must be *diligent* in this regard: "Therefore, beloved, looking forward to these things, be diligent to be found by Him in peace, without spot and blameless" (2 Peter 3:14).

When we come to the hearing or reading of the Word of God with the proper preparation of heart, with a careful examination of its truth, with a determined application of its message, when we meditate upon it and hide its words in our hearts, something dramatic will happen in our lives. We will be changed! This is the promise of God Himself: "So shall My word be that goes forth from My mouth; it shall not return to Me void, but it shall accomplish what I please, and it shall prosper in the thing for which I sent it" (Isaiah 55:11).

Probably there is no more sensational example of the life-transforming power of the Bible than the legendary story of *Mutiny on the Bounty*. In 1788 the *Bounty*, under Captain William Bligh, set sail for the island of Tahiti in the South Seas. After a voyage of ten months, the ship reached the Friendly Islands in Tonga, and the sailors became attached to the native girls. Upon receiving the order to embark, in April 1789 they mutinied, set the captain and a few men adrift in an open boat, and returned to the island.

Captain Bligh survived his ordeal and eventually arrived home in England. A punitive expedition was sent out, which captured fourteen of the mutineers. But nine of them had transferred to another island, where they formed a new colony. Here they degenerated so fast and became so fierce as to make the life of the colony a hell on earth. The chief reason for this was the distillation of whiskey from a native plant. Quarrels, orgies, and murders were a common feature of their life. Finally, all the men except one were killed or had died off.

Alexander Smith was left alone with a crowd of native women and half-breed children. Then a strange thing happened. In a battered chest, he found a Bible. He read it, believed it, and began to live it. Determining to make amends for his past evil life, he gathered the women and children around him and taught them too. Time rolled on. The children grew up and became Christians. The community prospered exceedingly. Nearly twenty years later, an American ship visited the island and brought back to Europe and England word of its peaceful state. This island was a Christian community. There was no disease, no insanity, no crime, no illiteracy, and no strong drink. Life and property were safe, and the moral standards of the people were as high as anywhere in the world. It was a veritable utopia on a small scale. What had brought about this astounding transformation? Just the reading of a book. That book was the Bible.[17]

# 6

## The Joy of Adversity

## (Philippians 1:12–26)

From: Turning Toward Joy—
Discover a Happiness That
Circumstances Cannot Change

*Whether in pretense or in truth, Christ is preached;*
*and in this I rejoice, yes, and will rejoice.*

I t was the bottom of the sixth inning. The Montreal Expos' most feared hitter, Tim Raines, was at the plate. The pitcher glared at the catcher and checked the runner on first base. Then kicking high, he pushed off the rubber and threw as hard as he could. It was the last pitch he would ever throw. A loud sickening crack was heard all over the stadium. Weakened by undiscovered cancer, the humerus bone in Dave Dravecky's pitching arm had snapped in two. "My arm felt like I'd been hit with a meat axe," said the San Francisco Giants' hurler. He grabbed his arm to keep it from flying toward home plate as he screamed, tumbling headfirst to the ground.[1]

While his baseball career was over, his adversity had just begun. After many examinations, the doctors told him that his pitching arm would have to be amputated at the shoulder to guarantee that the cancer would not spread to other parts of his body.

I can't imagine what Dave must have felt as the reality of that news set in. He was in the prime of his career, and under normal circumstances could have expected to play baseball for many more years. But now it was over.

Several weeks after his surgery, Dave Dravecky came back to Jack Murphy Stadium to say thanks to his many San Diego friends. He was greeted with a long standing ovation. As on every other speaking assignment since he came out of the recovery room minus his left arm, he glorified God and gave praise to the name of Jesus.[2]

The day after his appearance at the stadium, I read in the *San Diego Union* that he had received over seven hundred invitations to speak during the next year. The apparent tragedy in his life had begun to take on a look of victory!

God often has hidden purposes in the adversity He allows. I am reminded that several letters in the New Testament are called Prison Epistles. Paul wrote these letters, including the Letter to the Philippians, while he was incarcerated. The Book of Revelation was penned by the apostle John while he was in exile on the Isle of Patmos. It was in prison that John Bunyan saw the great vision that later became the immortal *Pilgrim's Progress*. The prisons of our lives can often become places of great opportunity and ministry. Charles Colson, the famed Watergate conspirator, concluded his book *Loving God* with this analogy:

> My lowest days as a Christian (and there were low ones— seven months worth of them in prison, to be exact) have been more fulfilling and rewarding than all the days of glory in the White House.[3]

And it was that way for the apostle Paul. When he referred in verse 12 to "the things which happened to me," he was reminding the Philippians that he had experienced some difficult days. He was writing to them in response to a letter from the Philippian church that had been carried to him by Epaphroditus. These believers in Philippi loved Paul dearly and were very concerned about his welfare. For two years he had been a prisoner in Caesarea and now he was a prisoner in Rome. Because Paul knew of their concern, he set out to put their minds at ease.

What were the things that happened to Paul? Although he did not itemize them in his letter, Luke has written the story in Acts 20—28, and Paul himself summarized his troubles in 2 Corinthians 11:23–27.

By his own testimony, we know that Paul had a great desire to preach the gospel in Rome.

- Acts 19:21—"After I have been there [Jerusalem], I must also see Rome."
- Romans 1:15—"So, as much as is in me, I am ready [eager] to preach the gospel to you who are in Rome also."
- Acts 23:11—"The following night the Lord stood by him and said, 'Be of good cheer, Paul; for as you have testified for Me in Jerusalem, so you must also bear witness at Rome.'"

When Paul prayed that he might have a prosperous journey to Rome in the will of God (Romans 1:10), I'm sure he had no idea how that prayer would be answered. As Warren Wiersbe has observed, he wanted to go as a *preacher* and ended up going as a *prisoner*.[4]

Paul's difficulties actually began to happen to him when he arrived in Jerusalem. It was there he was warned that afflictions and imprisonment awaited him (Acts 20:22ff).

In spite of the testimony of his dynamic conversion, he was falsely accused and nearly lynched by a religious mob and ended up in a Roman prison. He would have been beaten but for the fact that he pleaded his Roman citizenship. Everything about his imprisonment was a mockery. He was insulted and shamed.

And then there was the journey to Rome ... the storm at sea ... his life hanging in the balance. When finally he did arrive in Rome, it was not as he had hoped. He came with the condemned in chains, and waited for two full years before he knew the outcome of his appeal.

And yet Paul was still certain that this sorrow and suffering was part of God's plan for his life. When writing to the Corinthians, he said, "Therefore I take pleasure in infirmities, in reproaches, in needs, in persecutions, in distresses, for Christ's sake. For when I am weak, then I am strong" (2 Corinthians 12:10).

The words "take pleasure" mean "to think well," or "to have the right attitude." As he relayed his situation to his friends in Philippi, Paul clearly had the right attitude toward his troubles. His upbeat explanation has become a source of great encouragement to all who have walked through the valley. Here, then, from Paul's letter are seven proven principles that will encourage us when we face trouble.

## ADVERSITY PROMOTES THE PROGRESS OF THE GOSPEL (1:12)

When Paul talked about his present situation, he did not discuss his personal discomfort. He was not occupied with the inconvenience that imprisonment had caused him. His concern was for the gospel and its advance. He told his prayer supporters in Philippi that his imprisonment had actually put the gospel ahead of schedule in Rome.

When he described the advance of the gospel, he used the word "furtherance." This is a military term used by engineers who would prepare a road for an advancing army by removing obstructions such as rocks and trees. Paul viewed his imprisonment as the removal of barriers to the gospel in Rome. One writer expressed it this way:

> As Paul looks back over these events ... he stresses the masses of dark threads that the recent years had woven into the pattern of his life ... the animosities and bodily pains, the lies, misrepresentations and deceitfulness, the miscarriage of justice, the chains ... the mental turmoil of appealing to Caesar against his own people, the nearness of death and the loss of hope, the triumph of wickedness and the continued suppression of the truth. He invites us to take these things and look them in the face, for it is these which have resulted—contrary to what their surface appearance might have suggested— in the progress of the Gospel.[5]

Just as Dave Dravecky would never have received seven hundred invitations to speak about Christ's work in his life without his encounter with cancer, so Paul recognized that without his imprisonment, the influence of the gospel in Rome would have been retarded.

## ADVERSITY PROVIDES OPPORTUNITIES FOR WITNESS (1:13)

When the apostle spoke of his bonds being manifested in all the palace, he was referring to the Praetorian Guard which was a chosen division of crack imperial troops. They were paid well and given special assignments, one of which was to guard the prisoners who were waiting for an audience with Caesar. These guards would have been exposed to Paul's testimony as he shared it with them personally and as they listened to him share it with others.

Apart from his imprisonment, there would have been no way Paul could have approached the highest dignitaries in the palace in Rome. We know that some of them became Christians because of the final words of Paul in this very letter. He referred to "the saints ... who are of Caesar's household" (Philippians 4:22).

For twenty-four hours a day he was chained to a Roman soldier. Every six hours the shift changed, so Paul had four prospects for salvation every day of the week. During his two-year imprisonment, he would have been able to engage in almost three thousand witnessing opportunities with Rome's top military personnel.

If you compare Philippians 1:13 with Acts 28:30–31, you see that Paul had great freedom even though he was a prisoner: "Then Paul dwelt two whole years in his own rented house, and received all who came to him, preaching the kingdom of God and teaching the things which concern the Lord Jesus Christ with all confidence, no one forbidding him."

When he added to his mention of the Praetorian Guard the phrase "to all the rest," he revealed the fact that his imprisonment was making an impact on everyone in the palace. He had the opportunity to witness to other soldiers, household servants, and to government officials.

In her first book, Corrie ten Boom told of her experience in Ravensbruck prison during World War II. As she reflected on her own pain and suffering she came to understand that one of God's purposes was that her suffering should benefit others:

> God had brought me here for a specific task. I was here to lead
> the sorrowing and the despairing to the Savior. I was to see
> how He comforted them. I was to point the way to heaven to
> people among whom were many that would soon be dying.[6]

Marine Lieutenant Clebe McClary was permanently disabled when an enemy grenade exploded in his foxhole. His evaluation of his adversity is similar to that of Corrie ten Boom:

I don't think my suffering was in vain. The Lord has used
my experiences for good by drawing many lives to Him. It's
hard to see any good that came from the war in Vietnam, but
I don't believe our effort was wasted. Surely some seed was
planted for Christ that cannot be stamped out.[7]

Like the many others who have suffered after him, Paul allowed his
adversity to become a platform for the gospel. What the enemy hoped
would thwart the gospel actually advanced it. If for no other reason than
this, we should think twice before we complain about our difficult situations. It just might be that God is up to something eternal!

## ADVERSITY PRODUCES COURAGE IN OUR FELLOW BELIEVERS (1:14)

It is evident that Paul's imprisonment had an effect on his associates. He
was aware that many of them became very confident and bold because
they saw his courage. Bravery is contagious! Persecution can be productive! One has to wonder what would have become of the gospel, had it not
been for persecution. It was often the impetus to evangelism: "At that time
a great persecution arose against the church which was at Jerusalem; and
they were all scattered.... Therefore those who were scattered went everywhere preaching the word" (Acts 8:1, 4).

In seventeenth-century England, George Fox and the Quakers were
making their mark for the gospel and hundreds were being converted. In
the midst of the revival, while preaching at the Castle of Carlisle in the
north of England, George Fox was arrested on charges of blasphemy. After
his trial he was thrown into a filthy dungeon overrun with vermin and
criminals. No one was allowed even a glimpse of him. Some who tried
to bring him food were clubbed back by the jailers. But 150 miles away,
sixteen-year-old James Parnell, a cripple endowed with a brilliant mind,
heard about Fox's situation and walked the long miles to the prison.
Somehow he managed to get in, and he was never the same again. Says
Walter Williams, in his volume on Quaker history, "After he and George

Fox spent some time in fellowship together, the lad left Carlisle dungeon with heart aflame, and gave the rest of his life to Christ and the Friends Movement."[8]

In my lifetime I have witnessed the infectious impact of courageous suffering. The deaths of Paul Carlson, missionary to the Congo; Jim Elliot, missionary to Ecuador's Auca Indians; and Chet Bitterman, missionary to Colombia, have probably been responsible for more missionary recruits than any other recent motivating force.

## ADVERSITY PROVES THE CHARACTER OF OUR FRIENDSHIPS (1:15–18)

As Paul looked out upon the church, he saw encouraging things, but he also saw many discouraging things. He saw not only those who were supporting him in his trials, but also those who were taking advantage of his trials and attempting to "afflict" him. These were not false teachers, because Paul said they preached Christ. He rejoiced in the *message* they preached, but he was grieved by the *manner* in which they delivered it. They preached from envy and partisanship. Paul chose not to dwell on what they did to him; we don't know exactly what it was, but we do know that their private lives were not consistent with their public lives.

As Paul described those who were preaching for the wrong reasons, he used an interesting word. He said they were preaching out of *contention*. That word means "to canvass for office in order to get people to support you." Their aim was to get people to follow them. Paul's aim was to get people to follow Christ.

As he sorted this out, he tried to come to some resolution in the matter. He rejoiced that Christ was being preached, even if it was not as he wanted it to be. He knew that though Christ might not honor the motive of the messenger, He would honor and bless His Word.

# ADVERSITY PROVOKES GROWTH IN OUR LIVES (1:19–20)

> Two men are shot down in Vietnam and imprisoned in the infamous Hoa Lo prison. They are isolated, chained to cement slabs, and continuously beaten with rusty shackles and tortured for information. Yet although these men are receiving the same abuse, they form radically different beliefs about their experience. One man decides that his life is over, and in order to avoid any additional pain, commits suicide. The other pulls from these brutalizing events a deeper belief in himself, his fellow man, and his Creator than he's ever had before. Today Captain Gerald Coffee uses his prison experience to remind people all over the world of the power of the human spirit to overcome virtually any level of pain, any challenge, or any problem.[9]

Adversity separates men! It makes some better; it makes others bitter. Over eighty years ago, a well-known psychologist wrote:

> Most people live, whether physically, intellectually or morally, in a very restricted circle of their potential being. They make use of a very small portion of their possible consciousness, of their soul's resources in general much like a man who, out of his whole bodily organism, should get into a habit of using and moving only his little finger. *Great emergencies and crises show us how much greater our vital resources are than we had supposed.*[10]

As Paul faced the adversity of his circumstances, he saw the advantages. When he spoke of these events resulting in his salvation, he was not talking about his conversion to Christ, but about his continued growth in Christ. In 1:6 he plainly stated his conviction that God, who had begun that good work on the first day, would continue to perform it until the day of Jesus Christ. As he looked at his confinement, he saw it as another method of bringing him to his ultimate goal of Christian maturity. There were three things at work in his life accomplishing this goal.

First of all there were the *prayers of his friends*. Paul knew that the Philippians were praying for him. Earlier in this letter, Paul said, "I pray" (1:9). Now he was depending on the fact that they were praying also. In fact, in almost all of his letters, Paul cited the mutuality of prayer. What he himself practiced, he also profited from, as it was lived out in others.

In Romans he said, "I make mention of you always in my prayers.... Now I beg you, brethren, through the Lord Jesus Christ, and through the love of the Spirit, that you strive together with me in prayers to God for me" (1:9; 15:30).

In Ephesians he said, "[I] do not cease to give thanks for you, making mention of you in my prayers.... Finally, my brethren.... Praying always ... for me" (1:16; 6:10, 18–19).

In 1 Thessalonians he wrote, "Making mention of you in our prayers.... night and day.... Brethren, pray for us" (1:2; 3:10; 5:25).

In 2 Thessalonians he wrote, "Therefore we also pray always for you.... Finally, brethren, pray for us" (1:11; 3:1).

Often, when facing trouble, we are the focus of the prayers of God's people. It is through these prayers that we are able to survive our crises and go on to maturity. As members of God's earthly family, we should not forget to put the spiritual growth of others at the top of our prayer lists. When we are experiencing growing pains, it is good to know that someone is praying. I have always loved the stark contrast of the two phrases of this verse: "Peter was therefore kept in prison, but constant prayer was offered to God for him by the church" (Acts 12:5).

Second, not only was Paul sustained by the prayers of his friends but he was also encouraged by the *provision of the Holy Spirit*. His language is picturesque; this phrase literally means, "the full supply of the Holy Spirit."

If you have ever known the Holy Spirit drawing close to you in moments of crisis, then you understand why He is called "the Comforter."

David Jacobsen was a hostage in Beirut for seventeen months. He was head of the largest hospital in West Beirut when, one day in 1985, three hooded men wielding machine guns took him captive. He was taken bound and gagged from one hideout to another and spent most of his time on a cold dirt floor, chained to the wall. Once a day he was fed an unpalatable mush of water, rice, and lentils.

As an American, Jacobsen was hated by his captors. He was just a political pawn and was treated cruelly. Instead of breaking his spirit, however, this made him stronger. He wrote:

> I discovered that no one's faith was weakened by the hell we found ourselves in ... We hostages ... founded the Church of the Locked Door, a name we chose with some ruefulness. Grasping hands, we'd quote Scripture and pray. Oddly, our guards seemed to respect this ritual. Our togetherness in prayer showed me that when the Holy Comforter is called, He answers.[11]

Jacobsen was released in November 1986, but in his final forty-five days of captivity, he was alone in a six-by-six cell, his muscles and joints cramped by confinement and the damp, aching cold. Yet, he said, "The presence of God, the Great Comforter, was stronger than ever."[12]

Third, Paul's own *personal determination* was the third dynamic at work during this time of confinement. He was confident that he would come through this ordeal and see his friends in Philippi again. To describe his attitude, he used the term "eager expectation." This Greek word has three elements wrapped up in its meaning. It is made up of the words *away, the head,* and *to watch.* Together, they convey the idea of watching something so intently that your head is turned away from everything else. Paul had a single focus in his life. His eager expectation and hope were mixed with great determination.

- He was determined to keep a clear conscience. "That in nothing I shall be ashamed." Even though under pressure in a Roman prison, Paul was determined to live a holy and righteous life. He would not use his adversity as an excuse for a spiritual relapse.

- He was determined to keep a courageous testimony. "With all boldness, as always, so now." Paul was also determined to use his adversity as an opportunity to more loudly proclaim Christ. While many are silenced by adversity, Paul actually turned the volume up louder.

- He was determined to keep a Christ-centered focus. "Christ will be magnified in my body, whether by life or by death." From the human viewpoint, Paul's body was fairly useless to him, since he was chained to a soldier twenty-four hours each day. But Paul saw beyond all of that. He was determined that his body would be a vehicle for magnifying Christ. In one of his letters to Timothy, he described his situation like this, "I suffer trouble as an evildoer, even to the point of chains; but the Word of God is not chained" (2 Timothy 2:9). Guy King suggests some of the ways the body can magnify the Lord:

Christ magnified in the body—magnified by lips that bear happy testimony to Him; magnified by hands employed in His service; magnified by feet only too happy to go on His errands; magnified by shoulders happy to bear one another's burdens.[13]

When we magnify Christ, we do not do it *microscopically*. A microscope takes that which is little and makes it big. Our Lord is not little! Then we must magnify Him *telescopically*. We must take the Lord, who is far away from so many, and bring Him close at hand. Quite often the Lord uses the adversity in our lives as a lens through which He can be seen! In the process of it all, He is developing our character so that we can be worthy reflectors of his glory. Paul is teaching us that character cannot be developed in ease and quiet. Only through experiences of trials and suffering can the soul be strengthened.

Adoniram Judson, famous missionary to Burma, is an illustration of this attitude. After fourteen years on the mission field, what did he have to show for his labors? The graves of his wife and all of his children, imprisonments and diseases so awful that once he wrote, "If I had not felt certain that every additional trial was ordered by infinite love and mercy, I could not have survived my accumulated sufferings!" But he never thought of quitting. At the very lowest ebb of his career he prayed that "he might live to translate the entire Bible into the native language, and to preside over a native church of at least one hundred members."[14]

Helen Keller suffered an illness at eighteen months which left her completely blind and deaf. For five years she was isolated from the world and alone in darkness. Then with the help of Anne Sullivan, Helen fought back against her handicap. She never pitied herself; she never gave up. She once said:

> The marvelous richness of human experience would lose something of rewarding joy if there were no limitations to overcome. The hilltop hour would not be half so wonderful if there were not dark valleys to traverse.

## ADVERSITY PURIFIES OUR MOTIVES (1:21)

In what most scholars think is the key verse of this entire letter, Paul stated his life's motive and mission clearly. For him, to live was Christ and to die was gain. No wonder his life had such power and momentum. He forced every experience of life through the grid of his personal purpose statement. He knew what he was all about. The suffering of his present situation was not intolerable, because he saw it as a part of God's plan and his own stated purpose.

When we know who we are, and why we are here, and where we are going, we can confidently face each day; and even difficulties take on new meaning. Then, as Alec Moyter illustrates, everything becomes something for Jesus:

Two friends were talking together, one older and wise, the other younger and passing through a severe testing time. The older friend, with loving wisdom said, "No moment will ever again be like this; let there be something of Jesus in it." It is not something for Jesus if we dwell on our miseries; nor if we let opportunities pass without a word about our Lord; nor if we think that any hand other than His brought us to that place. It is something for Jesus if we think and speak about Him and His glory; it is something for Him if we acknowledge and trust His all-sovereign will.[16]

## ADVERSITY PREPARES US TO SEE LIFE AND DEATH IN PERSPECTIVE (1:22–26)

When a Christian faces adversity, especially if it is intense and prolonged, his perspective on life and death is brought into sharp focus. For Paul, the issue was not his desire to die in order to escape suffering. Paul loved life and accepted his imprisonment as a part of God's perfect plan for him. He also knew what God had planned for his future. As he contemplated his present joy and compared it to the promised joy of heaven, he found himself caught between two loves. H. C. G. Moule adequately summarizes his dilemma: "Life and death look to us like two evils of which we know not which is the less. As for the apostle, they look to him like two immense blessings, of which he knows not which is the better."[17]

In other words, Paul saw life and death as equally desirable. If he continued to live, he would come to know and love and serve the Lord more fully. If he died, he would completely and finally and perfectly know Him. He was caught between his *desire* to be with Christ personally and his sense of *duty* to help the Philippians. Paul's selfless servant heart is unmatched, outside of Christ Jesus. William Hendriksen's chart visualizes the dilemma which the apostle faced as he compared the advantages of life and death:

| Remaining Here | Departing to Be With Christ |
|---|---|
| a. A temporary residence | a. Permanent abode, a tent dwelling |
| b. Suffering mixed with joy | b. Joy unmixed with suffering |
| c. Suffering for a while | c. Joy forever |
| d. Being absent from the Lord | d. Being at home with the Lord |
| e. The fight | e. The feast |
| f. The realm of sin | f. The realm of complete deliverance from sin, positive holiness.[18] |

Looking back over the apostle's statement about trouble, we discover that there are indeed advantages to adversity:

1. Adversity promotes the progress of the gospel
2. Adversity provides opportunities to witness
3. Adversity produces courage in our fellow believers
4. Adversity proves the character of our friendships
5. Adversity provokes growth in our lives
6. Adversity purifies our motives
7. Adversity prepares us to see life and death in perspective

A woman whose heart was crushed by a tragedy, which happened through no fault of her own, wrote her pastor, "Your advice to stop asking *why* helped a lot. And your sermon yesterday helped to make us able to say, 'We will,' and leave it in God's hands. We will let Him use even this, till His plan is perfected." And then she added this bit of verse, which better than anything I have seen summarizes the message of this section of Paul's Letter to the Philippians:

*The things that happen unto me*
*Are not by chance, I know,*
*But because my Father's wisdom*
*Has willed to have it so.*
*For the "furtherance of the gospel"*
*As a part of His great plan,*

*God can use our disappointments*
*And the weaknesses of man.*
*Give me faith to meet them bravely,*
*Trials I do not understand,*
*To let God work His will in me—*
*To trust His guiding hand.*
*Help me to shine, a clear bright light,*
*And not to live in vain—*
*Help me hold forth the Word of life*
*In triumph over pain.*[19]

*Only let your conduct be worthy of the gospel of Christ,*
*so that whether I come and see you or am absent, I may hear*
*of your affairs, that you stand fast in one spirit, with one mind*
*striving together for the faith of the gospel, and not in any way*
*terrified by your adversaries, which is to them a proof of*
*perdition,  but to you of salvation, and that from God. For to*
*you it has been  granted on behalf of Christ, not only to believe*
*in Him, but also to suffer for His sake, having the same conflict*
*which you saw in me and now hear is in me.*

—PHILIPPIANS 1:27–30

# 7

## GUARDING AGAINST GUILT

### YOU CAN WIN THE BATTLE AND LIVE VICTORIOUSLY

From: Slaying the Giants in Your Life—
You Can Win the Battle and Live Victoriously

R obert Garth was running the RACE and he felt ready to break away from the pack.

Not that he hadn't been slow off the starting blocks. Robert had been born into a poor family in Detroit. His house was small and his clothes were shabby and shameful to him. But at age fifteen, Robert had found the key to help him escape his limitations. His young body was built for speed; he could run like the wind. And that gift had bought him a ticket to the Junior Olympic tryouts. If he ran well, then his dreams might come true—for him and for all his brothers and sisters. All the fastest sprinters in the region would be at these trials. But he thought of his stained shirt and torn jeans. Now, at his defining moment, how could he walk in rags among the best and the brightest?

It was the night before leaving for the Junior Olympic Trials. Robert sat brooding before the television set, thinking about his gray life. Somehow his thoughts began to drift toward the warehouse where he did a few odd jobs for cash. He began to think about Joseph Moceri, the man who paid him. Mr. Moceri always pulled a thick wad of bills from his back pocket when the job was done. He counted them out carefully as he peeled them off, one by one. It was always cash—and the man was always alone. Those facts suggested certain possibilities, unpleasant possibilities that Robert couldn't stop thinking about.

A picture began to form in Robert's mind—a picture of Mr. Moceri coming into work the next morning, a picture of a shadowy figure lurking behind the door with a blunt object, of the figure knocking Mr. Moceri unconscious and sprinting out the door with the money—sprinting away with the remarkable speed of a track star.

It was an ugly picture, but there was another one that pulled at him. This was a picture of himself at the trials wearing bright, stylish clothing fresh from the best store in the neighborhood.

The next morning at five o'clock, Robert was on his way to the warehouse. He eased behind the door and waited. That's when events began to quickly play out. But they didn't play out in a way that was consistent with the pictures he'd seen in his mind. They didn't play out as they did on TV thrillers. They played out, instead, to disaster.

Mr. Moceri strolled through the warehouse with a coffeepot in his hands. He was moving more slowly and cautiously because of his burden. Robert crept toward him from behind. At the last possible moment, his foot brushed some object on the floor and made a noise—just enough noise to destroy Robert's life. Mr. Moceri quickly whirled around to see a young friend he knew well, one raising a blunt instrument above his head. Sadly, Mr. Moceri said, "Please. I'll give you whatever you want."

Robert hadn't prepared himself for a face-to-face confrontation. This was all wrong, and he panicked. He swung the club furiously at Mr. Moceri's head, knocking him to the floor. Then he knelt and thrust his hand into the unconscious man's pockets, pulled out $67, and hurried away.

That afternoon, Robert was on his way to the Junior Olympics. He knew nothing of the ambulance that rushed Mr. Moceri to the hospital, nor did he know Mr. Moceri would die that night. The next day, he learned it all. That was the beginning of the nightmare.

Robert Garth's performance was less than exceptional at the trials. He came in fourth in the 200-meter sprint, a race he'd been certain he could win. And just like that, the trials were over. It was time to go home.

Back in Detroit, Robert tried to pick up his life where he'd left off. He'd always been pretty popular at school. But it was no good now; nothing felt the same. There was always the secret that isolated him. He had to face it—he was an unrecognized murderer.

His focus on the track was gone. His formerly good grades plummeted. From the awful chaos in his mind there was no escape, with one exception; there was alcohol. Robert hadn't been much of a drinker in the past, but now he drank as often and as heavily as he could, seeking the blessed oblivion that blocked out his memories, if only temporarily.

Somehow he made it through high school; maybe he could turn the corner. The awful incident was behind him, wasn't it? The important thing was to keep running, to put some miles between himself and the terrible event. In time, perhaps he could forget. Marriage would help. Robert and his high school sweetheart announced their engagement and planned the wedding.

The marriage lasted three years, producing a daughter and nothing else good. The union never had a chance at success, really. The young bride couldn't understand her husband's bleak, morbid moods. What had happened to the old Robert she had loved? Finally, Robert's wife filed divorce papers, packed up her belongings, took their daughter, and moved away.

Robert had few options. He moved back home briefly, but it was only another dead end. He and his father couldn't get along. So he climbed even deeper into the bottle.

He tried other things—moving to another city, moving home again, new jobs, new starts. The track star was running, always running, but there didn't seem to be a finish line and certainly no trophies; just a dark, endless track and a cup of sorrow. The bleak face that greeted him in the mirror had thirty years on it now. There was no trace left of the athletic fifteen-year-old. He often found himself wandering through the city streets like a crazy man, mumbling bitter words to himself. The murder, all those years ago, was still on the books, unsolved. No one suspected the identity of the assailant. Everyone had forgotten.

Everyone except himself. And one night, walking among the alleys, it occurred to him that he was tired of the knowledge—or at least, of knowing it alone. Perhaps he should end it all. Then there would be peace. There would be no more knowing.

But he couldn't do it. Deep inside, something directed him toward the other option—the one even more frightening than suicide. Instead of letting nobody know, it only seemed right to let everyone know. And just like that, Robert found that his feet had changed direction. They were leading him now, he realized, toward police headquarters. Those feet, once so quick, took him slowly through the door and up to the desk.

There, before the clerk, Robert cleared his throat and stated that he'd like to confess to a fifteen-year-old murder.

## The Invisible Giant

Guilt is a giant with interesting powers. This giant is the most invisible, but the heaviest one of all. There are people all around us who are being slowly crushed, slowly suffocated by the giant of guilt. It kills slowly but with excruciating pain. Think of Judas, hanging from a tree; Shakespeare's Lady Macbeth, with blood on her hands that would never wash away; the expectant woman who aborts her child and lives with remorse for the rest of her life. There are so many stories I could tell, and you could add to the list. But I believe the most powerful one of all is found in the Bible. It plays out in the books of history and then moves through pain and resolution between two psalms. It's the psychodrama concerning a man named David.

David had it all—every good thing life has to offer—and he knew it. For starters, he ruled the greatest nation in the world. He was not only God's anointed, but also the people's choice. Once he had been an obscure young shepherd; now he was the most important man alive.

He could sing beautifully and play musical instruments. He could dance artistically. He was a military hero and a conqueror of armies and antagonists of titanic stature. David had the heart of an artist, the soul of a priest, the mind of a philosopher, and the body of a warrior. Perhaps it was an embarrassment of riches, too much for any one man to be given. In any case, David had finally found an enemy he feared: midlife. He'd grown up in the fields where lions dwelt. He had come of age fleeing for his life, hiding in caves from a jealous king. Whole armies had pursued him. Now he'd made it to the top, but he was bored and restless. He needed a new giant to conquer. Sadly, he found one that got the best of him.

David found himself restless on the battle lines, where he was spending time with the troops. At home, he found he couldn't sleep and he took a stroll on the palace roof. It was there that a sight in the courtyard below caught his eye. There was a woman, a strikingly beautiful one, bathing in the twilight. David couldn't take his eyes away; afterward, he couldn't take his thoughts away. Instead, he sought her out. It all led, of course, to an act of adultery that quickly gave way, as always, to remorse. He sent the woman home and tried to move on. But the whole incident escalated into a nightmare when word came that Bathsheba was pregnant. Everyone knew that her husband was away at battle. They also knew who was home from that battle. David realized his moral authority as a godly king would quickly erode if the truth came out. What could he do?

David settled on a solution that made a transgression into a tragedy. He sent for the husband of Bathsheba, a man named Uriah. David invited him to his quarters for dinner and wine, then sent him down to spend time with his wife. No matter what happened between the couple, this would create a window of opportunity that would erase any suspicion that Bathsheba's child was illegitimate.

But David hadn't allowed for one contingency: the innocence and goodness of the husband. Uriah said, "King David, I wouldn't feel right about spending time with my wife tonight. After all, the other soldiers in my unit are in the trenches right now. Here I am eating at a fine table, drinking palace wine—it's not right for me to enjoy all these luxuries." And so he slept that night on the steps of the palace.

David's plan had gone awry. He couldn't think of what else to do. Finally he gave Uriah a note to carry to the general. The note decreed that Uriah should be sent to the very front lines, the bloodiest ground, then deserted by the troops and left to die. This would produce a pregnant widow who could be quickly married.

After all the wine and the feast, David was sending Bathsheba's husband back to war carrying his own death warrant. Murder and intrigue had been added to adultery. David knew the gravity of his bloody deeds, and he was sentenced to the penalty of living with himself over the next year. In the meantime, we have two records of what transpired in his soul: Psalm 32 and Psalm 51. They should be read in reverse order; 51 shows the excruciating pain of his guilt, and 32 shows his resolution and renewal.

Both psalms give us an intriguing window into David's spiritual journey. And they reveal to us a legacy of silence, sorrow, and secrecy—the telltale marks of the guilty.

# THE AGONY OF GUILT: PSALM 32

### Silence

When the damage has been done and the guilt sets in, our first impulse is silence. Listen to this somewhat awful description:

*When I kept silent, my bones grew old through my groaning all the day long.* (Psalm 32:3)

What else is there in times of guilt, but silence? We can't talk to people, even those closest to us. We can't talk to God. Psalm 66:18 tells us that "if I regard iniquity in my heart, the Lord will not hear." This was no small thing for David, a man who kept counsel with God constantly on every subject. Now a gulf of silence stretched between them. The man after God's own heart found himself exiled from it.

Sometimes the silence can be deafening, can't it? The only sound was David's groaning, and he tells us that his very bones became old through this period. His soul was suffering, and his health began to follow suit—something you can always count on happening.

### Sorrow

No one is more eloquent than David on the dimensions of suffering. He writes:

*For day and night Your hand was heavy upon me; my vitality was turned into the drought of summer.* (Psalm 32:4)

A great army stood at his beck and call. A palace and a kingdom obeyed his every whim. But his conscience could not be ruled.

David was trapped inside his own guilt. Sorrow overcame him, sapping his life of all its considerable vitality. There was no reason to dance. There were no words to sing. The only poetry he had was the poetry of grief.

*Secrecy*

As we've seen, guilt is a force of isolation. He couldn't talk to friends. He couldn't talk to God. He was worse than an adulterer—he was someone who would murder to avoid negative publicity. Only Bathsheba and Joab, his trusted adviser, knew the truth. The king spent a year living with an intolerable secret, in psychological exile from God and from people. David, by constitution an open and transparent man, had to face agonies he had never before encountered.

Finally God reached into David's world to offer a way out. He provided something profoundly loving and terribly painful. He sent an accuser.

## THE ACCUSATION OF GUILT: 2 SAMUEL 12:1–7

The whole story is laid out for us in the Book of 2 Samuel. It tells us that the voice of God came to a man named Nathan who, for all intents and purposes, was David's pastor. He served as the palace prophet. And now Nathan was sent by God to confront sin and corruption at the highest political level. It was a frightening assignment, but it came with the territory.

Nathan was bold, being a prophet, but this was a daunting task all the same. How does one confront a king? Nathan achieved his goal in a very clever way. He told David his own story by way of misdirection, changing the terms and settings. He related current events in the comfortable distance of a parable.

Two men lived in a city, he said, one rich and one poor. One had the finest flock in the kingdom, the other only one little ewe that was something of a family pet. The little lamb was a part of the family, eating from their hands and drinking from their cups. No more than a little lamb, but a beloved one in the life of a poor family.

Meanwhile, the rich man was entertaining a visitor. Dinnertime came around, and the host didn't want to make a withdrawal from the wealth of his own herd. Instead, he thought of the poor man, out there living in that little hut—the man with the single scrawny lamb. He took the man's pet by force, and served it as dinner for his visitor.

David the king sat back and listened with absorption, caught up in the story—for to him, it was no more than a story. He never anticipated the twist in the punch line. He never equated wool with women, or misers with monarchs. All David saw was an outrage to civility. He blurted out to Nathan, "As the Lord lives, the man who has done this shall surely die!" (2 Samuel 12:5)

Nathan, of course, knew that this was a compelling ruling from the king, who was sentencing himself to death.

"David," said Nathan, no doubt pointing a bony finger at the very face of the ruler, "You are the man."

What a moment it must have been, as the truth came home to roost. It must have been a stake through the heart. It must have been a public humiliation. And it must have been, in some sense, a relief. Now the thing was out on the table. At least the furtiveness, the secrecy, was over. The solitude of the secret was the worst part. Now there would be public repercussions, but David had come to a place where he could accept that. It was high time to set his house in order.

## THE ADMISSION OF GUILT: PSALM 51

Psalm 51 is already one of the most absorbing passages in all of God's Word, but perhaps one of the most intriguing portions is the superscription, that little introduction that often accompanies a psalm. This particular one reads: "A Psalm of David when Nathan the prophet went to him, after he had gone in to Bathsheba."

In other words, we have here the aftermath of Nathan's confrontation. David has been humiliated and confronted with the full gravity of his wickedness. What does a man say to God at such a moment? How does he handle the awful state in which he finds his soul?

### He Accepts Full Responsibility for His Sin

It all begins with owning up. Many of us are masters of shifting the blame. It's a natural human impulse, and scapegoats come cheap.

But not David. If you browse through Psalm 51, you're going to find personal pronouns again and again: I. Me. My. Mine. In the passage below, which encompasses the first three verses of the psalm, I've indicated those words with italics:

> Have mercy upon *me*, O God . . .
> Blot out *my* transgressions.
> Wash *me* thoroughly from my iniquity,
> And cleanse *me* from *my* sin.
> For *I* acknowledge *my* transgressions,
> And *my* sin is ever before *me*. (Psalm 51:1–3)

There's no mistaking who takes the rap, is there? It's refreshing to see. Today, it's easier to blame our subordinates, or the board of trustees, or the media, or stress, or society, or an unhappy childhood. Most of us don't herd sheep anymore, but we keep plenty of scapegoats on hand.

Don't overlook the importance of this starting point. The journey of recovery starts here or nowhere. You've got to own up to what you've done. President Truman kept that famous plaque on his desk that said, "The buck stops here." David, a commander in chief himself, knew the significance of that philosophy. To push away guilt is to ensure, ironically enough, that it goes nowhere. You must embrace it to distance yourself from it.

### He Acknowledges the Sinfulness of Sin

Another pet coping device we often use is to minimize the transgression. "Oh, it was no big deal," we say. Think of the rationalizations David might have used: I was dealing with stress. I simply made a poor decision, but it was an isolated incident. It was a learning opportunity, really. The man was bound to die in battle anyway—I'm his commander, after all. The woman was beautiful, and the king is entitled to beautiful wives. A king must be a little ruthless to be successful in today's tribal environment.

Most people would carefully choose words that mitigated the damage and toned down the rhetoric. David's vocabulary, however, isn't like that at all. He chooses four significant words to take in the scope of his actions.

- The first is transgressions (verses 1, 3). The word is one of moral gravity; it means a revolt against the law. "Lord," David is saying, "I've rebelled against Your laws."
- The second is iniquity, a word capturing the perversity of man's nature.
- The third is sin, a word needing no introduction. It means "to miss the mark."
- The fourth is evil, which sums up the whole sordid mess—a vile thing worthy only of condemnation.

***Transgressions. Iniquity. Sin. Evil.***

When you've failed to live by God's standards, listen carefully to your language. Ask your spouse or your best friend to listen for you. Do you use words with the gravity of these four, or do you use words like stress and circumstances and unavoidable and this is how God made me?

The concept of confession comes into play. Confession is all about naked honesty before God or before fellow Christians. It means describing our actions with the same words God uses, and no dissembling or distortion. Confession will not allow us to foolishly hide, as Adam and Eve did in the Garden; it will force us to change from the inside out. "The sacrifices of God are a broken spirit, a broken and a contrite heart—these, O God, You will not despise" (Psalm 51:17). David knew what it meant for his actions to be despised by God. The act of confession was intensely painful and thoroughly liberating.

It's helpful here to make a side trip to Psalm 32. In verse 5 David looks back at his painful prayer of confession, and he makes this observation about it: "I acknowledged my sin to You, and my iniquity I have not hidden. I said, 'I will confess my transgressions to the Lord,' and You forgave the iniquity of my sin."

David is describing a breakthrough moment—the moment in which we come clean, acknowledging the awful truth. Finally we can say we have done something right. Finally the door is open again to transactions with our heavenly Father.

In 1973 Dr. Karl Menninger, a psychologist, wrote the book *Whatever Became of Sin?* But his prophetic title is truer now than it was nearly thirty years ago. The word is out of step with the times, isn't it? There are no sins, only "personal decisions." Actions once forbidden are now the subjects of TV sitcoms. And if someone does happen to do something our culture can't accept, then it's shrugged away as a result of nature or nurture. In every era between the biblical world and this one, sin was despised. One might be so conscious of a serious sin that he agonized over losing his salvation. If those generations needed a better grasp of grace, it is our time that needs a better sense of sin—its blackness, its filth, its ability to exile us from the presence of our loving Father.

Sociologist James Davison Hunter observes that schoolteachers no longer say things like, "Stop it, please! You're disturbing the class!" No, that would be too "judgmental" by current standards. If Johnny is involved in some destructive activity in the classroom, today's young teacher is more likely to say, "What are you doing? Why are you doing it? How does doing it make you feel?"[1]

We can only grimace when Hunter points out that the word "sin" has retreated mostly to dessert menus. Butterscotch Binge and Fudge Fandango are sinful, according to the menus. And that's supposed to be a good thing. But when it comes to lying and adultery—we fudge, of course. We choose careful euphemisms for discussing our iniquities. "I didn't lie. I presented a subject interpretation," or "I ended the marriage so we could better fulfill our independent goals."

By scrubbing the word "sin" out of the vocabulary of everyday life, we've actually deprived people of the doorway to healing. There's no way to be made well unless we first acknowledge the reality of sin. Apart from this, your situation is hopeless.

### He Addresses His Confession to God

David then addresses the true victim. He writes:

> *Against You, You only, have I sinned, and done this evil in Your sight.* (Psalm 51:4)

That prayer is very wise. After acknowledging the reality of sin, the second step is to turn our face toward God. All sin is an offense first and foremost against Him, even when there's a human victim.

David knows painfully well how Bathsheba has been manipulated—used sexually, made a widow and subsequently the bride of her husband's killer. David knows that Uriah has been deprived of his very life. Even Joab has been wronged, for he was forced to compromise his integrity by following the orders of his king. And we must also mention the little boy born to David and Bathsheba, who was yet another victim of David's ruthlessness. All of these have borne the brunt of David's sin.

But confession must first be directed above. David recognized that at the root of every sin, from the pettiest offense to murder, is an insult to the God who created us and sustains us every moment of our lives. Before the sin claims any victims, it has already been an injury to the person of God, who set out laws to guide us. David therefore said to God, "against You and You only I have sinned." At the deepest level it's "only God," and that's why, when it comes to forgiveness, it's also "only God." No one else can redeem except Him. If you sin against me I can forgive you personally, but I can't remove your guilt. I can't give you that deeper level of forgiveness, because I can't remove the offense against the Lord. Only He can do that.

David acknowledged his sin; he addressed his confession to God.

## THE ANSWER TO GUILT: PSALM 51:2–12

### Removing the Sin

Now David turns his attention to the issue of cleansing.

*Wash me thoroughly from my iniquity, and cleanse me from my sin.* (Psalm 51:2)

Five verses later, he adds, "Purge me with hyssop, and I shall be clean; wash me, and I shall be whiter than snow." Have you ever been out after a day's outdoor work in the summer heat, and you long for a bath or shower more than anything else? David feels that way inside. He knows the full extent of his filthiness, and he knows that only God can wash the filth deep within.

"Blot out all my iniquities," he pleads in verse 9. Again and again he repeats this idea. This is more than lip service—this is genuine, remorseful petition. He speaks of his sin and God's forgiveness with the same depth of intensity. If moral degradation is unthinkable, then forgiveness is all the more blessed. David is humble, honest, and wholehearted. Sin is a stain to the soul, and the king uses the same Hebrew word for cleanse that might have been applied to the cleansing of a leper—serious cleansing indeed. "I'm a leper of the soul," he says of himself with relentless honesty. "Make me clean again."

In verse 7 we find this word "hyssop." An interesting Old Testament custom is worth relating here. Purity, as we know, was a crucial issue to the Jews. The law required that when a person came into contact with a corpse, he had to be ceremoniously cleansed with hyssop. David is thinking of Uriah. He has been dealing in death, and he must be cleaned to satisfy the fullest demands of the law.

"Lord," he continues, "blot out all my iniquities." Why blot? Most sins were handled in the manner of transactions. If you committed some offense, you could perform some kind of sacrifice to make atonement. But there were two sins with no remedy: adultery and murder. David had committed both of these, and they were written in God's great book in red letters. There was nothing David could do, no sacrifice to make, no atonement to seek. The accusing page was beyond his reach. All he could do was fall upon the mercy of God to blot out that red ink. Wipe it away completely, Lord!

No priest, of course, could do that. Only God had the solvent, then and now.

### Restoring the Joy

Unfinished business of the soul takes its toll on our lives. David had not, prior to now, confronted the demons within him. He had not come to terms with them, and he had paid the price in misery for a year. For twelve months, the very vitality of his life had been seeping away. Now he comes to God and asks Him to do more than offer forgiveness. He asks God to restore his joy. In verses 8 and 12 he writes, "Make me to hear joy and gladness, that the bones which You have broken may rejoice . . . Restore to me the joy of Your salvation, and uphold me with Your generous Spirit."

Notice David doesn't ask for his salvation to be restored; that will come next. What he wants back is the joy of it, the liberation and freedom of living the redeemed life. We can't lose our salvation, but we can certainly lose some of the fringe benefits. Some of us do things that displease God, and we never face up to them. The time comes when we realize our lives are grim and joyless. When that happens, we need to check the backlog for unconfessed sin. Something is standing between God and us, and we need the joy of our salvation restored. The non-Christian, of course, would never know the difference; he or she has always lived without God. But the believer who "backslides," as we used to say, is aware of something missing—the unique, boundless joy of walking in the Spirit.

### Renewing the Fellowship

"Do not cast me away from Your presence," David writes in verse 11, "and do not take Your Holy Spirit from me."

Imagine it: cast away from the presence of God. This would be the description of a soul eternally lost—a soul castaway! David prays to avoid such a destiny. He pleads with God not to remove His Holy Spirit from him.

The Bible tells us that on the day when David was crowned king, God removed His Spirit from Saul and filled David instead. The new king was mindful of Saul's great sin and the ugly consequences. Saul had become a soul castaway, and God had finally set him adrift. You can imagine that these things are running through David's mind as he offers this prayer. Please, Lord. Don't let me go the way of Saul. Don't set me adrift! Don't take Your Holy Spirit from me.

### Refocusing on the Future

"Uphold me with Your generous Spirit" (verse 12). David is asking God to bolster him in the future, to help him learn from his tragic mistakes. He never wants to go through this again. Having dealt thoroughly with the sin, brought it before God, experienced cleansing, and sought the restoration of joy, the time comes to look to the future.

There's a beautiful spiritual principle known as a covenant. Covenants often follow times of forgiveness and restoration. We say, "Lord, I can see the folly of my ways. You've saved me from myself. Now it's time for me to make a solemn promise that I'll be responsible for my actions. I'll never let this happen again." It's a time to put it into words. It's a time to write it on paper. It's a time to hold yourself accountable. But it's also a time to seek deeper strength from God. Uphold me, Lord. Let me depend so thoroughly on Your guidance that such a failure will be unthinkable in the future.

In Psalm 32, we see how David's thinking has changed. "Blessed is he whose transgression is forgiven, whose sin is covered. Blessed is the man to whom the Lord does not impute iniquity, and in whose spirit there is no deceit" (verses 1–2).

The word "blessed" is another word for happy. Happy is that man whose sin is forgiven. The truth here is so incredible, so revolutionary, that your life is bound to be changed forever if you will only grasp it. No sin outweighs the forgiveness of God. If I were you, I'd read that sentence slowly, several times; I'd contemplate it carefully.

Someone reading this book might have committed a murder in the past—you could be reading from a prison cell. Some of you have committed adultery. Many of you have damaged and betrayed those closest to you, just as David did. The only two things I know for certain about you are that you've sinned seriously and that God's mercy is even more powerful. It's a great, boundless sea that will engulf the worst atrocities we can imagine. It doesn't matter what others may tell you or how they may make you feel. It doesn't matter how you yourself feel about it.

What matters is God's response, for He's the ultimate victim of every sin ever committed. And He sent His Son to pay the price for each one of them. His message to you is, "I no longer know your guilt. I don't want you to know it, either. I want you to live in a new way with Me, in a fellowship so rich that it will overflow and overcome your old sinful tendencies."

## THE BURDEN OF A LIFETIME

When we read David's appalling story, we react as he did when he heard the sheep tale. We say, "This is an outrage! The man must die!"

And then, like David, we realize with a shock that we're talking about ourselves. We, too, have multiplied our transgressions. We would do well to face up to the full magnitude of our guilt, as David has, and embrace the full magnitude of His forgiveness. I learned that lesson in the school of experience.

As a high school student, I worked for a hardware store in Cedarville, Ohio. Fred Lutenberger ran the store—a fine man and a tough taskmaster. He sent me to the attic to clean the oily metal shavings from pipe threading, and each night I came home filthy. The work wasn't fun; I felt I was getting the lowest assignments.

One day I was hard at work when a customer came in to make a purchase. No one was there to help him but me, so we made the twenty-dollar transaction. Stuffing the bill into my pocket instead of the cash register, I returned to my labor. I was in a hurry to be finished. When I arrived home, I found the store's twenty dollars still in my pocket. It hadn't been theft on my part—just an honest mistake. And yet, I got to thinking. This was a lot of money for those times. I was a teenager without much, and here was this boss underpaying me for hard labor. Why, he required overtime and didn't pay me for it. I was able to create in my mind a complex rationale for keeping the money.

So I kept the money and went on about my life. But the strangest thing happened. I didn't think about the money except in those times when I wanted to do something for God. And then the issue of the twenty dollars always sprang into my mind. It weighed upon me. But the problem was that any way I could think of to make restitution would embarrass me, as well as my father, who was the president of a local Christian college. Like David, I had entangled myself in a mess. My new rationale was that I was protecting my father from embarrassment by not returning the money.

Time passed; I attended seminary and married. Soon we accepted our first ministerial calling in Haddon Heights, New Jersey, working with youth. One day I received an invitation to speak to the young people at a Bible Club camp. So I set off alone for Upper Darby, Pennsylvania, in my car. During that trip, the old incident of the twenty dollars arose from the grave where I'd attempted to bury it. All the suppressed guilt came back, and I was overwhelmed with remorse. On a car trip alone there's a lot of time to think and nowhere to hide. You can't turn the radio loud enough to drown out a conscience.

I found myself computing the interest on twenty dollars over the intervening years. Soon I pulled over in a small town and pulled sixty dollars in traveling money from my pocket. I stuffed it all into an envelope and made out the address, without any note, to that old hardware store in Cedarville. An anonymous restitution. Now, I thought, I can have peace.

I'd repaid the money. I'd even been on the generous side in estimating the interest. But there were things I hadn't done, too. I hadn't confessed the sin. I hadn't asked for forgiveness. I hadn't moved through the steps that David laid out for us in these psalms. I found that the blot on my hand hadn't washed away.

More years passed, and I became a pastor in Fort Wayne, Indiana. One day the hardware dealers came into town for a convention. So there I stood at the pulpit when the sanctuary door swung open and in came Mr.

and Mrs. Fred Lutenberger. It was as if Nathan himself were coming down the aisle of my church, pointing his bony finger right at me.

The Lutenbergers found a seat in the third row. I can assure you I didn't do my best preaching that day. I couldn't help wanting the service to be over as soon as possible. After the sermon, there was a brief invitation. Then I came down and found the couple. "Come with me," I whispered as I took each of them by the hand. I led the Lutenbergers to my study and asked, "Do you ever remember receiving an envelope with sixty dollars and no explanation?"

Fred Lutenberger nodded and looked at his wife. "Yes, as a matter of fact. That was a strange thing."

Then I lost my composure. I began to weep as I told them the whole story. I'd been carrying the burden for all these years. A little thing—a few dollars—is enough, over time, to bring about misery, even destroy a life. I confessed everything, and begged for the Lutenbergers' forgiveness. They quickly wrapped their arms around me and told me they loved me. They thanked me for doing the right thing. And I felt such joy that it's difficult to put into words. I felt light enough to dance. An old, heavy weight had been lifted, and I was free.

> *Blessed is he whose transgression is forgiven, whose sin is covered.* (Psalm 32:1)

In a little cell in Detroit, Robert Garth, former track star and confessed murderer, marked time. He was at peace even as the detectives were in turmoil, racing around to check facts and pore over old files.

Robert's shocking story did check out, of course—every detail. Only one element made no sense to the detectives: Why would a murderer, who'd committed a perfect crime, come forward to implicate himself fifteen years later? He'd pulled it off; no one had known.

But someone had known, of course; the person who mattered most of all. Now that person was free, at least from the solitude of the secret. He was actually able to concentrate on the book that someone had handed him: a Bible. The section of the Book that drew him irresistibly was the

Book of Psalms. It was as if someone had been recording his thoughts over the years, an x-ray of his soul. This King David had wandered down the same dark alleys of guilt, the same boulevards of despair—but he had found a way out. Robert read about a God of forgiveness who could shoulder the heaviest, deadliest burden. He found the promise of true liberation. David was a murderer like himself, and God loved him nonetheless.

It was too good to be true, but Robert knew in his heart it was true. He couldn't contain his joy, and finally his feelings overflowed in a great shout that echoed through the barred corridor. He'd have to be careful about that—they already thought he'd taken leave of his senses just for confessing. He didn't want to be moved to a psychiatric ward.

The trial judge, seeing Robert's remarkable remorse, was lenient. This defendant was his own accuser; he might have escaped, but he had made a full confession and accepted the consequences. The sentence was a short one for a murder case.

"My time in prison," Robert would later say, "was easy—compared to the fifteen years I lived with that crime in my mind . . . Nothing they could ever do to me, even incarcerating me for the rest of my life, could measure up to the imprisonment of my own guilt during the fifteen years of hiding my sin."

Guilt is a giant of terrible weight. But Robert finally brought down that giant with a shout of joy. For the first time in years, his feet felt light again—light enough to sprint all the way to the throne of the One who forgave him.[2]

Now he was truly ready to run the race and claim the prize. Let's you and I run beside him.

# 8

---

# WHEN YOU ARE AT YOUR WITS' END

---

FROM: WHEN YOUR WORLD FALLS APART—
SEEING PAST THE PAIN OF THE PRESENT

## PSALM 107

1   Oh, give thanks to the Lord, for He is good!
    For His mercy endures forever.

2   Let the redeemed of the Lord say so,
    Whom He has redeemed from the hand of the enemy,

3   And gathered out of the lands,
    From the east and from the west,
    From the north and from the south.

4   They wandered in the wilderness in a desolate way;
    They found no city to dwell in.

5   Hungry and thirsty,
    Their soul fainted in them.

6   Then they cried out to the Lord in their trouble,
    And He delivered them out of their distresses.

7   And He led them forth by the right way,
    That they might go to a city for habitation.

8   Oh, that men would give thanks to the Lord for His goodness,
    And for His wonderful works to the children of men!

9   For He satisfies the longing soul,
    And fills the hungry soul with goodness.

10  Those who sat in darkness and in the shadow of death,
    Bound in affliction and irons—

11  Because they rebelled against the words of God,
    And despised the counsel of the Most High,

12  Therefore He brought down their heart with labor;
    They fell down, and there was none to help.

13  Then they cried out to the Lord in their trouble,
    And He saved them out of their distresses.

14  He brought them out of darkness and the shadow of death,
    And broke their chains in pieces.

15  Oh, that men would give thanks to the Lord for His goodness,
    And for His wonderful works to the children of men!

16  For He has broken the gates of bronze,

And cut the bars of iron in two.

17 Fools, because of their transgression,
And because of their iniquities, were afflicted.

18 Their soul abhorred all manner of food,
And they drew near to the gates of death.

19 Then they cried out to the Lord in their trouble,
And He saved them out of their distresses.

20 He sent His word and healed them,
And delivered them from their destructions.

21 Oh, that men would give thanks to the Lord for His goodness,
And for His wonderful works to the children of men!

22 Let them sacrifice the sacrifices of thanksgiving,
And declare His works with rejoicing.

23 Those who go down to the sea in ships,
Who do business on great waters,

24 They see the works of the Lord,
And His wonders in the deep.

25 For He commands and raises the stormy wind,
Which lifts up the waves of the sea.

26 They mount up to the heavens,
They go down again to the depths;
Their soul melts because of trouble.

27 They reel to and fro, and stagger like a drunken man,
And are at their wits' end.

28 Then they cry out to the Lord in their trouble,
And He brings them out of their distresses.

29 He calms the storm,
So that its waves are still.

30 Then they are glad because they are quiet;
So He guides them to their desired haven.

31 Oh, that men would give thanks to the Lord for His goodness,
And for His wonderful works to the children of men!

32 Let them exalt Him also in the congregation of the people,
And praise Him in the assembly of the elders.

33    He turns rivers into a wilderness,
      And the watersprings into dry ground;
34    A fruitful land into barrenness,
      For the wickedness of those who dwell in it.
35    He turns a wilderness into pools of water,
      And dry land into watersprings.
36    There He makes the hungry dwell,
      That they may establish a city for habitation,
37    And sow fields and plant vineyards,
      That they may yield a fruitful harvest.
38    He also blesses them, and they multiply greatly;
      And He does not let their cattle decrease.
39    When they are diminished and brought low
      Through oppression, affliction and sorrow,
40    He pours contempt on princes,
      And causes them to wander in the wilderness where there is no way;
41    Yet He sets the poor on high, far from affliction,
      And makes their families like a flock.
42    The righteous see it and rejoice,
      And all iniquity stops its mouth.
43    Whoever is wise will observe these things,
      And they will understand the lovingkindness of the Lord.

*The Lord's our rock, in Him we hide,*
*Secure whatever ill betide*
*A shelter in the time of storm*
*The raging storms may round us beat*
*We'll never leave our safe retreat,*
*A shelter in the time of storm.*

—Ira Sankey

When I was first diagnosed with cancer, I went to certain special people for counsel and comfort. One of these was Dr. Marv Eastlund of Fort Wayne, Indiana. I knew he was a man who would fill three critical roles: first, as a close, trusted friend of many years; second, as a career physician of excellence; third, as a fellow struggler who had grappled with serious illness in his own life. I leaned on his support, advice, and brotherly encouragement; I'll never forget his ministry to me.

Dr. Eastlund's bend in the road was a pancreatic disorder. I've asked him to tell you about the medical misadventure that landed him flat on his back for several weeks at the Mayo Clinic.

There are certain kinds of change none of us ask for, and none of us receive with open arms. In my life, pancreatitis was an uninvited visitor—the last item that would ever have appeared on my agenda. I was thoroughly miserable when the doctors broke the news to me about it.

The dreadful disease moved into my life like a tornado, demolishing my control over my life, my career, and all my plans for the future. My first reaction was intense anger, to be honest. I resisted this outrageous medical intrusion and fought it with all the energy I could muster. One of my main weapons was denial. I insisted on keeping my usual schedule and simply ignoring the pain.

That was a losing battle, as I'm sure you can imagine. The pancreatitis won. I soon reached my pain threshold, and I could no longer pretend that my body was fine and healthy. I was filled with anger. Who could I blame? I could find no scapegoat, so I blamed myself. Anger gave way to discouragement and self-pity. I wallowed in my own misery for extended periods of time, fully realizing that I was sick—really sick— and that my life would never again be the same. What response was there for me but despair and gloom? I became consumed with my own problems. And if there was any small thread of hope left within me, the repeated hospitalizations snuffed it out.

Discouragement gave way to depression. There were days I could do nothing but sit and stare. My family tried desperately to encourage me, but I made certain they didn't succeed. I was investing a good bit of energy in my negative emotions, and I didn't want to cheer up. Life was unfair. The future was hopeless.

And yet deep within me, there was the nagging question of my faith. I couldn't give up the life commitment I had made to God. He meant too much for me to simply turn away from Him. So I was being torn by great spiritual conflict: How could a believer experience the thoughts and emotions I was feeling? Why had God let me sink into anger, discouragement, and depression? If my faith was as strong as I'd always thought it was, why then—how, then—could I now be questioning His very existence? Where was He? Why didn't He answer my pleas?

My faith was on very rocky ground indeed. Physically, mentally, and spiritually, I had come to my wits' end. I had nowhere to turn. So I lay down on my back one day, sighed deeply, and stared up at the ceiling.

And as I did that, I realized that my eyes were fixed in the right direction—up. I was looking toward heaven. *Up* was the

only direction a bed patient could look. And with new resolution, I realized I had to be faithful to Him and keep trusting Him. I could not turn away. As distant as He seemed at
times, I realized that my pain and despair only served to draw
me closer to Him than health and happiness could ever have
brought me.

Through the pain, I began to know Him better. I found a
friend in God, a *genuine* Friend I had never known before.

I see my problems differently now. When life closes in, I
know that the only way out is the way up.

*God is a genuine friend*—Dr. Eastlund found that out, and the psalms
repeat that rich theme over and over.

## PICTURES OF HELPLESSNESS

Psalm 107 celebrates the friendship and the faithfulness of God. It's a
beloved hymn of thanksgiving for His deliverance. We can find, in the section spanning verses 4 through 32, four word pictures of circumstances
faced by God's people along their journey. These four separate pictures
have a common overlapping theme: the human feeling of helplessness.

We'll be taking a close look at these fine pictures. As we do so, I invite
you to imagine you and me walking through the Bible's great gallery of
art. It is a fabulous museum, filled with inspiring portraits and fantastic
renderings in every corner. We've begun with the beautiful landscapes of
the tranquility of the Garden of Eden, the towering summit of Sinai, and
the pastoral beauty of Canaan. We've seen portraits of prophets, priests,
and patriarchs. Finally, as we enter the building known as the Book of
Psalms, we come to Room 107. It's a thought-provoking gallery. We'll need
to spend some time here in contemplation.

Here are four paintings carefully rendered by the artist whose goal is to
portray four great challenges of life. I'll be serving as your tour guide for
this particular room, and I ask you to keep up with the group and, please—
no flashbulbs! As we study the paintings, I will pause briefly at the first

three to make some general comments. Then we'll engage in an in-depth exploration of the fourth and final painting. This one is the culmination of the other three, a masterpiece filled with emotion and symbolism that will astonish you. We will spend the majority of our time there, and I predict you'll be coming back to gaze at the painting on your own time and again.

But let's begin our tour, shall we?

*Painting #1: The Desert*

The first painting is a landscape, but it's not one you're likely to see from the brush of your typical painter. This landscape happens to be a desert.

We might call this one "Wanderers in the Wilderness." The title would draw its inspiration from a description found in verses 4 through 9 of Psalm 107. There we read about the experience of being lost in the desert. Of course, we realize that not all deserts are composed of sand, and we can be lost without losing our physical bearings. Listen to the word picture painted by the psalmist: "They wandered in the wilderness in a desolate way; they found no city to dwell in. Hungry and thirsty, their soul fainted in them." We grow thirsty just hearing these words.

Many have lost their way in a dry wilderness, devoid of meaning and purpose. For some, the desert is loneliness. Others are lost in a cycle of routine futility. Still others become dislocated in a desert of affluence, which turns out to be a drier and thirstier land than they ever expected. The wanderers trudge through the sand without hope or help, seeking the true spiritual home that always eludes them.

As we move to the next portico, we find a different scenario.

*Painting #2: The Prison*

The desert may have seemed an odd subject for a painting, but verse 10 offers one even less likely. It is a group portrait of prisoners, "those who sat in darkness and in the shadow of death, bound in affliction and irons."

Leonard Griffith writes, "People are like prisoners, trapped in the dungeon of their own moral folly, the victims of evil rather than the doers of it. They started out with freedom of choice, but they continued to choose the wrong thing." But that freedom will be fleeting when we choose evil. The wrong choices become patterns of behavior that finally master those who made the choices. "The drug addict would give anything to be set free from the chains of his habit, but it has him hooked and he knows that the end of it will be his death. . . . In his sober moments, the alcoholic hates himself for the hell that he creates in his own home, but his bottle is like a chain, and he knows that he cannot break loose from it."[1]

So there are prisons of addiction—gambling, drugs, and alcohol—but there are also prisons of abuse or of improper relationships. People are taken prisoner by their own conduct.

Not all prisons are of our own making, however. Some of us are trapped by difficult circumstances from which there seems little hope of escape. These prisons might have been constructed by other people's evil, by persecution, or by matters over which they have no control. We don't have to be at fault to become hopeless captives. Our painting shows the desolation of imprisonment, and it saddens us to look upon this canvas. We take one more look, and we move on.

*Painting #3: The Hospital*

Now we come to the portrayal of a familiar but forbidding setting, that of a hospital. In verses 17 through 22, we find something not too different from an ICU. Are you surprised to find that in the Bible? Look closely at the picture painted for us in these verses: "Fools, because of their transgression, and because of their iniquities, were afflicted. Their soul abhorred all manner of food, and they drew near to the gates of death" (verses 17–18). This is a ward of illness and affliction, and it serves as a corridor that opens into the darkness of death.

Not every illness, of course, is caused by sin. But the people here have poisoned themselves with their own transgressions. They are suffering, ready for the release brought only by death. There in the ward they lie, waiting only for their final moments on this earth. That's the story laid out for us in the third of the four paintings. We take in its gloomy canvas and move to the last picture. This one is larger than the others, and it captures our full attention.

*Painting #4: The Storm*

The picture causes us to catch our breath. It captures perfectly the power of nature in all its unleashed fury. As our eyes move across the canvas, we know what it means to be clinging to the deck of a ship that is caught in a terrible storm. We take the forces of nature for granted—until we become their helpless prey.

We know how the disciples felt, violently tossed in the nighttime waves and fearing death before Jesus came. We know how the passengers of the *Titanic* felt on a far calmer night—but one in which the greatest ship ever built was no match for a stray block of ice. We're gazing at the portrait of a furious tempest:

> Those who go down to the sea in ships, who do business on great waters, they see the works of the Lord, and His wonders in the deep. For He commands and raises the stormy wind, which lifts up the waves of the sea. They mount up to the heavens, they go down again to the depths; their soul melts because of trouble. They reel to and fro, and stagger like a drunken man, and are at their wits' end. Then they cry out to the Lord in their trouble, and He brings them out of their distresses. He calms the storm, so that its waves are still. Then they are glad because they are quiet; so He guides them to their desired haven. Oh, that men would give thanks to the Lord for His goodness, and for His wonderful works to the children of men! Let them exalt Him also in the congregation of the people, and praise Him in the assembly of the elders.
>
> (Psalm 107:23–32)

# A Closer Look at the Storm

*The Place of the Storm*

These sailors realize their small stature, their seeming insignificance, out on the open sea. There is no land in sight. There is no one to rescue those in peril on the sea.

You may never have crossed the ocean on a large ship, but the picture will remain just as powerful for you—for we all know what it's like to be caught in one of life's many storms. You realize immediately that towering waves and billowing storms can come in many forms.

When I've encountered the storms of my own life, I've taken encouragement from this psalm. It has always been when I've ventured out onto the open sea, when I've been taking a great step of faith and moving beyond the borders of safety, that I've been caught by the treacherous winds. I feel certain that I'm pursuing the will of God for my life, but my faith is sternly tested by the wind and the rain. That's when I have thought about the assurances of Psalm 107. At the end of this chapter, I'll tell you how this psalm became permanently etched on my soul.

For now, let's consider Jesus and the small circle of men around Him. They understood the terror of the tempest. They also understood the mystery of deep waters. We know this from Luke 5:4–6, when Jesus commanded Simon Peter to "launch out into the deep and let down your nets for a catch." Simon grumbled a little about this, reminding the carpenter from Nazareth that the professionals—men who knew their trade—had been fishing all night, and they hadn't caught a thing. Nevertheless, Simon said if that's what Jesus wanted, the boys would take one more shot. And you know the rest. After one more trip, the nets were overflowing, literally bursting with fish.

The message? Great works are done in deep waters. If you're diving for pearls, you have to move out of the shallow end. Many of us never learn that lesson; fear restricts us to the comfort zone, where we miss out on untold adventures. But Jesus tells us to launch out into the deep—in risk taking, in the pursuit of excellence, and in the knowledge of Him. We walk to the edge of all our light, and that next step into the blackness holds the destiny God has for us. But it also holds whatever dangers lie in the darkness. We know that, we realize the risks, and perhaps we'll never take that one terrifying step that makes the miracle possible.

It's not simply biblical sense—it's common sense as well. If you're in the business world, you realize that. Play it safe, and you'll never build a business. Launching a new firm is launching out into the deep. The storms are certain to come, and the winds will howl. You'll be out on the edge, all by yourself in an unsteady boat. Perhaps your business will fail despite all your best efforts and intentions. But you'll never know unless you cast the net.

No one ever said it would be easy out in the deep waters. No one ever guaranteed fair weather and smooth sailing. It's your choice—stay along the shore and you'll always be safe from drowning and disaster. But you'll also never know the blessings of the deep things of God.

*The Producer of the Storm*

What's wrong with this picture? What seems unusual about the storm depicted in this psalm?

"For He commands and raises the stormy wind, which lifts up the waves of the sea" (verse 25). The pronoun *He* is capitalized. Now we realize the striking thing about this storm. As great as the power of the wind and the waves may be, there is something—Someone—more powerful in the background, behind it all. It is God—the God who sends the rains.

Did you step back from the canvas when you realized that detail? Are you shocked? We're much more comfortable crediting God with calming storms than with causing them. And yet we must take the Scripture at its word. The Bible teaches us that He is Lord of all—and that includes the storms that serve His purposes along with everything else.

Let's take care before blaming God for every storm, however. Sometimes we've done just fine on our own bringing on those dark clouds. We make the mistakes, and God's place is simply to let us discover how deeply we need Him when we're just about to go under the waves. So we're not referring to those self-induced tempests. We're talking about storms brought about expressly by divine intention. And those do exist.

Job understood that. He had a disciplined understanding that character is a function of trial, and even trials were deeply tied to His friendship and faith in God. He said, "He knows the way that I take; when He has tested me, I shall come forth as gold" (Job 23:10). *He knows.* Job found strength in the knowledge that God knew him intimately, and he set out with the understanding that tests would deepen that friendship. When the storms came, he was prepared. Even during the most excruciating pain, Job knew God was in control of his problems. He knew that pain had a purpose.

Listen to this expression of the same understanding in Psalm 66: "You brought us into the net; you laid affliction on our backs. You have caused men to ride over our heads; we went through fire and through water; but You brought us out to rich fulfillment" (verses 11–12). Have you felt people "riding over your head" at your workplace recently? Have you been through fire and water in family problems? A devoted believer will pray for God's deliverance from problems, but a wiser one will pray for God's use of them.

Even Jonah—rebellious, dispassionate Jonah—knew Who was behind the storms. When God sent him on a mission, he booked passage on a ship and headed in the opposite direction as quickly as he could. The belief that he could run away demonstrated an appallingly limited view of God. His God was too small! But the ensuing tempest enlarged his perspective. Here was a God who could trouble the sea. Job realized that he could run, but he couldn't hide. The Lord sent the storm just as He sent Jonah. Jonah was God's messenger to the Ninevites, but the storm was God's message to Jonah.

Why did He send the storm in your life? Is it intended to cut off your flight from God, as in the case of Jonah? Is it to draw you closer, as in Job's life? If you're weathering a storm, you can be certain the winds are no random weather front. They blow for a clear purpose. As you're caught up in a tempest, ask God to help you be caught up in His purposes.

*The Peril of the Storm*

"They mount up to the heavens, they go down again to the depths; their soul melts because of trouble. They reel to and fro, and stagger like a drunken man, and are at their wits' end" (Psalm 107:26–27). What an image God paints on the canvas of our minds here!

In his masterful paraphrase, *The Message,* Eugene Peterson rewords the passage like this: "You shot high in the sky, then the bottom dropped out; your hearts were stuck in your throats. You were spun like a top, you reeled like a drunk, you didn't know which way was up." This is a riot of mixed metaphors, of course, in the service of a strong point—the "you" in this passage is spinning wildly out of control! Have you ever lost control of an automobile on an icy highway? If so, you know this feeling well. These passengers of the rocking ship are at their wits' end.

By the way, did you know where the expression "at your wits' end" came from? Right here in the psalms. These people have been outwitted. They've come to the end of all their ideas and strategies. The tempest has mastered their vessel. The ship has set off to navigate the winds and the waters, but that's all been turned upside down. The wind and the waters are now navigating the ship. The passengers can do little but watch—and pray.

*The Prayer in the Storm*

Unfortunately, prayer seems to be our last port in a storm. It should be the first. But the people of this passage do turn to God in verse 28: "Then they cry out to the Lord in their trouble, and He brings them out of their distresses." Have you ever noticed the inverse relationship between depth of crisis and length of prayer? You could almost create a mathematical formula to demonstrate that the calmer things are, the lengthier and more eloquent our prayers tend to be. But the greater the storm, the shorter and simpler we pray—starting with this classic prayer adopted by many devout and troubled believers over the centuries: "Help!"

When we were living in Fort Wayne, Indiana, the driveway of our little house emptied out into a busy highway. For us, a simple trip to buy groceries was a guaranteed adventure. One day, I was sitting in the passenger seat while Donna backed out into traffic—and never saw the approaching car. But I did, right at the last moment. I looked up, anticipated the collision, and blurted out, "Lord—help!" Yes, the car hit us; but it barely missed the side of the car where I was seated, and I escaped a serious injury. I assure you I have several prayers more inspiring and articulate than "Lord—help!" But it was just the thing for that occasion—precisely the right length.

The seafarers of the psalm may have called out the same words, and probably more than once. Their circumstances have certain similarities to the characters in the other paintings. Let's look at the first picture again. The desert wanderers, hopelessly lost, "cried out to the Lord in their trouble, and He delivered them out of their distresses" (verse 6).

How about those prisoners in their cell? What are they saying? "Then they cried out to the Lord in their trouble, and He saved them out of their distresses" (verse 13).

Meanwhile, back in the sterile, deathlike hospital ward, what are the patients saying? "Then they cried out to the Lord in their trouble, and He saved them out of their distresses" (verse 19).

In the storms, in the wilderness, in captivity, and in illness, people desperately seek an escape. And Dr. Marv Eastlund has said it for all of us: The only way *out* is the way *up*. No matter what the problem may be, no matter what trouble may ensnare us, there is only one path to safety. The only hope is to reach beyond ourselves to Someone stronger than we are, and stronger than the shackles that bind us. Only One can fill that requirement. And even the proverbial atheist in the foxhole realizes it in the depths of his heart. Even the most thoroughgoing skeptic will finally come to that point of absolute desperation and look up to the heavens to cry, "Lord—help!"

God's part in the storm is a sensitive topic for us right now—it hits a little too close to home, for many of us are being tossed around by ill winds at this very moment. We fear that if we stopped to consider that God may be the Author of the storm, we might be overcome with anger at God. And yet I imagine arriving in heaven when my day comes, and hearing my Lord admit that He has used storms quite frequently to drive me to my knees. I'll be capable of handling the knowledge of it then, and He'll smile and say, "That one was a real corker, wasn't it, David? That crisis you went through that particular year? I really had you going! But now you can see that it brought you back into My camp at just the right time. You weren't paying as much attention to Me in those days, remember? You were drifting, and where might you have finally ended up if I hadn't stepped in and done something to get your attention? Remember how it all paid off? I'm sure you never realized how that whole crisis prepared you for the good things to follow!" And for the first time, I'll be able to laugh about some sore spot or other; we'll laugh together, but in a joyful way.

God certainly hates everything that causes us pain, whether it may be imprisonment or illness or a storm of some kind. But He knows that lesser pain is a necessary part of avoiding far deeper pain later. It hurts to pull out a thorn, but the pain of leaving it would cause the deeper agony of infection. God knows that He has to pull out a few thorns occasionally, and we'll cry out in pain and even anger at Him. But it's all for a purpose.

God knows, even if we don't, that we're not self-sufficient. He loves to bring us to our knees in fresh dependence on Him. If only peacetime prayers carried the intensity of storm-tossed prayers! If only we could seek Him with the passion that possesses us when we feel trapped and desperate. God hears those passionate prayers. And He provides the peace that can be found nowhere else.

### The Peace in the Storm

"He calms the storm, so that its waves are still. Then they are glad because they are quiet" (verses 29–30).

Have you ever noticed the wonderful purity of silence after a prolonged cacophony of noise? The tyranny of sound suddenly loses its hold on us, and the ensuing quiet seems to liberate the spirit. It's truly a peace that passes understanding. We refer to this phenomenon as "the calm after the storm." It's about comfort and relief. Deep inside us, we realize that the Bringer of the storm is also the Master of it; He can take it away in the blink of an eye. When we realize He is great enough to send and remove storms, we fall down in worship.

When the people of the psalm were being battered by the storm, they cried out in fear and helplessness. And God responded. He calmed the storm and stilled the waves. And that idea quickly reminds us of the stories of Jesus. The events played out in Psalm 107 foreshadow the remarkable episodes we find in the Gospels. The disciples, having chosen to pursue the Teacher and the adventure He called them for, found themselves in the middle of turbulent experiences, challenges for which they must have felt ill-prepared. We can read these accounts and realize the Lord was allowing the storms to break loose because He wanted them to learn lessons that would serve them well later. They would face persecution. They would face hostility and terrible odds against an intimidating goal. They could not learn the lessons and build the strength in any other classroom than the stormy seas.

On one occasion, the disciples climbed into a boat to travel across the Sea of Galilee. Jesus boarded with them, crawled into the back, found a nice spot, and went to sleep. As they traveled far out to sea, suddenly the weather changed. A storm front quickly rolled in, and it looked like a serious one. Here were the disciples, hopelessly far from safety; surely they were going to die together. According to Matthew 8, Jesus awoke, took a good look around, and asked why His friends were so worked up. He also dropped in a stinging remark about the weakness of their faith. Then he stood in the boat, rebuked the winds and the sea, and watched the calm settle as far as the eye could see.

That's Matthew's story. But it's rewarding to discover what Luke adds to the picture. Always the astute observer of human emotions, he shows us the dimension of fear the disciples experienced. It is in Luke's account that we find out how some of the men came to Jesus and jostled Him awake, gasping, "Master, Master, we are perishing!" (Luke 8:24)

These fishermen and tax collectors and assorted commoners were shaking the arm of the Lord of glory, the One who created the winds and the waves and the sea that had them so frightened. If they had realized the full import of this, they wouldn't have demonstrated so much panic in the way they roused Him. They might even have been looking forward to the show Jesus was capable of putting on as He stilled the storm. But they were fully expecting to die. I've always been impressed by this story, and years ago I scribbled a little note next to it in the margin of my Bible. My note reads, "We are far more secure in the storm with Jesus in our boat than we will ever be on the shore without Him."

And I still believe that. If you've opted to pursue the adventure of following Jesus, you've already discovered that the journey doesn't occur in a luxury limousine. He will lead you to and through some rough places. It may be that you've found yourself in the "old gospel ship," rocked by the waves and thrashed by the downpour as lightning and thunder boomed all around you. The moment may come when you say, "I didn't sign up for this! I know I sang, 'Wherever He leads, I'll go,' but can't we at least check the weather report first? How could He lead me into a storm like this one?"

Just cling to the knowledge that you could be in no safer place than a storm of His making. You are safer and more secure in the tempest with Jesus than you could ever be in the calmest place without Him. That calm, you'll come to realize, is an illusion; and the storm is for a good purpose and a short duration.

Speaking of storms, my friend Ron Mehl told about a woman who was caught in a frightening storm in the middle of the Atlantic Ocean. She was aboard a luxury liner carrying a large number of children. The woman saw that everyone else was panicking, running to and fro through all the passages. All this was upsetting the children, so she gathered them together and began telling them Bible stories to keep them calm. The children became quiet, captivated by the wonderful stories.

The ship made it through, safe and sound. As the captain made his rounds, he saw the woman laughing and talking with the children. She had stayed calm through the storm, and she was calm now. He was puzzled. "How did you keep your cool when everyone else was falling to pieces?" he asked her. "Have you been through something like this before?"

"It's simple," said the woman. "I have two daughters. One of them lives in New York and the other one lives in heaven. I knew I would see one or the other of them in a few hours and it didn't make any difference to me which one."

Does that story seem a trifle sentimental and unrealistic to you? It shouldn't. It simply describes the mind-set of the serious believer—the follower who takes Jesus at His Word. If you feel such a story is simply sentimental, you may feel the same way about heaven and the concept that God is in control. Grace through the storm is a function of believing that the Creator of the storm is also the Deliverer from it. He is also the One who can bring us peace and strength when all those around us are falling to pieces.

He is our Deliverer, and that fact is gloriously portrayed in living color in every canvas of the eternal gallery known as Psalm 107. The first painting shows desert wanderers—those who can't find the path. "And He led them forth by the right way, that they might go to a city for habitation" (verse 7). *A city for a habitation*—the very words that define hope and peace when you've been lost in the desert.

Then we revisit the darkened prison. What happens to the captives? Someone comes to unlock their cell and show them the sunlight again. "He brought them out of darkness and the shadow of death, and broke their chains in pieces" (verse 14).

Over in the hospital, patients hover near death—only to be healed miraculously. "He sent His word and healed them, and delivered them from their destructions" (verse 20).

Downpour or desert, dungeon or disease—the specific facts of the crisis ultimately don't matter. For God is in control. Wherever we are, whatever we may be up against, when we cry out to God in our trouble, He will hear us. He will calm the waters. And the time may come when He will even let us know the reasons He unleashed them.

## The Purpose of the Storm

"So He guides them to their desired haven" (verse 30).

The Lord didn't stop at delivering the people from the storm. He took them where they needed to go. There's only one twist: The storm may change our idea of a destination. Crises never leave us the same as they found us. Those of us who love and trust God through the worst times—those of us who are receptive to what He might be trying to teach us—find that our hearts have changed by the time the stillness replaces the storminess. We will be far more in tune with His desires. Our goals will have moved closer to His own.

If you doubt that point, you might want to ask Jonah a few questions. Was he a different man after the whale spit him up onto the shore? Were his purposes closer to God's purposes after he discovered what can be wrought from disobedience? He came out of the belly of a whale and hit the ground running. There were no roads that could deliver him to Nineveh fast enough.

God changes our *want-to* in the midst of His storms.

### The Praise After the Storm

What is there for us in that time when the calm returns but to praise our God? And how we wish everyone we know, and all men and women on the face of the earth, would join us in worship and exaltation. He is greater than any of the forces of nature.

"Oh, that men would give thanks to the Lord for His goodness, and for His wonderful works to the children of men! Let them exalt Him also in the congregation of the people, and praise Him in the assembly of the elders" (verses 31–32).

We've been hopelessly lost in the barren wilderness, and suddenly we find ourselves in an oasis. What do we do? We give thanks. "Oh, that men would give thanks to the Lord for His goodness, and for His wonderful works to the children of men! For He satisfies the longing soul, and fills the hungry soul with goodness" (verses 8–9).

We've been imprisoned by addiction or abuse or past memories or another cruel master—when we discover a Master who is loving and who frees us. What do we do? We give thanks. "Oh, that men would give thanks to the Lord for His goodness, and for His wonderful works to the children of men! For He has broken the gates of bronze, and cut the bars of iron in two" (verses 15–16).

In the first two word-pictures in Psalm 107, we offer thanksgiving to the Lord for what He has done. But in the last two pictures, the image changes.

We've been desperately ill, waiting only for death. How do we respond to healing? We come together for worship. "Oh, that men would give thanks to the Lord for His goodness, and for His wonderful works to the children of men! Let them sacrifice the sacrifices of thanksgiving, and declare His works with rejoicing" (verses 21–22).

And finally, we make it through the storm. God brings us through, and what do we do? We assemble for thanksgiving, praise, and worship. "Oh, that men would give thanks to the Lord for His goodness, and for His wonderful works to the children of men! Let them exalt Him also in the congregation of the people, and praise Him in the assembly of the elders" (verses 31–32).

Is it really important to include other people in this celebration? Shouldn't it be enough simply to thank God quietly, in the privacy and sincerity of our own hearts?

I hear that sentiment more and more frequently these days. "I don't really need to worship God in a church," people say. "I can worship Him just as well by myself, working in my garden on a Sunday morning, or up at my lake cottage."

It sounds convenient, but it's not very biblical. We're told all through Scripture to come together in the assembly for the exaltation of God together. "In the presence of the elders," that is, of the leaders, we give praise to God. Together we become something greater than we could ever be individually. Together we offer an entirely different brand of worship than we offer in solitude. Together we are the living body of Christ.

## From Raging Storm to Rejoicing

I have turned to Psalm 107 in my Bible through the years, and its meaning for me grows as I advance in age. This psalm, I feel, has my name written on it. I've felt that way ever since something that happened early in my ministry at our current church.

I've been pastor at Shadow Mountain Community Church for more than nineteen years. But in the early years of my time here, I held two jobs. I accepted a call not only to pastor the church, but also to become the president of Christian Heritage College. I had a strong feeling of God's leading in holding both positions. But I never saw the storm front that was moving in. Eight years ago, the college was seriously ill, hanging on by a thread.

During one particular summer we had run out of resources, the tuition money was gone, and existing funds were insufficient to carry us through to the fall. The church had underwritten us, but now those resources were no longer available. The church had simply given all it could give. Nearly every week, I attended meetings in which we agonized over what to do. Slowly but surely, we were edging toward the idea of simply closing the doors of the college. We even met with another Christian college to explore the possibility of a merger. I remember wondering if this was what God had in mind—but I could feel no peace about it.

One day I was filled with a sense of the storm. I felt like the waves were crashing over us, and that we were drowning in the waves. I didn't know what to do. I gathered our senior staff, and we all traveled to a local Christian camp called Pine Valley. It was vacant, and the caretakers allowed us to use one of their conference rooms. Our group gathered around the table to pray, but I still felt a deep sense of despair and hopelessness. No options were appearing; our prayers weren't being answered, or so it seemed. We'd tried everything we could think of trying.

And then I came to Psalm 107.

It was the storm. My feeling of enduring a storm reminded me of the imagery in the psalm. So as we sat there in the conference room at Pine Valley, I opened my Bible and I read this passage to the group. I told the senior staff, "There is one crucial thing we can never forget. Together we have chosen to do business in the great waters—deep waters. Not many churches have schools, but we have several. We have a preschool, three elementary schools, a junior high school, a high school, and a college. We've pursued these out of obedience to God's leadership. It's not supposed to be easy. We've launched out into the deep, and we shouldn't be surprised to find ourselves caught in the storm."

We talked about the challenge at hand, and I returned to the theme of the psalm. "What we have to do is to *cry out to the Lord*. We have to ask God to move into the midst of this situation and do something that only He can do."

I've experienced few events like that one, and I'll never forget what followed. We began to pray around the table with very intense, heartfelt emotion. It was one of those powerful, spiritually charged atmospheres that come about when needy Christians get serious about seeking God's deliverance. There were tears; there was pleading. There was a knock at the door.

It was the proprietor of the camp. She motioned for me to come out into the hall, where she told me, "You need to call your office."

I found a pay phone and called Glenda at the church office. She said, "Are you sitting down?"

I said, "Glenda, I'm in a phone booth."

"Well if you can't sit down, hang on," she began. And this is what she told me. She said the women down in the college mailroom had been routinely opening mail. They came across a strange envelope—it contained no letter. No letter at all, but it did have a check inside—*a check for half a million dollars.*

I went back into the meeting with my eyes filled with tears, and everyone was anxious. They wanted me to tell them who had died. I said, "No one has died! Let me tell you what has happened. We've been sitting here in this room, in the midst of a storm. We've been crying out to God for His help, and He heard our pleas. He reached out to us in our trouble and brought us into a place of peace."

To say that we began to praise God would be an understatement. When you come out of a storm in which all had seemed lost, and God does something magnificent, the worship is unforgettable!

That's known as a happy ending. Do you still have doubts that your story will have one? Perhaps the storm is raging for you as you read these words. Perhaps you're lost in a wilderness of shattered hope, or shut away in a prison of debt. Perhaps you face a hospital ward of health concerns, or family problems are rocking your boat and you feel you'll be lost forever.

Wherever you are, whatever the crisis may be, there is an important principle at work. If you feel helpless, you've become eligible for the assistance of God. You need only cry out for His salvation. He will do the rest in His time, *and He'll do it well.*

When the storm is over, you'll be a new creature—wiser, stronger, and ready to serve Him. The sea will be calm, the breeze will be soft, and the silence will present itself as a sanctuary for you to exalt His name and sing His glorious praises. If He can control the storm, what other wonderful works might He bring to pass in your life?

With that exciting thought, you'll cast off and launch out into the deep waters.

# 9

---

# LONELY SAINTS

---

From: OVERCOMING LONELINESS

*I'm alone Lord*
*alone*
*a thousand miles from home.*
*There's no one here who knows my*
*name*
*except the clerk*
*and he spelled it wrong,*
*no one to eat dinner with*
*laugh at my jokes*
*listen to my gripes*
*be happy with me about what happened*
*today*
*and say that's great.*
*No one cares.*
*There's just this lousy bed*
*and slush in the street outside*
*between the buildings.*
*I feel sorry for myself*
*and I've plenty of reason to.*
*Maybe I ought to say*
*I'm on top of it*
*praise the Lord*
*things are great*
*but they're not.*
*Tonight*
*it's all*
*gray slush.*[1]

Every year during football season a lot of Americans spend many enjoyable hours with their favorite team. And then the season's over. It's gone. There's a letdown and a feeling of loss.

That's a picture of life, isn't it? The things that have no eternal value, but are just temporal—they go, they end, and only a kind of emptiness is left when it's all over.

Things of eternal value don't leave that feeling. Our relationship with the Lord never leaves an empty feeling. In Jesus Christ we find rest, joy, and happiness regardless of whether or not something happens or whether our teams win.

People face different kinds of loneliness. A particular kind of loneliness comes to us when we have lost a loved one. It touches us at the very core of our lives. Some readers of this book have recently lost someone in their immediate families—a husband, a wife, a child, a grandparent—and an aching loneliness is in their hearts because of it.

Separation from friends causes loneliness too. Missionaries often speak of that. They know what it's like to be on the other side of the world, facing crises, with no one there to help. Nobody is close enough to them to understand what they're experiencing.

Another kind of loneliness can take place when you're with others— in the midst of a large crowd or even when you're surrounded by people you love. The feeling that no one cares creeps in and you crave affirmation from someone that you matter.

Christians are sometimes called upon to take positions that are unpopular, that do not meet with the approval of the majority. We feel very much alone then, and because of these experiences we can identify with a man in the Bible who for fifty years carried on a public ministry that was not appreciated.

Jeremiah, God's prophet through the reign of five different kings, watched terrible things happen to those to whom God had called him to minister. The first few verses of his prophecy, the Old Testament Book of Jeremiah, identify the three major kings under whom he served: Josiah, Jehoiakim, and Zedekiah. Two other men were king for only three months each. During this time period, Jeremiah watched disorder on a national level because of political upheaval and corrupt leadership. He saw disturbing social problems and dissension tear his people apart. Discontent and despair seemed to be the mood of the times. But Jeremiah continued to minister as a prophet of God in the land of Judah, no matter how unpopular, opposed, condemned, ridiculed, and scorned he was.

On one occasion he was stoned and thrown out of his home town. On another occasion he was disgraced and beaten in public. Another time he was imprisoned, and once he was thrown into a pit and left for dead. Eventually he wrote *Lamentations*, a book of poetry often called a collection of funeral poems. They are the outpouring of his grief at the destruction of the holy city. Because of them he has been called the "weeping prophet." If you haven't read Lamentations recently, read it and you'll come to know and understand a lonely, hurting man.

Jeremiah ministered during the last years of Judah's history, from the thirteenth year of King Josiah until the destruction of the nation. The decline of Judah greatly depressed him. He said,

> *An astonishing and horrible thing*
> *Has been committed in the land:*
> *The prophets prophesy falsely,*
> *And the priests rule by their own power,*
> *And my people love to have it so.*

(Jeremiah 5:30–31)

The prophets were not speaking from God, the priests were using their sacred mission for personal gain, and the people didn't object. That kind of corruption was to their fancy.

Jeremiah looked out over his nation and saw a whole generation of backslidden people who had fallen away from their godly moorings. They had walked a road away from God. "The harvest is past," he said. "The summer is ended, and we are not saved!" (Jeremiah 8:20) As he looked at the awful apathy among the people who were supposed to be God's people, depression swept his soul.

One of the key words in the Book of Jeremiah is *backslide*. Over and over again, Jeremiah mentions the backsliding of God's people. For example,

> *Your own wickedness will correct you,*
> *And your backslidings will reprove you.*
> *Know therefore and see it is an evil and bitter thing.* (2:19)

*The Lord said also to me in the days of Josiah the king: "Have you seen what backsliding Israel has done?" (3:6)*

*Then I saw that for all the causes for which backsliding Israel had committed adultery, I had put her away. (3:8)*

*Return, you backsliding children, And I will heal your backslidings. (3:22)*

Jeremiah cried out against all this, but his cries fell on deaf ears. These people had lifted apathy and indifference to new heights.

Lord Macaulay, who was a British historian, wrote these words about somebody else, but they fit the man Jeremiah. He said: "It is difficult to conceive any situation more painful than that of a great man, condemned to watch the lingering agony of an exhausted country, to tend it during the alternating fits of stupefaction and raving which preceded its dissolution, and to see the symptoms of vitality disappear one by one until nothing is left but coldness and darkness and corruption."

Just as this man did with his country, Jeremiah stood in the nation he loved, among the people to whom God had called him, and watched the awful moral decline that ultimately placed the people in captivity. Jeremiah went to his grave having seen the death of his nation.

It is one thing to watch a nation fall; it's another to watch its people be totally insensitive to the inevitable. It was the disinterest of the people that broke Jeremiah's heart. He grieved about their sad spiritual state and spent a great deal of time weeping.

*Oh, that my head were waters,*
*And my eyes a fountain of tears,*
*That I might weep day and night*
*For the slain of the daughter of my people!*

(9:1)

*But if you will not hear it,*
*My soul will weep in secret for your pride.*

(13:17)

*Let my eyes flow with tears night and day,*
*And let them not cease;*
*For the virgin daughter of my people*
*Has been broken with a mighty stroke, with a very severe blow.*

(14:17)

In the Book of Lamentations we find instance after instance of Jeremiah weeping for a nation that had been reared on the precepts of God and had turned from them. God had raised him up, made him a prophet to pronounce God's judgment and the way of deliverance, but the people would not listen. Their ears were closed; they refused to hear. As Jeremiah thought about that in the night watches, loneliness overwhelmed him. He was alone, deserted and friendless, God's representative in a decadent society. The desertion of his friends distressed him.

*See, O Lord, that I am in distress;*
*My soul is troubled . . .*
*They have heard that I sigh,*
*With no one to comfort me.*
*All my enemies have heard of my trouble;*
*They are glad that You have done it.*

(Lamentations 1:20–21)

*I did not sit in the assembly of the mockers,*
*Nor did I rejoice;*
*I sat alone because of Your hand,*
*For You have filled me with indignation.*
*Why is my pain perpetual*
*And my wound incurable,*
*Which refuses to be healed?*

(Jeremiah 15:17–18)

Jeremiah felt what all of us are prone to feel in such situations. He was ready to disown it all. He had what we call in the modern vernacular his own, private pity party. And thinking back over what we've already learned about this lonely man, we cannot really blame him; from the human standpoint, he wanted to die. He was ready to quit. He was all by himself, and you can feel the ache of his heart as he writes. Each of us has had some kind of experience at one time or another, an experience with isolation, and can imagine how Jeremiah felt. I don't know what finally was the last blow, but one day Jeremiah decided he had had enough; all of it was too much for him.

> *Cursed be the day in which I was born!*
> *Let the day not be blessed in which my mother bore me!*
> *Let the man be cursed*
> *Who brought news to my father, saying,*
> *"A male child has been born to you!"*
> *Making him very glad.*
> *And let that man be like the cities*
> *Which the Lord overthrew, and did not relent;*
> *Let him hear the cry in the morning*
> *And the shouting at noon,*
> *Because he did not kill me from the womb.*
> *That my mother might have been my grave,*
> *And her womb always enlarged with me,*
> *Why did I come forth from the womb to see labor and sorrow,*
> *That my days should be consumed with shame?*
> (Jeremiah 20:14–18)

Jeremiah was so distraught he wished he had never been born; He had hit bottom and didn't want to go on.

Someone wrote a paraphrase of these verses. I don't know who it was, but he must have been a modern-day pastor writing on a Monday morning. It vividly expresses Jeremiah's despair: "I had no idea when you called me into Your office that it would be like this. I pictured myself preaching great sermons, perhaps working a miracle now and then. I foresaw some opposition, but I thought I would override it in calm victory. You never mentioned my destruction or the number of those who would despise me. You neglected to mention that everyone in Jerusalem would mock me constantly. I'm the laughing stock of all Judah! Everyone points or smirks or laughs or snarls at me when I walk down the street, even the smallest children. I *quit!*"[3]

Do you ever talk like that? Have you ever said, "I quit!" Then you can understand Jeremiah, He wanted to disown the whole thing. Everyone at one time or another has wanted to quit.

> *Oh, that I had in the wilderness*
> *A lodging place for travelers;*
> *That I might leave my people,*
> *And go from them!*
> *For they are all adulterers,*
> *An assembly of treacherous men.*
>
> (Jeremiah 9:2)

What was Jeremiah saying? "I wish I had a motel room in the wilderness so that I could get away from this hassle. If I did, I'd do it tomorrow. If I could just get in my car and drive away from it all, leave it behind me, oh, what a good feeling that would be!"

Do you ever feel like that? James Conway, in his book *Men in Mid-Life Crisis*, speaks of how he sometimes feels as a pastor, husband, and father. He feels stretched to the breaking point, unable to satisfy all the demands put on him. He doesn't have the same reasons for his despair as Jeremiah, but his loneliness and longing for relief are just as genuine. He also, from time to time, wants to quit.

> I feel like a vending machine, dispensing products. Someone pushes a button, and out comes a sermon. Someone punches another button for a solution to a personal or administrative problem. The family pushes buttons, and out comes dollars or time involvement. The community pushes other buttons, and I show up at meetings, sign petitions, and take stands. It is

easy for a man . . . to feel that he is trapped with obligations to everyone, and the frustration is that he can't get out.[3]

Jeremiah wanted to quit, but he didn't. He was faithful to what God had called him to do. For fifty years he stayed by the stuff, so to speak, not appreciated. Nobody came by and said, "Boy, it's tremendous what you're doing to save our nation." But, though he had his low moments, though he wanted to run, he was faithful.

I'm glad the Bible has recorded his emotions. Reading his words and knowing his emotions makes us feel better about our own. Knowing that a man of the Bible felt complete despair and overwhelming loneliness puts our feelings in perspective. Some people say the Bible paints plastic men, straw people, but it doesn't. It shows them the way they were: real flesh and blood individuals whose feelings sound a lot like ours.

What Jeremiah did, you and I can do. The things that were true in his life can be true in our lives. How did he do it? Four stabilizing factors kept Jeremiah secure and at the task to which God had called him. These four concrete principles caused him to be victorious.

First, *he had a conviction of his calling.* Did I say conviction? Well, at first he said, "Okay, it seems like no matter what I do, whenever I open my mouth, somebody doesn't like it. I'll tell you what—I'm not even going to talk. I'll just be quiet. I know when to shut up. I won't even mention the Lord's name." That's what he wanted to do, but his conviction was too great. He couldn't be quiet.

> *But His word was in my heart like a burning fire*
> *Shut up in my bones;*
> *I was weary of holding it back*
> *And I could not.*
>
> (Jeremiah 20:9)

How did he get such conviction? He came to the realization that God had called him. If you look carefully at the first chapter of Jeremiah, you will understand why that call was such an important part of his life.

*Then the word of the Lord came to me, saying:*
*"Before I formed you in the womb I knew you;*
*Before you were born I sanctified you;*
*I ordained you a prophet to the nations."*

(Jeremiah 1:4–5)

These verses tell us four things about his calling. God *knew* Jeremiah before he was formed; God *formed* Jeremiah in the womb; God *sanctified* Jeremiah and set him apart for His service; God *ordained* Jeremiah. God said, "You're my man, Jeremiah; you do it." Even his name, Jeremiah, carries out God's command. It means literally "whom Jehovah appoints." Jeremiah realized that he was an appointed servant called by God. In the midst of the discouragements of his life and the problems of his society, the thing that held him in place and kept him going was the realization that he was where God wanted him and doing what God wanted. Though he didn't understand the circumstances, He was convicted about his calling. He couldn't quit.

When I was considering going into the ministry, my father said, "David, if you can do anything else, do it." That was rather strange advice for a man to give his son, I thought, when I knew he'd been praying all his life that I'd be a preacher. What he meant was if my call to the ministry was not so strong as to blot out all desire for any other vocation, when trouble came, as it surely would, I would vacillate. I would want to quit. He was telling me to be sure of my calling, to be convicted about it.

My father's advice does not apply only to those who would be pastors. It applies to everyone no matter what God has commissioned us to do. For instance, some of you may be college students who face financial difficulty and academic pressure. You could be thinking about how great it would be to have a job so that you could earn money and do the things you want to do. The pressure is on, and you want to quit. But if you really believe God called you to go to school, you won't quit.

Every person has a calling from God—every one of us. Whatever yours is, you'd better be sure of it. If you know that's where God has put you, it will help you when tough times come.

So reason number one for Jeremiah's steadfastness when he wanted to quit was his *conviction of his calling.* He wanted to get out, but something in him drove him on. That something was the knowledge that God had put him in that place, given him a job to do, and implanted His word in him.

The second principle that gave Jeremiah victory was, he had *confidence in his companion.*

> *For I heard many mocking:*
> *"Fear on every side!"*
> *"Report," they say, "and we will report it!"*
> *All my acquaintances watched for my stumbling, saying,*
> *"Perhaps he can be induced;*
> *Then we will prevail against him,*
> *And we will take our revenge on him."*
> But the Lord is with me as a mighty, awesome One.
> *Therefore my persecutors will stumble, and will not prevail.*
> (Jeremiah 20:10–11, emphasis added)

Jeremiah said, "I know they're after me. I know even my friends are trying to get me. But I've got the Lord; He's my companion."

Do you remember what Jeremiah said when God asked him to go into the ministry? He said, "Lord, I can't do it. I'm a child. I'm not mature enough." But the Lord answered his objection with these words: "Do not be afraid of their faces, for I am with you to deliver you. . . . They will fight against you, but they shall not prevail against you. For I am with you." (Jeremiah 1:8, 19)

Just like Jeremiah, we need companionship. We need fellowship. God has built these needs into us. It isn't true that all we'll ever need throughout our lives is Jesus. We need the companionship of other people too. But in those moments when we are between friends, in those dark caverns of being all alone, we have the Master Companion who stays with us through it all.

> *Now, thus says the Lord, who created you, O Jacob,*
> *And He who formed you, O Israel:*

*"Fear not, for I have redeemed you;*
*I have called you by your name; You are Mine.*
*When you pass through the waters, I will be with you;*
*And through the rivers, they shall not overflow you.*
*When you walk through the fire, you shall not be burned,*
*Nor shall the flame scorch you.*
*For I am the Lord your God,*
*The Holy One of Israel, your Savior."*

(Isaiah 43:1–3)

The third principle is that Jeremiah had a *commitment that went beyond his circumstances.*

*Blessed is the man who trusts in the Lord,*
*And whose hope is the Lord.*
*For he shall be like a tree planted by the waters,*
*Which spreads out its roots by the river,*
*And will not fear when heat comes,*
*But its leaf will be green,*
*And will not be anxious in the year of drought,*
*Nor will cease from yielding fruit.*

(Jeremiah 17:7–8)

When you put your roots down deep in trust in God, when your faith is in Him, your confidence goes beyond the circumstances.

How many Christians vacillate with the circumstances? Jeremiah said, "In the midst of all these problems and troubles and difficulties, my trust is in the Lord. It doesn't matter whether it's summer or winter or what. I don't need to be anxious because I have a commitment that goes beyond these circumstances."

Do you have that kind of commitment? Or are you in the everyday hassle so many people experience—up and down, up and down in reaction to circumstances?

*And let us not grow weary while doing good, for in due season
we shall reap if we do not lose heart.*

(Galatians 6:9)

*He who continually goes forth weeping,
Bearing seed for sowing,
Shall doubtless come again with rejoicing,
Bringing his sheaves with him.* (Psalms 126:6)

*Be steadfast, immovable, always abounding in the work of the
Lord, knowing that your labor is not in vain in the Lord.*

(1 Corinthians 15:58)

Someone has said, "Integrity is carrying out a commitment even after the circumstances in which it was made have changed." Have a conviction of your calling, confidence in your companion, and a commitment beyond your circumstances.

Finally, Jeremiah had a *chorus of celebration.*
   *Sing to the Lord! Praise the Lord!
   For He has delivered the life of the poor
   From the hand of evildoers.*

(Jeremiah 20:13)

How could a person in a situation like Jeremiah's possibly sing to the Lord? He did it with faith.

Doctors speak of the "threshold of pain," the level of awareness at which a person feels pain. Some people have a high threshold; others have a very low threshold. When you take an aspirin, it has no effect on your physical problem. All it does is raise your pain threshold so that you must experience more pain before you are aware of it. The aspirin makes you feel better because you don't feel how bad you feel.

Joy is like that. Happiness and joy are spiritual aspirin. When you are filled with the joy of the Lord, the hurts around you don't touch you so quickly.

I have found that psychologically, music raises my threshold of pain. On days when I am discouraged, I'll go home, turn on the stereo, and begin to listen to music. God uses that to assuage my soul and bring me out of pain. Is it any wonder that Saul required David to come and play for him on the harp to bring him out of his depression? That's what music can do in our hearts.

Medical specialists have now established that feelings of joy raise the threshold of pain. A delightful book by Norman Cousins, called *The Anatomy of an Illness as Perceived by the Patient*, was on the best seller list. It is Cousins' story. He was told he had one chance in five hundred to live and decided to make the most of his life. In effect he said, "If I'm going to die, I don't want to die in surroundings like these." He left the hospital and rented a hotel room, a plush hotel room, and began laughing. He secured tapes of some old "Candid Camera" TV shows along with other humorous films and watched those comedies every two hours from morning till night. And he began to get better.[4] He demonstrated the truth of the Old Testament statement: "A merry heart doeth good like a medicine" (Proverbs 17:22 KJV). Many times, the joy of praise and thanksgiving to God will dissipate the hurt you feel, for, as Ezra said, "The joy of the Lord is your strength" (Nehemiah 8:10).

Are you joyful? Do you have anything you're praising God for? I learned a long time ago that there is always something for which I can give thanks. On the very worst day I still can be glad about something.

The principle of the power of joy is demonstrated in the story of Anne Frank. Perhaps you recall that Anne and her family were prisoners in their home during the Second World War. They suffered greatly with unimaginable hardship and difficulty. Anne kept a diary of their experience, recording the fear of discovery they lived with every day. But along with the descriptions of the danger and despair, Anne recorded the feelings in her heart. Somehow, despite the suffering, she found joy. In 1944, when she was a young girl, she wrote, "Nearly every evening I go to the attic, and from my favorite spot on the floor, I look up at the blue sky. As long as this exists, I thought, and I may live to see it—this sunshine, the cloudless skies—while this lasts, I cannot be unhappy. Riches can all be lost, but that happiness in your own heart can only be veiled."[5]

We have something more than blue sky and clouds. We have Jesus Christ living in us. Though the world may crumble around us, He is the blue sky; He is the light from on high that thrills and encourages our hearts. I can look beyond my circumstances into the face of the one who loves me more than I know, the one who would never allow me to go through anything that is not for my own good. And I say to myself, and to you, be convicted of your calling, have confidence in your companion, be committed, sing a chorus of celebration.

*And don't quit.*

Q. What were the problems Jeremiah encountered?

Q. How did Jeremiah overcome these problems?

Q. Can you apply what happened to Jeremiah to your own experiences?

Q. What would you say is the best cure for unhappiness?

Q. How can you obtain and keep a good mental attitude?

Q. In the face of adversity, it is hard to feel positive. What activities make you feel positive?

Q. Who can you turn to for help? Remember, you always have the Lord.

Q. How can you follow the example of Jeremiah?

Q. How did Jeremiah deal with the socio-political problems he faced?

Q. What or who is the key to happiness?

# 10

## STAY
## CONVINCED

FROM: LIVING WITH CONFIDENCE
IN A CHAOTIC WORLD—
WHAT ON EARTH SHOULD WE DO NOW?

I 've thought long and hard about world conditions, but I was still taken back by the headline of a recent opinion column by the Israeli journalist, Eitan Haber. It blared: *World War III has started!* Haber was writing about the success of North Korea's nuclear program, and he warned that the test missile fired recently by the North Koreans landed squarely in the prime minister's office in Jerusalem.[1]

The world is quickly reaching a point of no return, Haber suggested, especially when it comes to the Middle East. Experts believe the Iran–North Korean nuclear axis is now even stronger than when it was when it was formed in 2007. North Korea appears ready to supply nuclear weapons in exchange for subsidized oil from a nuclearizing Iran that is threatening to destroy Israel.[2]

With rogue states like Iran and North Korea grabbing the headlines, it's easy to forget that somewhere in the world right now there's a nuclear weapon already waiting to go off: maybe in a bunker in Pakistan, an armory in India, a silo in Israel, or stashed away in an Afghan cave. Perhaps below ground in Russia or on a firing range in China. God forbid it's sitting in a suitcase on the docks of New York City.

Depending on who you believe, about twenty-five thousand nukes are scattered around the world.[3] The top Russian defense expert under Yeltsin revealed that nearly 40 percent of so-called suitcase bombs were unaccounted for.[4] Israel itself is believed to possess numerous nuclear weapons.

Elizabeth Zolotukhina, editor of the Case Studies Working Group with the Project on National Security Reform, recently warned that purveyors of nuclear materials are communicating with customers using sophisticated new methods not readily apparent to Western intelligent officials. The nuclear black market, she warned, is becoming more professional by the day, and is surprisingly strong and resilient.[5]

*National Defense Magazine* recently ran a chilling article entitled, "7 Deadly Myths About Weapons of Terror," warning that smuggled nukes cannot be easily detected at U.S. ports. Our ability to spot small amounts of nuclear components is "over-hyped," said the report.[6]

All it takes is one explosion, and history will never recover.

It's a horrific thought, but what if a nuclear explosion occurred somewhere in the world tomorrow? What would people do? Where would people turn? What if a gathering of world leaders were attacked by terrorists? These are apocalyptic questions, but we're living in apocalyptic times. I'm not an alarmist, but sometimes I do feel alarmed.

And then I remember Romans 13:11, a verse with a clarion call from the Lord to be ready for the return of Christ. Here we find a clear strategy for living proactively as appalling things transpire around us. No weapon on earth can blast this verse out of the Bible; rather, these words tell us how to respond internally and intentionally to the times in which we're living.

Let me express to you the importance of this verse to me. The volume preceding this one, *What in the World Is Going On?*, has been the best-selling title of all my books. I've been asked to sign many copies, and on every occasion, after signing my name, I've written *Romans 13:11* on the flyleaf in hopes that the book's owner will turn to that verse and be compelled by its truth.

In this book, you'll notice that the conversation, like a boomerang, always comes back around to Christ's return. Now we have a chapter in which that subject is fully front and center. As I was deep in God's Word, researching the topic of what in the world we should do, I found that the Bible itself comes back to this topic over and over. In good times or bad times, God wants us to be alert concerning this issue, and never to fall asleep like negligent sentries on the tower of the fort. As we see our culture in decline, we know we are at war with the enemy; we need to be more vigilant than ever.

Read and reflect on Paul's words for us:

> And do this, knowing the time, that now it is high time to awaken out of sleep; for now our salvation is nearer than when we first believed. The night is far spent, the day is at hand. Therefore let us cast off the works of darkness, and let us put on the armor of light. Let us walk properly, as in the day, not in revelry and drunkenness, not in lewdness and lust, not in

strife and envy. But put on the Lord Jesus Christ, and make no provision for the flesh, to fulfill its lusts. (Romans 13:11–14)

In words terse and blunt, you might say that Paul's message is, *Live like you were dying*. That phrase was Tim McGraw's choice from the title song of one of his albums. In part, the lyrics are:

> I loved deeper, and I spoke sweeter,
> I gave forgiveness I'd been denying.
> Someday I hope you get to live
> Like you were dying.[7]

Meanwhile, Carnegie Mellon University Professor Randy Pausch was invited to be a speaker in an ongoing series asking thoughtful lecturers to assume they were giving their last presentation—to lecture as if they were dying. As it turned out, this was really the case with Pausch, who would be a victim of pancreatic cancer at forty-seven. He delivered an unforgettable talk that became a book with more than ten million readers, *The Last Lecture*.[8]

The country singer and the university professor hit a common chord: the importance of living on purpose, of moving through life with a sense of urgency based on something higher than the pursuit of pleasure. How much more should this apply to those of us who follow Christ?

If the church seems to be snoring through the fire alarm, it's not the first time. Listen to a few critical blasts from the past:

- "It has been a year of very limited spiritual fruitage, and great destitution; the church has fallen asleep."—Charles Brown, Midwestern evangelist[9]
- "I am sure I need not unroll a page of history and ask you to glance your eye down it except for a second; for again and again you will see it has occurred that the church has fallen asleep, and her ministers have become . . . destitute of zeal, having no ardent passion."—Charles Haddon Spurgeon[10]

- "It is not correct to say that the Church 'fell asleep' in the last century, simply because it had never been awake." —Henry Richard[11]

- "What is the present condition of the evangelical church? The bulk of Christians are asleep. I do not mean that the bulk of Christians who come to evangelical churches are not converted because if I meant that I would say they were dead and never had been born again. But I say they are asleep. It is possible to be morally asleep yet mentally, intellectually, physically and theologically alert. The present condition is that we are asleep."—A. W. Tozer[12]

In my last book, I quoted an observation by Vance Havner that bears repeating: "The devil has chloroformed the atmosphere of this age . . . we need to take down our 'Do not disturb' signs, snap out of our stupor, come out of our coma, and awake from our apathy."[13]

Tozer again: "God's alarm has been going off for years. Are we listening? Let's wake up—you and me!"[14] From the pages of Scripture, written so long ago, that alarm has never ceased. It calls us to snap out of the reverie of what to watch on TV tonight, where to find a good pizza. We can almost hear the voice of Jesus in the garden at night, imploring His disciples, "Watch and pray, lest you enter into temptation . . . Behold, the hour is at hand" (Matthew 26:40, 45).

Romans 13 offers four keys to resisting the seductiveness of this world.

## WE ARE TO WATCH VIGILANTLY

First, Paul tells us that "now it is high time to awake out of sleep; for now our salvation is nearer than when we first believed" (Romans 13:11). In the golden days of radio, the thriller program called *Lights Out* always began with a voice intoning, "It . . . is . . . *later* . . . *than* . . . *you* . . . *think*," pronouncing each word in synchronization with the chimes of a clock.

In a less sensationalistic manner, Paul is saying just that. The word for *time* here is *kairos*, which refers to the kind or quality of time; a season or an opportunity. This is not the same as *chronos*, which is actual, chronological time. Time is the theme of this passage, as evidenced by five references to the subject.

Throughout the Bible we are admonished to know the times and the seasons. In the Old Testament, a group was appointed for the specific purpose of discerning the times: "the sons of Issachar who had understanding of the times, to know what Israel ought to do" (1 Chronicles 12:32).

That crucial task, "understanding the present time," is Paul's theme here. The present time is the age of salvation that has come in the person of Jesus Christ. Paul consistently sets a dividing point between this age, which began with Christ's first coming, and the age to come, which will be ushered in when He comes again (1 Corinthians 1:20; 2:6, 8; 3:18; 2 Corinthians 4:4; Galatians 1:4, 14; Ephesians 1:21; 1 Timothy 6:19; Titus 2:12; Matthew 12:32; and Hebrews 6:5).

Reckoning with the future is always a part of wisdom. Many of us hire financial planners to help us prepare for the future and manage our money in a way that will provide security and (if we are believers) glorify God through our giving. In any time or season, it's always wise to factor the future into our plans. But now, all the wires have been tripped in God's warning system and we're on red alert. We must increase our watchfulness.

On one occasion Jesus scolded His critics: "You know how to discern the face of the sky, but you cannot discern the signs of the times" (Matthew 16:3). In other words, they watched for rain or for the setting sun, but not for spiritual signals. Today's technology lets us consult seven-day weather forecasts with reasonable accuracy. Doctors can predict that certain diseases may occur, even before they are manifest. Some even spend their lives compiling data on stars many light years distant, and forecast the life cycle of those stars. But all the while, we are remarkably blind to the workings of the Holy Spirit in our very lives. We are hypnotized by the rhythm of life and culture, as if this moment has no bearing on eternal reality.

Some laugh at the very suggestion of spiritual barometric readings. As we have seen, Peter encountered these mockers: "Scoffers will come in the last days, walking according to their own lusts, and saying, 'Where is the promise of His coming? For since the fathers fell asleep, all things continue as they were from the beginning of creation'" (2 Peter 3:3–4).

You've heard this just as I have. With more than a little smugness, the skeptics smile and say, "That hysteria has always been with us. Every decade someone opens his Bible and declares that the End Times are upon us. Funny how those same prophecies are so flexible they work in every generation. And still no Rapture."

The same kind of skepticism was expressed on the eve of the stock market and mortgage meltdowns. To be sure, there were voices telling us there would be terrible economic consequences to the way we were conducting our business. But they were laughed off as "economic doom prophets." Talk to the Wall Street gurus today and you'll see them wince a bit before quoting, "Past performance . . . is not a predictor of future performance."[15] Some lessons have to be learned the hard way.

## THE IMMINENCE OF OUR LORD'S RETURN

When we speak of the imminence of Christ's return, we're using the idea of time that Paul does—not chronological, but seasonal. We're not setting a date. We're speaking of the fact that all is in readiness, and there's no reason it couldn't happen today. Snow could be in the weather forecast, but no meteorologist would be able to tell you it would start falling on your yard at 3:15 in the afternoon. He could only tell you that it was imminent because all of the necessary conditions were in play for snow to arrive. With Christ, we're talking about prerequisites rather than precision.

I can identify with the frustration of Dr. Paul Kintner of Cornell University. He says his students "show a deep indifference" when he lectures about an event he and other reputable scientists at the U.S. National Academy of Sciences deem imminent—a violent storm on the surface of the sun that "could conceivably be the worst natural disaster possible" on Earth—worse than even Hurricane Katrina. He adds, "It is terribly difficult to inspire people to prepare for a potential crisis that has never happened before and may not happen for decades to come."[16] Just because a highly probable event has not yet occurred is no guarantee that it will never happen.

Since NASA scientists are a pretty conservative group, if they are warning of a probable catastrophic geomagnetic storm occurring soon and without warning, there must be reason for concern.

One such solar storm, known as the Carrington Event, occurred in 1850, and it provides a cautionary note for us today. Just before daybreak on September 2 of that year, brilliant red, green, and purple auroras burst throughout the skies as far south as the tropics, which "produced enough light to rival the brightness of the sun itself." Visually, the effect was awe-inspiring; pragmatically, there was chaos. The electric grid, such as it was at that time, was fried. Telegraph was the state of communication art at the time, and telegraph operators were shocked by flying sparks. Paper was set on fire and messages were sent even after machines were unplugged.

Scientists aren't comfortable with the implications of something like that happening in the context of today's technology. Everything from drinking water, fuel delivery, and ambient environmental controls like heating and cooling would be severely impacted. It is possible for sun storms to cause devastating results on Earth. NASA watches the skies for signs of supersolar flares that could create havoc throughout the world.[17]

Paul urges us to watch the skies for entirely different reasons. His idea of salvation, compared to our typical conception today, is like a wide-screen HDTV picture compared to a wavy black-and-white one on a 1950s picture tube. We tend to simplistically think of salvation as a passing moment, the one when we accept Christ. Even then, we consider it to be a simple intellectual decision that affiliates us with a religion and serves as a simple ticket to heaven's gate—something to tuck away and forget about, like that life insurance policy or birth certificate.

Paul, on the other hand, uses a dynamic word for salvation that comes in three tenses—three dramatic dimensions. Past salvation is the moment when we say yes to Christ, are sealed by the Holy Spirit, and have our sins washed by the blood of Christ, with that debt declared paid in full, so that we are seated with Him in the heavenly places. And that's just the past part.

Present salvation is an ongoing growth process, as spiritual molecule by spiritual molecule we are conformed to the image of Christ through the redeeming work of the Holy Spirit. Through prayer and the Word, we learn to experience victory in Christ, issue by issue.

Then, most thrilling of all, there is a future salvation. That is the event Paul is describing in Romans 13 and elsewhere. There will be a day when we are finally freed from the presence of sin. As there can be no sin in heaven, no impurity in God's holy presence, it must finally be eliminated for good. We will see that happen, and I can't imagine how wonderful it will be.

This is threefold salvation. It began when I trusted Christ, and the penalty was removed. It continued as I began walking with the Lord, and more and more I learned how to be victorious over temptation and in trials. Salvation will be complete when Jesus takes me unto Himself in the future, when sin is judged and destroyed, and eternal life begins for us. And that day, Paul tells us, "is nearer than when we first believed."

No one could have a more prophetic name than me: *David Paul Jeremiah*. But I'm not a biblical prophet. Even so, reading this verse gets us all involved in prophecy. We are included in the whispers of heaven, telling us to stand by, something wonderful is in the wings . . . and objects in the biblical mirror are closer than they may appear.

## THE INCENTIVE OF OUR LORD'S RETURN

Our love for Christ is incentive enough for us to await His return. But Paul gives us more. He tells us that in light of these expectations, we have work to do: "Knowing the time, that now it is high time to awake out of sleep" (Romans 13:11).

We define sleep as the suspension of consciousness. It can also mean allowing one's alertness, vigilance, or attentiveness to lie dormant—the human body doing absolutely nothing. We could use some of the same language to describe today's church—the Christian body doing absolutely nothing. At least this is true concerning the matter of His return.

The catastrophic events in our present day world seem to have little or no impact on our individual or collective sense of urgency.

Charles Spurgeon preached to Victorian England about the same problem: "You can sleep, but you cannot induce the devil to close his eyes . . . The prince of the power of the air keeps his servants well up to their work . . . if we could, with a glance, see the activities of the servants of Satan, we would be astonished at our own sluggishness."[18]

Paul wants to astonish us out of our sluggishness with his words of urgency. And once he has our attention, he tells us what to do: "Owe no one anything except to love one another, for he who loves another has fulfilled the law" (Romans 13:8). He follows with a summary of the Ten Commandments (Exodus 20). You may remember that the first four commandments tell us how to love God; the final six tell us how to love people. Here in Romans, Paul is emphasizing the final commandments—the relational ones. He concludes, as Christ does in the gospels, that love is the grand summation of them all.

Love, in other words, takes care of the bill. If you have it, you will owe none of those debts Paul says to avoid because if you love your neighbor, you won't steal from him or lie to him. Love is the grand shortcut to fulfilling God's commandments. The Old Testament system works on the basis of detailed restrictions: *Thou shalt not.* The gospel, however, offers a streamlined and proactive way to live. We don't have to worry so much about what we should *not* do because we are busy with what we *should*, which is one simple thing: love those we would ordinarily not love. Simple, yes, but radical and foreign to this world. As the Scottish preacher Alexander Maclaren puts it, we become "a new thing . . . a community held together by love and not by geographical accidents or linguistic affinities, or the iron fetters of the conqueror."[19]

What does this have to do with the second coming of Christ? Love is an incentive for making right choices under duress. The next time you're stuck in traffic, think, *Do I want to be honking my horn and shaking my fist at the instant I'm suddenly looking into the eyes of my Lord?* Paul is saying, "Get your relationships in order. He could be here before you finish reading this sentence." One writer stated it well: With every passing day, we "pitch our moving tent a day's march nearer home."[20]

## We Are to War Valiantly

What else can we do? "The night is far spent, the day is at hand. Therefore let us cast off the works of darkness, and let us put on the armor of light" (Romans 13:12). Paul is about to make a rather aggressive point about the way you and I are to live our lives.

*Put off Darkness.* When Paul tells us to *cast off* darkness, he chooses a decisive verb. It means to deliberately, purposefully, significantly, and permanently put aside the things of darkness. But what kind of darkness? He refers to the residue of the old, pre-Christian life; the difference between a child of God and the natural man, who is still walking in the shadow. By rights the old man should have no hold on us, but just the same, we fall into his patterns. We speak harsh words. We tell lies. We judge each other. We cannot stand each other's successes, and we often act like it is our duty to keep others in their place.

Paul is warning us that while Christ is accepted in a moment, sin remains our foe for a lifetime. We give in to the "little" temptations; we make a concession here, an exception there, and before we know it, we've conceded a great deal of authority to sin. We must put off darkness deliberately and purposefully, and do the same tomorrow and each day. Every victory of the redeemed will make us stronger while every concession draws us deeper into the slavery of sin.

Therefore, just as we are vigilant in watching for the return of Christ, like a guard on the wall, so must we be on constant guard against the encroachment of the old ways. We can't allow the devil to get his little toe into the door. The good news is that "the night is spent," as Paul poetically expresses it. "The day is at hand." The devil has played all his cards, and we have the victory of Christ on our side. As good soldiers, then, we buckle on the "armor of light" and prepare to make our stand.

*Put on the Light.* How do you put off the darkness of a room? That's easy—you flip a switch, and light makes darkness flee. There was no electricity in Paul's time, so he uses military language: "Put on the armor of light." This is the New Testament picture for walking in fellowship with God. "If we walk in the light as He is in the light, we have fellowship with one another" (1 John 1:7). Because we are saved, and indwelt by the Holy Spirit, we push back the assault of the rulers of darkness with the decisiveness of a great soldier.[21] In chaotic times, the battle rages wildly. More than ever we need to strap on that armor; more than ever we need to know our allies from our enemies. A soldier may stand on the wall, but he never sits on the fence.

About sitting on the fence: a new Barna Research report suggests that three quarters of American Christians believe God is the "all powerful, all-knowing Creator of the Universe who rules the world today." So far, so good. The problems come when the subject turns to Jesus, Satan, and the Holy Spirit. Thirty-nine percent believe Jesus sinned during His time on earth, and 58 percent of Christians do not believe that the Holy Spirit is a living being. Strangely, nearly 60 percent don't believe Satan is real, while 64 percent believe that demons can affect us. Apparently demons are more believable to some people than the work of the living, indwelling Holy Spirit.

Consider also that one out of every three Christians believes the Bible and the Koran teach the same truths. We have to conclude that most of these have read neither book. Do you see now why we speak of the need for believers to wake up?[22]

I would say that the poll results suggest that we're not sitting on the fence at this point; we're helping the enemy tear down the fence entirely. Barna has concluded that American Christians tend to stretch the Bible to fit their everyday experiences. What we are called to do is to face our everyday experiences with the undiluted, uncompromised wisdom of the Word of God. We are soldiers, not defectors.

## WE ARE TO WALK VIRTUOUSLY

Now we are ready for Paul's third admonition as we watch vigilantly and war valiantly; we must also walk virtuously. "Let us walk properly, as in the day, not in revelry and drunkenness, not in lewdness and lust, not in strife and envy" (Romans 13:13). Paul often lists traits, good and bad. Again, this list is not an exhaustive one. But it's enough to give a good indication of someone who is not walking in the light. We have two checkpoints here:

- *We are to reject public sins of the night.* "Drunkenness and revelry" is Paul's first category, and it's not difficult to understand what kind of sin he means: disorderly social behavior. Thinking of warfare again, Paul may have envisioned the soldier who goes into the city on leave and abuses alcohol. The next day, he is worthless to the army. Paul's message: "You're in the army now. Don't disgrace the uniform."

- *We are to renounce private sins.* What about who we are when no one is looking? Paul warns us against "lewdness and lust, strife and envy." These are usually the most dangerous sins of all because they hide in the human heart. We can't be held accountable by others for what they can't see, but we can become useless to God. The self-centered person becomes concerned with ego more than Christ, and ego can be defined as Edging God Out. Paul wants us to be aware of sin in its daily and nightly manifestations, its assaults from the inside and the outside.

## WE ARE TO WAIT VICTORIOUSLY

So far we've encountered a lot of soldierly discipline. Here's the payoff. All these things that Paul asks us to do are possible and positive. The strength and the strategy are both available to us—the strength through the Spirit, the strategy through the Word. Once we determine to live this way, we are happier, healthier, and far more productive.

But how do we get from where we are to where we want to be? Many Christians live in quiet defeat every day. Perhaps you would include yourself in that category. So many good people love the Lord, attend church regularly, and try to pray, all the while having a sense that there *must be more.* A. W. Tozer wrote about the spiritual craving people were feeling even in his time: "The hungry sheep look up, and are not fed. It is a solemn thing, and no small scandal in the Kingdom, to see God's children starving while actually seated at the Father's table."[23]

Maybe you're reading some of the chapters of this book while thinking, *Of course I would love to experience more of God, but I just don't ever seem to get there. My days are a series of small defeats, clusters of sin I can't overcome, and prayers that seem to bounce off the ceiling. Is there a way to get past the obstacles and live the kind of life you're describing?*

And the answer, as you might expect, is yes. Nobody has to live a disappointing Christian life. If you'll think about it, there are people we observe who are living in victory. We know it can be done because we've seen it—and we know that God is not partial in His dealings with men. This next section of Romans 13 gives us a genuine, hands-on strategy to live the kind of life we'd like to be living when Christ returns. Romans 13:14 has two calls to action. Read the verse again, and you'll see what they are: "Put on the Lord Jesus Christ, and make no provision for the flesh, to fulfill its lusts."

Yes, it's true that these steps are easier to talk through than walk through. How do you "put on Christ," and how do you "make no provision for the flesh"? Let's take them one at a time, and let me offer you an outlook that has helped me.

- *Putting on Christ.* Ray Stedman suggests this approach: "When I get up in the morning, I put on my clothes, intending them to be part of me all day, to go where I go and do what I do. They cover me and make me presentable to others. That is the purpose of clothes. In the same way, the apostle is saying to us, 'Put on Jesus Christ when you get up in the morning. Make Him a part of your life that day. Intend that he go with you everywhere you go, and that he act through you in everything you do. Call upon his resources. Live your life IN CHRIST.'"[24]

- *No Provision for Flesh.* What about the second warning? It concerns avoiding any temptation to gratify the desires of the flesh.

Harry Truman's biographer, David McCullough, recounts an example from Truman's life. The president was in the midst of talks with the USSR and Great Britain. The question at hand was what to do with postwar Germany, and there was great deal of anxiety and stress. After one really tough day, according to a Secret Service agent, Truman was ready to head back to his quarters. An Army public relations officer jauntily asked him for a ride. Truman, always the down-to-earth type, gave him a seat in the car. As a thank-you gesture, the stranger offered to get Truman anything he wanted from the city's thriving black market. He suggested a few of the products he dealt in: cigarettes, watches, whiskey, women—with a leering emphasis on that final one.

The smile was gone from President Truman's face. He replied, "Listen, son, I married my sweetheart. She doesn't run around on me, and I don't run around on her. I want that understood. Don't ever mention that kind of stuff to me again."

When they arrived at the yellow stucco house assigned for his use at the conference, Truman left the car with no further word to the now humbled officer.[25]

There's an old Native American saying that goes like this: "Call on God, but row away from the rocks." The idea is to put yourself in the best situation to succeed, and as far away as possible from the place of failure. Some people need to erase a few streets from their maps. Still others need to install software to protect their eyes from certain Internet destinations. When you're on a diet, you don't loiter at the ice cream parlor. That's what Paul means by making no provision for the flesh.

According to a *National Review Online* article, Americans rent eight hundred million pornographic videos and DVDs every year. A *vast*

*majority* of men between the ages of eighteen to thirty-four frequent pornographic websites monthly. Among those addicted to pornography are
a great number of people professing to be followers of Jesus Christ. We
can only wonder if they've received the information that, according to
research, pornography actually produces changes in the brains of users—
changes that affect one's ability to give or receive genuine love.[26]

I find these facts extremely disheartening, even tragic. Don't you? So
many children of God, blessed benefactors of the blood of Christ and the
surpassing love of God, are choosing to hand themselves over to a new
kind of slavery. We have the opportunity to walk in the light, but we
wander off into dark alleys. We damage the precious minds God has given
us, the very temples in which the Holy Spirit dwells.

The Bible tells us to run from four things: idolatry (1 Corinthians
10:14); youthful lusts (2 Timothy 2:22); materialism (1 Timothy 6:17)
and sexual immorality: "Flee from sexual immorality. All other sins a
man commits are outside his body, but he who sins sexually sins against
his own body. Do you not know that your body is a temple of the Holy
Spirit, who is in you, whom you have received from God? You are not your
own; you were bought at a price. Therefore honor God with your body" (1
Corinthians 6:18–20 NIV).

Ray Stedman spells it out in language no one can misinterpret: "'Flee
immorality'—that is the advice everywhere in the Bible. Do not try to
fight with it; do not try to overcome it; do not try to suppress it. Get away!
These are subtle, powerful forces, and the widespread destruction we see
in lives around us is simple testimony to the subtlety with which they can
conquer us."[27]

The devil has a broad arsenal of weapons. But we are not helpless. We
can strap on the armor of light (Ephesians 6), and Satan will flee. We can
take simple steps to avoid the relentless temptations that are bearing down
on us. Most of all, we can ask God to help us. The power of the cross is the
most awesome force in the universe. Paul writes, "I have been crucified
with Christ; it is no longer I who live, but Christ lives in me; and the life
which I now live in the flesh I live by faith in the Son of God, who loved
me and gave Himself for me" (Galatians 2:20).

Just knowing—*really* knowing—that Christ lives in you is half the battle. You can experience that power every single day. I'll never forget the first time I saw the film *The Passion of the Christ*. A group from our staff attended a premiere in Dallas. Like most people at that time, we had heard publicity and controversy about the film, and we had no idea what to expect. It was, of course, just a movie, and we'd seen any number of other movies about Jesus. In short, we were totally unprepared for the cinematic experience that was ours in that darkened church. I've spent much of my life studying the gospels, reading and praying and reflecting on the meaning of the Cross. But I had never seen it like this—not even close. We sat and watched a bloody, gory, graphic depiction of what the Lord endured for our sake.

Yes, we knew it was only a movie. We knew the blood was not real. None of that made any difference at all. God spoke to us in the very deep corners of our souls—places that hadn't before been touched in such an emotional way. It wasn't just the crucifixion, but the beatings, the spitting, and the pathetic mockery of Jesus. We were hearing the words in true Aramaic, as they were spoken two thousand years ago. I would never have thought any film could affect me so powerfully.

You may remember what movie theaters were like, all across our country, as the lights came on after that film—awed silence; stifled sobs. As we returned to California on the airplane, there was silence among us. We were each left to our private thoughts and reflections, processing what we had seen; talking to God about it. My own prayer was, "Lord, help me to live my life from this moment onward in such a way that I never do anything to hurt You or to break Your heart. Not after what You have done for me."

That's the power of the Cross, isn't it? It stands on that rock at Calvary, even today, casting its shadow across an entire planet, and across twenty centuries until it engulfs every one of us with its unquenchable power. To let ourselves experience that cross—to stand weeping before it with Mary and John and the centurion and millions of Christians through the ages—is to be radically and entirely changed from the inside out. To catch, even through a glass darkly, a fleeting glimpse of Christ and His incredible love for us, is to devote ourselves wholeheartedly to giving Him our lives in return.

In another movie from a few years ago, we cover a span of fifty years through a series of flashbacks. The four Ryan brothers have all bravely gone off to fight in World War II. When information surfaced that the other three brothers had died within days of one another, a senior official in Washington DC orders a special mission to bring Private James Ryan home from the front. Because Ryan's unit is listed as missing in action, it becomes a search mission, as well. Captain Miller assembles a seven-man rescue squad that succeeds in locating Ryan who refuses to leave his unit, despite the news of the death of his brothers. Most of the men on that mission lose their lives in the effort to save Ryan or in a subsequent battle between Ryan's unit and the enemy forces. As if holding Ryan responsible for the great sacrifice made on his behalf, the mortally wounded Captain Miller pulls the stunned private toward him and with his final breath says, "*James, earn* this—*earn* it!"

Then the scene flashes forward to the present where James Francis Ryan, now in his eighties, is seen paying homage at Captain Miller's grave at Omaha Beach in Normandy, France. Overcome with emotion and perhaps some guilt, he says to the grave marker, as if to Miller and the rest: "I hope . . . I've earned what all of you have done for me."[28]

We all know that no one could ever merit such a great sacrifice; no one could ever do enough to earn the incredible price of the gift of a rescued life. No gift is ever earned, especially the gift of life.

That is the truth about salvation as well; we can never earn it. There is zero mathematical possibility that a sinful life can ever, under any circumstances, make a good exchange for the one perfect and holy life that was ever lived; no way human blood can equate to the blood of God's Son. We can't earn it. But what we can do is to know what Christ has done in the past, to know He is with us right now, and to know that He is physically coming back soon. We know those things with our minds. But do we know them with our hearts? Or are we dozing?

A recent headline called the recent nuclear developments by North Korea and Iran a wake-up call to the world. Well, the world has had an endless series of wake-up calls over the past decade.

If we're not out of bed by now, we may be unconscious.

I believe Christians all over the world are wide awake and more aware of the times than we've ever been. As followers of Christ, we must be alert, watchful, and vigilant, with one eye on the headlines and the other on the eastern skies.

That's what Paul is shouting: "Awake! Awake! He's coming! Live every single moment for Him as if you knew this would be your last on earth and the sweet moment of reunion. Do nothing you wouldn't want to be doing when the Lord of the universe comes to claim His bride. The victory will be overwhelming—let's put on the armor of light and take our stand."

# 11

## COMING TO CARRY ME HOME

FROM: ANGELS—WHO THEY ARE AND HOW THEY HELP...WHAT THE BIBLE REVEALS

P EOPLE DIE. For thirty years now I've ministered to those who were dying. I've been with them in the process, and I've been in the room after death has occurred. I've watched their loved ones mourn over their loss, trying to hold on to a body where there was no longer any life.

But recently I've learned more about what actually happens in the process between seeing these people holding on to life one minute, then seeing them with no life at all the next.

I've come to believe from Scripture that angels take believers home to heaven when we die. I have to tell you honestly that this is the first time I've been really convinced of that. I had always wondered about it. But now I realize there's strong justification for believing it.

Not long ago I preached the message of this chapter at the funeral of the mother of someone on our ministry staff. Mrs. Huntsman was ninety-five years old. Her husband is still living.

During the service I spoke about what happens when a believer dies, and how the angels come to get that person.

After the service, I walked down to greet and comfort Mr. Huntsman, and to tell him I would be praying for him. As I leaned over and spoke to him, he answered so loudly you could hear him all over the chapel (apparently he had turned down his hearing aid). "Oh, Pastor Jeremiah," he said, "it's the part about the angels I love. I just love that about the angels coming to get Gladys."

I was glad it was a comfort to him, and I wish I'd understood it earlier and been able to offer it to others. The loss of a friend or family member can be the deepest darkness known to God's people on earth. In pain the psalmist cried out to God, "You have taken my companions and loved ones from me; the darkness is my closest friend" (Psalm 88:18). But the Scriptures offer hope for us in those dark times.

Before we look closer at what the angels have to do with our death, let's look at death itself.

## WHAT IS DEATH?

The word death means "separation." In the New Testament it's the Greek word *thanatos*. Physical death is the separation of the spirit and soul from the body. We'll be more like the angels then, because we'll have lost the part of us that angels don't possess—our physical bodies. After death we no longer exist in both the physical and spiritual realms, but in the spiritual realm alone.

After a person dies his body is only a corpse—"the body without the spirit is dead" (James 2:26). The person's body will only decay, but his spirit and soul will go to be either forever with God or eternally apart from him.

God places great value on the death of the believer. "Precious in the sight of the Lord is the death of his saints" (Psalm 116:15). John in his vision heard heaven itself pronouncing this preciousness:

> Then I heard a voice from heaven say, "Write: Blessed are the dead who die in the Lord from now on."
> "Yes," says the Spirit, "they will rest from their labor, for their deeds will follow them." (Revelation 14:13)

"To die is gain," Paul said (Philippians 1:21).

Christians who grow in their relationship with God understand this blessedness of death. As a Dallas Seminary student I started my ministry career working as an intern chaplain at Baylor Hospital. I often went with the head chaplain to the family room to help someone deal with death. A few times I had to go by myself, when I was on duty alone. I got to the point where I could walk in the room where the family was and within two or three minutes know if I was dealing with Christians or non-Christians. It was uncanny. Death for a believer is difficult and challenging and nothing anybody wants to deal with. It's hard and scary and painful. But it's not despair. It isn't the end.

Not long ago a 34-year-old man in our church died of cancer, and I preached his funeral. I must confess it's been a lot harder for me to do that since I've had cancer myself.

The cancer had ravished his body in a short period of time. Before he died I visited him at his home. His wife was there, as well as his young son. We sat together in their living room. He talked about going to heaven just as if it he were going to the grocery store. It overwhelmed me. He was telling his little boy, "And when I get there, this is what it's going to be like. I know I'll miss you a lot, but just think what Daddy's going to get to do!"

I had never seen anything quite like it before. It was another indication to me that Christians die differently. There's no question about it. The way believers face death is one of the strongest evidences of the reality of our faith.

## ANGELS FOR OUR FINAL JOURNEY

So where do angels enter in? Scripture gives us comforting precedence for their special service to us the time of our death.

Our Lord told a fascinating story in Luke 16 of two men who were as different as they could be. Jesus began their story in such a way as to make the most of the contrast:

> There was a rich man who was dressed in purple and fine linen and lived in luxury every day.
>
> *At his gate was laid a beggar named Lazarus, covered with sores and longing to eat what fell from the rich man's table. Even the dogs came and licked his sores.*
>
> *The time came when the beggar died and the angels carried him to Abraham's side.*
>
> The rich man also died and was buried. In hell...he was in torment....

Only a gate separated these two men. Lazarus begged on the outside, the rich man lived lavishly on the inside. But Lazarus knew God, and the rich man didn't.

Notice especially the contrast in what happened after their deaths. The rich man "died and was buried." Period. Next we see him in hell.

But when Lazarus died, "the angels carried him to Abraham's side." ("Abraham's side" was a picture in the Jewish mind of the feasting and joy we'll know in eternity.) In his lifetime the beggar had licking dogs as his companions, but at his death the angels were honored to convey him into heaven. And they weren't just with him; they "carried him."

Lazarus was regarded as one of the most inferior of persons in this life, but that didn't disqualify him from having an angel escort through eternity's doorway. Lowly Lazarus was awarded this privilege, and apparently so was the highest of men — the Son of Man himself.

Scripture hints that Jesus may have been carried by angels into heaven on the day of his ascension. In Mark 16:19 we read that "he was taken up into heaven." Luke writes that while Jesus was "blessing" his disciples, he left them and was taken up into heaven" (24:51). Based on a respected alternative rendering in the Greek text, the King James Version translates the sentence this way: "While he blessed them, he was parted from them, and carried up into heaven." In Acts 1:9 we read, "After he said this, he was taken up before their very eyes...." Angels may have had this privilege of taking or carrying Jesus up on his return trip home.

Why would angels come to provide this service to us at the time of our deaths?

One reason may be related to the fact that Satan is described as "the ruler of the kingdom of the air" (Ephesians 2:2). Perhaps we must cross this "kingdom of the air" in going from earth to heaven. Our temporary home here and our permanent home there may be separated by an immense stretch of enemy territory. It's a trip angels must take often, so it will be a great comfort to have them at our side as we traverse it ourselves.

In *Somewhere Angels*, Larry Libby gives children another reason:

God wants you home so much he'll send his own angel to meet you. And don't be surprised if the angel is wearing a big smile.

# 12

## Staying in Love for Life

### Song of Solomon 8:5-14

From: What the Bible Says About Love,
Marriage, & Sex—The Song of Solomon

I magine this: a husband and wife who haven't had an argument since 1946.

But wait. Even in '46, they had already been married for more than two decades. Add six decades plus to that. They've been married for eighty-three years, as of this writing. Clarence and Mayme Vail are getting pretty good at this thing.

When the couple married in 1925, Calvin Coolidge was president, Babe Ruth was all the rage, and movies had no sound. Clarence was eighteen that year, his bride only sixteen. They had been sweet on each other since eighth grade, and their parents gave them their blessing to go ahead and marry. No marriage in modern history has lasted longer. We might have to go back to Abraham and Sarah to find a better marriage story.

Like so many other couples with staying power, the Vails seem nonchalant when asked for their secret. There is no magic formula, they insist; they simply made a sacred vow at the altar, and they have regarded those vows quite seriously. As for the absence of arguments, Mayme credits her husband: he's the strong, silent type who by nature isn't given to bickering.

The Vails originally moved into a one-room home. Together they endured the Great Depression, the Second World War, several other wars, and unprecedented cultural and technological revolutions. The only true challenge, as they saw it, came in 1948 when Clarence came down with tuberculosis. Staunch Catholics, the couple prayed hard and clung together. Mayme made a vow to God that if her husband pulled through, she'd attend Mass every day for the rest of her life.

Clarence was spared, and Mayme was as good as her word for sixty years until her health made it impossible to attend church daily. Together the couple finally moved into a retirement home in 2007. From there, they try the best they can to follow the exploits of their one hundred and eighty-six descendants. That number was not a misprint. You see, the Vails have six children, thirty-nine grandchildren, one hundred and one great-grandchildren, and forty great-great-grandchildren. They are a one-couple family tree with deep roots. The Bible told them to be fruitful, and apparently they took that one pretty seriously, too.

Clarence naps frequently these days, but Mayme is said to look young for her age; she could easily pass for ninety. She makes quilts, as she's done all her life; she receives two Masses per week; and she continues to care for her beloved husband, eighty-three years into the wonderful, always surprising adventure of holy matrimony.[1]

Their commitment is inspiring, of course, but we know there is something more than simple commitment at work here. We are committed to many things without the obvious delight that the Vails have shown with each other. Honoring a commitment is a powerful concept, a question of obedience and integrity. But what about love? Isn't love truly the glue that holds a marriage together? Isn't it the reason why we get married in the first place? If commitment is the engine of a strong marriage, love is the fuel that makes it run so smoothly.

Let's think about love, the great mystery, the core emotion of this world.

In the late 1800s, Henry Drummond wrote a little essay called "The Greatest Thing in the World" that became a classic devotional book. Reviewing 1 Corinthians 13, he concluded that love is ultimately the secret of life, and that we cannot truly live until we truly love. Therefore love is "the greatest thing in the world," life's ultimate secret, given that God Himself is love (1 John 4:8). When we begin to take hold of His love *for* us, His love takes hold *of* us. We begin to love other people in His supernatural, humanly impossible manner. It is an awesome power the world can never reproduce, because this love doesn't come from earth.

That is the kind of love we read about in Scripture. But this four-letter word has become victimized by its careless use in a society that defines it as a feeling that comes and goes, something we "fall" in or out of, or even a generic fondness, as in "loving" pizza or "loving" a television show. How sad that we don't reserve a separate word for divine love, as New Testament Greek does: *agape* love. There is something more than a generic fondness about the kind of love Christ showed for us on the cross; the kind of gracious love God has stubbornly maintained for us through all our centuries of disobedience; even the kind of love we see in a godly couple that remains joyfully together through life. This love is powerful stuff!

The best definition I know of *agape* love is giving ourselves to someone with no strings attached and for no expected reward. If I can love you even if you do the worst and I gain the least, if I love you just because I love you—well, that's a supernatural love. It rises above human nature, because it is not our way but our Creator's.

If you think about it, every other emotion we have is turned inward. What makes love unique is that it shows the possibility of self-sacrifice, which is the image of God in us. This is at the very core of the kind of marriage we've described in this book. There is no response to love but to accept it, because it is a gift and not a transaction—except for the one case when it is reciprocated *in kind*, at which time it becomes something holy, a two-way relationship of self-sacrificial love. This is marriage, and it is indeed beautiful.

As we read the New Testament, we understand *agape* love in the person of Jesus Christ, the ultimate model of self-sacrificial, unconditional love. Then we begin to see it manifest itself in human relationships, particularly in that passage known as 1 Corinthians 13. In two hundred seventy one words, Paul defines God's kind of love with poetry and precision. John Wesley and many other historic leaders of the church regard 1 Corinthians 13 as the greatest chapter in all of the Bible.

In reading that chapter, we discover Paul has written a kind of job description of *agape*—what love actually does. The chapter is filled with action verbs. Love is not a feeling or a reaction. It is not passive but active, a force to be reckoned with. Love gets busy.

Other emotions come naturally: fear, desire, sadness, and the rest. A small child will feel all of these things. But *agape* love must be adopted as an act of the will—ultimately it isn't an emotion at all, though it does involve emotions. Pulitzer Prize-winning writer Katherine Anne Porter has written: "Love is taught, always by precept, sometimes by example . . . Love must be learned, and learned again and again; there is no end to it. Hate needs no instruction, but waits only to be provoked."[2]

Gary Thomas adds, "Love is not a natural response that gushes out of us unbidden . . . but hate is always ready to naturally spring forth."[3] People don't love selflessly unless they are taught to walk in obedience to God.

We see it in the final verses of the Song of Solomon, the passage that completes our exploration of this fascinating book. Once again, I'm amazed at the things our Bible does that no other book can do. In this case, we find seven principles in this Old Testament chapter that correspond to the words Paul was to write centuries later in his letter to the Corinthians. I was amazed by the parallels, and I was left to wonder whether Paul actually reviewed the Song before he wrote the epistle. I do know this: The same Holy Spirit inspired both passages, so we shouldn't be surprised by how perfectly they dovetail.

## THE STABILITY OF LOVE

*Song of Solomon 8:5*

"Who is this coming up from the wilderness, leaning upon her beloved? I awakened you under the apple tree. There your mother brought you forth; there she who bore you brought you forth" (8:5). Apparently the getaway rendezvous has ended. Solomon and Shulamith are in the royal chariot, hurrying through the desert on their way back to the palace, "coming up from the wilderness." The wife leans upon her husband in the closeness of intimacy. They may be talking casually, recalling the places they've been and the times they've enjoyed. They're refreshed by their escape from the world and their time together.

How about the apple tree reference? Earlier, Shulamith has spoken of Solomon as being "like an apple tree among the trees of the woods . . ." (2:3) In 8:5 we find another repetition of that motif. Love is something like a fruit tree, a gift that keeps giving: abundant, nourishing, and tasteful. What we think of when we see a tree, however, is sturdiness and stability. Solomon and Shulamith knew that a cedar from Lebanon could live for hundreds of years, while kings and kingdoms rose and fell. What living thing could be sturdier? The first Psalm speaks of the man who delights in God's law: "He shall be like a tree planted by the rivers of water, that brings forth its fruit in its season, whose leaf also shall not wither; and whatever he does shall prosper" (Psalm 1:3)—a tree used as a picture of endurance and consistency.

Now listen to Paul speak of one of the qualities of love: "Love never fails" (1 Corinthians 13:8). Don't you love those words? They sound lofty and magnificent—until you give them a little thought. Love is failing in every direction, wherever we look! Nearly every family has a broken relationship somewhere or other. Who says love never fails?

There is a difference, of course; no one said *marriage* never fails. Paul uses the word *ekpipto* which means "to collapse," or "to fall down," or "to be lowered in value." God's love doesn't collapse or fall down. The world's idea of love, a passing feeling, can and will collapse. Emotions aren't built on anything substantial, but agape love is eternal. Its leaf shall not wither; it never fails because God never fails.

What a marvelous job this poet has done in describing it:

> *When the last day is ended,*
> *And the nights are through;*
> *When the last sun is buried*
> *In its grave of blue;*
> *When the stars are snuffed like candles,*
> *And the seas no longer fret;*
> *When the winds unlearn their cunning,*
> *And the storms forget;*
> *When the last lip is palsied,*
> *And the last prayer is said;*
> *Love shall reign immortal*
> *While the worlds lie dead![4]*

Would you like to have a love that reigns immortal? Such a love would not only hold your marriage together, it would make it powerful and fulfilling. Embrace Christ and you will know this love; follow Him and it will overflow into every relationship you have. That is a sturdy love, a love with stability.

# The Security of Love

*Song of Solomon 8:6*

Shulamith says: "Set me as a seal upon your heart, as a seal upon your arm" (Song of Solomon 8:6).

A seal in that day was not only a sign of ownership but a sign of great value. You would never set a seal upon something of little worth; you would carefully mark it as your property. Today, you wouldn't install an expensive burglar alarm on your garden shed, but you would on a fine home.

Shulamith wants to claim ownership of Solomon's heart, to have her name engraved upon his soul. As they ride back to Jerusalem in the chariot, she leans upon him, near to his heart where she feels secure. Back at the palace, he will undoubtedly be whisked away by chattering advisors. Shulamith wishes she could be set upon his heart, sealed in such a way that no one could come between them.

Security has proven to be a constant theme in this book, hasn't it? The idea has come up four different times. We don't think about the word very much, but a secure feeling is essential to marriage. It provides us peace that we need. Women in particular need to feel the security that a good marriage will bring. As one commentator has written, "The seal was two-fold: inner feelings and outer behavior. She didn't want any other woman to catch her husband's attention, and she didn't want her husband to be looking at any other woman."[5] It's about love, yes, but it is also about security.

Shulamith already knows she has his love, but she wants to reaffirm it. During their vacation, she has had him all to herself, and she doesn't want to let go of that sense of perfect belonging when the two are back in Jerusalem society and beautiful women are all around.

First Corinthians 13:7 tells us that love "endures all things." That means that in genuine love, we have true security. Ultimately, we find it in knowing God. Among human relationships, our greatest security is found in the partnership of marriage. At the altar, we vow that we will endure all things together: "in sickness and in health, for richer for poorer, 'til death do us part." Love endures all things, and what a comfort that is in the times in which we're living.

I've mentioned my friend Gary Smalley, a fine writer and speaker. He has also raised a fantastic son who, along with his wife Erin, is following in his dad's footsteps. Greg Smalley is willing to be transparent in sharing about his own life issues. This story from his marriage is a good example.

Greg tells how he and Erin had an issue related to his busy travel schedule. Greg would leave for a speaking tour, and while he was gone, all three kids would pile into the bed and sleep with their mother. Then, when he came back home, it was difficult to shoo them all back to their own rooms. It could often take days to break them of the habit again. Greg finally decided to lay down the law with his family. He gathered his kids and told them that, while he was gone, they could sleep in his room until one night prior to his return. Then they had to go back to their own beds.

Several weeks passed, and Greg was once again coming home from a trip. He was met at the airport by Erin and the children. Since this was before September of 2001, the group was able to proceed to the arrival gate. The plane had a late arrival, so there were hundreds of people standing around the tunnel from which Greg finally emerged. His son Garrison came running toward him shouting at the top of his voice, "Hi Dad! I've got some good news! Nobody slept with Mommy while you were gone!"

Greg adds, "If only you could have seen the looks."[6]

I hear a story like that and know immediately that there's security in that marriage. They feel free to share such an amusing incident because they belong to one another, and there's solid trust. How many couples today really have absolute mutual trust in each other? If an atmosphere of suspicion or jealousy ever permeates a marriage, that marriage can't approach what it is designed to be. We need the security that Shulamith and Paul are describing.

# THE STRENGTH OF LOVE

*Song of Solomon 8:6*

The next comment is a striking one, as powerful in its wording as anything in Scripture: "For love is as strong as death, jealousy as cruel as the grave; its flames are flames of fire, a most vehement flame" (8:6). Compare that one to a New Testament passage from Paul: "For I am persuaded that neither death nor life, nor angels nor principalities nor powers, nor things present nor things to come, nor height nor depth, nor any other created thing, shall be able to separate us from the love of God which is in Christ Jesus our Lord" (Romans 8:38-39). Shulamith says that love is as strong as death; Paul says that love is stronger. Christ, of course, spans the difference.

However, Song 8:6 is also a perfect match with 1 Corinthians 13:13: "And now abide faith, hope, love, these three; but the greatest of these is love." In all three passages, we see the staying power of love.

Notice that Shulamith describes the strength of her love for Solomon using two similes and one metaphor. It is "as strong as death," "as cruel as the grave," and is "a most vehement flame."

- **"Strong as Death"** is an interesting expression because it seems so unlikely. Death is dreaded, love is desired. Death is an ending, while love as described here is eternal—symbolized by the endless circle of the wedding ring. But "just as death cannot be subdued," writes Patterson, "so love is also invincible and cannot be repressed."[7] Again, the best example is God's love. That's an amazing picture of the unbreakable strength of the love of Christ, from which nothing can separate us.

But we can love with the love of Christ, too. *Agape* love never lets go. It's unlike the kind of love the world advertises. In counseling married couples over the years, I've probably heard this statement two dozen times: "But Pastor, you don't understand. I just don't love her/him anymore."

Those words are offered as the ultimate get-out-of-marriage-free card. "The feeling is gone, so I will be, too." It's a far cry from the eternal thing Paul describes that is stronger than death, greater than faith and hope.

I remember an occasion when someone played the "I don't love her anymore" card and I chose to confront it squarely. I replied, "I see. So you've chosen to disobey God."

"What did you say?"

"You've decided to disobey God."

He said, "What do you mean?"

I said, "It reads this way. Are you ready? *Husbands love your wives.* Which part of that don't you understand?"

"Well, *you* don't understand. I just don't have any feeling for her."

I explained that feelings don't enter into this discussion for the reasons I've already offered in previous chapters. Love is not a feeling but an act of joyful obedience. My friend said, "But let me tell you what my wife did . . ."

"It won't change anything. It still says right here, *Husbands, love your wives.* I don't see any loopholes."

Gary Thomas calls it both cruel and self-condemning when a husband admits he doesn't love his wife. The husband believes his declaration comes across as an indictment of her, as if it were her responsibility to somehow account for his loving feelings. Instead, "put in a Christian context, it's a confession of the man's utter failure to be a Christian."[8]

The solid truth is that God has given you your spouse *and* the love you need for that spouse. If you attempt to reject either or both of those precious gifts, then it's a simple matter of disobedience—no one can stop you from leaving, but don't try to describe it in terms of an emotion gone missing and a free option for walking away. Neither is relevant.

There was a time when this epidemic was a male-based thing. But we've seen it equal out a bit in recent years. Women are saying, "I don't love him anymore." The same concept of disobedience applies, and the same solution: Stay and start loving.

- **"Jealousy Is As Cruel as the Grave."** This sounds initially like a negative statement. In truth, the Old Testament often describes a righteous kind of jealousy, as odd as that sounds. When God says he is a "jealous God," as He does often in the Old Testament, He is speaking of wanting every bit of our devotion, as He has every right to. The difference is in what you want and why you want it. Envy is unrighteous; this kind of jealousy is the desire to preserve what already belongs to you. Jealousy "is possessive and exclusive,"[9] and it is "a righteous concern and protective care."[10]

Don't get carried away with this new idea of "godly jealousy." Godly jealousy means that you do your utmost to keep your spouse's attention focused on you—to protect your spouse from any temptation to be unfaithful.

God is jealous for us. He's jealous for our purity, for our honesty, and for our obedience in marriage.

- **"Flames of Fire, a Most Vehement Flame."** This metaphor is so designed as to emphasize the intensity of the flame. Think of a forest fire that rages out of control. Love is a powerful fire that burns in our hearts. Because it is supernatural, it is a compelling force to the degree by which it takes us by surprise. Daniel Akin observes: "The love God kindles in a marriage over which He is Lord is such a fervent and fiery flame that nothing on earth can extinguish it or put it out. . . . This is a passionate love, a red-hot flame."[11]

## THE STUBBORNNESS OF LOVE

*Song of Solomon 8:7*

Love is stable, secure, and strong, but also a stubborn thing. This is another word we often use in a negative way, but we would all agree there is a time for rightful stubbornness, just as there is a righteous jealousy. We've already mentioned God's stubborn love for us over the centuries of our disobedience. Praise His name that He is willing to be stubborn rather than wishy-washy about that. Shulamith writes, "Many waters cannot quench love, nor can the floods drown it" (8:7). Staying with the metaphor of fire, imagine someone throwing bucket after bucket of water upon a campfire, but the flames keeps leaping back into place. That's the image of stubborn love that will not be quenched, that suffers whatever comes its way but is never discouraged.

We know something about wildfires in California. Huge tankers are often employed to drop massive amounts of water on these fires. We're told that much of the time, the fire wins out. The fire evaporates a good bit of the water before the water can envelope the flame.[12] Fire is a stubborn force, difficult to subdue.

Those of us in the ministry see our share of misery and hear more than our share of sad stories. But I will also tell you that we witness incredible demonstrations of the power of God's love. There are so many stories of spouses whose love was only heightened and enflamed by the misfortune a partner faced. When we fall in love, we don't count on a spouse to become a paraplegic after a tragic automobile accident. We don't count on our beloved to enter a long bout with cancer, or suffer some other life disaster. But love never abandons need; in fact, it proves itself by coming into its own in such times. I've told you about Mayme Vail, who walked to church every day for sixty years to thank God for letting her care for a husband stricken with tuberculosis. I have seen the love of God poured out to a spouse who could not respond in any way. We see these things and we know love is real; we know its Author is real, or to what could we attribute such a power?

Love is the eternal flame, a fire from heaven that never becomes ash. "Loving is not primarily what you receive but what you do—and do even when boredom, resentment, or hunger for novelty tells you life can be better somewhere else."[13]

## THE SACRIFICE OF LOVE

*Song of Solomon 8:7*

Frederick Buechner has defined our next term in this way: "To sacrifice something is to make it holy by giving it away for love."[14]

He is describing one of the true secrets of godly love. Jesus described it, then demonstrated it: "Greater love has no one than this, than to lay down one's life for his friends" (John 15:13). In other words, to give what is difficult to give is a proof of love; to give one's life is the ultimate gift and the ultimate proof. In marriage, sacrificial love is the key to staying in love for a lifetime.

Listen to how the Song of Solomon makes use of this concept: "If a man would give for love all the wealth of his house, it would be utterly despised" (8:7). The idea is that a man would be laughed out of the neighborhood for trying to buy love with his possessions. We all know that love cannot be bought or sold, only given.

Craig Glickman adds one qualification: "But if you cannot give all the wealth of your house to gain love, is there anything you can give to attain it? There is. But it's much more costly than the sum of one's possessions. It is the gift of oneself. Solomon and Shulamith gained love only when he gave himself to her and she gave herself to him in return. Two priceless gifts made one priceless love."[15]

This concept is also covered by 1 Corinthians 13:3: "And though I bestow all my goods to feed the poor, and though I give my body to be burned, but have not love, it profits me nothing." We can actually sacrifice without love, but we cannot truly love without sacrifice.

Real love, then, is the giving of oneself, which is already a sacrifice. There will be more and more as love and commitment grow. There comes a time when sacrifice becomes the default position in a loving relationship. We are constantly willing to give up something in order to bless the one we love.

## The Self-Control of Love

*Song of Solomon 8:8-10*

Marriage also includes the quality of self-control. As we read through our passage in the Song, we suspect there has been a change of scene. Solomon and Shulamith are no longer alone. Shulamith's brothers are on the scene.

We can't be certain about the nature of the occasion— perhaps some kind of festival or reunion.

We remember how the brothers once made Shulamith work in the vineyard. (See 1:6.) Her father is never mentioned; he may have died earlier and left his sons to carry on the family work. Now the brothers are remembering the time when their sister was a little girl: "We have a little sister, and she has no breasts. What shall we do for our sister in the day when she is spoken for?" (8:8) Siblings are often playful together after they're grown, reminding each other of this or that amusing incident. Now, at a time when Shulamith has become a beautiful queen, perhaps they're recalling the girl at a time before puberty, when she roamed the orchards as a tomboy. Even then, they could foresee the beauty she would become. What would they do to protect a little sister's honor until the right man came along?

Her brothers observe that she will become either a "wall" or a "door" (8:9). A wall is stationary and represents moral strength; a door swings open and closed and represents moral laxity. The first option is the one for which loving brothers would hope. If she is a "wall," that is, if she guards her chastity, they will honor her with a battlement of silver. If she behaves as a "door," she will have to be shut behind boards of firm cedar—that is, locked away for safekeeping.

The brothers are acting as a good father would act then and now. What dad hasn't had a thought of putting his daughter somewhere safe from boys with dishonorable intentions?

Virginity is a delicate gift from God. If only young people could be allowed to hold onto that understanding without the world pushing them into decisions they'll regret. The norm today is that virginity is something to be cast off like baby teeth, and that waiting for marriage is abnormal behavior. The truth is that men and women who save themselves for marriage have something beautiful that their friends have denied themselves. A bride and groom with self-control can present their bodies to one another as gifts of purity. Isn't that worth the wait?

Shulamith's brothers are ready to affirm and celebrate good moral decisions on their sister's part. They're willing to take disciplinary measures if they note danger signals.

Now, after these two verses of nostalgic indulgence, Shulamith brings her brothers back to the present: "I am a wall, and my breasts are like towers; then I became in his eyes as one who found peace" (8:10). She is no longer that little girl, but a mature, healthy, and morally pure young lady who has observed the discipline of delayed gratification. The latter part of the verse is particularly beautiful. As Solomon sees a virtuous young woman before him, she in turn sees the peace and joy in his eyes.

Lost virginity can never be recovered. But let us remember that it can be forgiven—by God and by a spouse. Once a couple is married, this factor of self-control is no less important. The husband and wife reserve themselves for each other exclusively. They maintain a kind of virginity in relation to the world as they give themselves joyfully to each other. From then on, self-control protects a faithful and devoted marriage.

## THE SELFLESSNESS OF LOVE

*Song of Solomon 8:11-12*

Love is a challenge, and each of these attributes reflects that. But this final factor is perhaps the most difficult of all: the challenge of selflessness, which is the most familiar component of genuine, godly love. In one way or another, all the other attributes have this one at their core.

Our world, of course, cannot comprehend selflessness. In the 1970s, *Looking Out for Number 1* became a bestselling self-help book, and at the time the title provoked a bit of discussion and controversy. It would seem less shocking today because self-absorption is the way of the world. Again, it's not difficult to see the connection between this philosophy and the age of widespread divorce. Married love requires emotional maturity, disciplined perseverance, and a willingness to put the other person first. When two people "look out for number one," and number one happens to be the person in the mirror, there will be trouble. When number one is the other spouse, they're onto something.

Shulamith is still reminiscing with her brothers. She says, "Solomon had a vineyard at Baal Hamon; he leased the vineyard to keepers; everyone was to bring for its fruit a thousand silver coins. My own vineyard is before me. You, O Solomon, may have a thousand, and those who tend its fruit two hundred" (verses 11-12).

What is happening here? It seems likely that Solomon owned the vineyards in which Shulamith labored as a child. Her family had paid the annual rent of one thousand silver coins. Had the girl not been put to work outdoors—had they found reason to lock her away behind those boards of cedar—she and her future husband might never have met.

Shulamith reminds Solomon that he may have as many as a thousand vineyards, but she has only one. She is speaking of herself metaphorically, of course. Her vineyard is herself, kept pure for his delight all this time. In a teasing way, she is saying, "So where is my rent? Where are my thousand silver coins?"

"Those who tend its fruit," are, of course, her brothers who have cared for her until the day when her groom came to bear her away. She has forgiven her brothers, and she signals that by saying they're due two hundred coins for their watch-care over her life. They have brought Solomon a profit of fruit in his vineyards; they have brought him a precious gift in their protection of their sister. She comes to him now with character, integrity, and purity.

Solomon now whispers, "You who dwell in the garden, the companions listen for your voice—let me hear it!" (verse 13) Craig Glickman observes: "Her voice is a song in the gardens, dovelike music in a paradise. When she sings from her heart, her words touch his heart, and the melody resonates through his soul."[16]

The Song of Solomon is thus coming to its ending with a song of Shulamith. Their love has come of age like the grapes in the vineyard, sweet, and full of life and health. Shulamith responds to her husband's invitation with one of her own: "Make haste, my beloved, and be like a gazelle or a young stag on the mountains of spices" (verse 14). It's not the first time she has compared him to a gazelle or a young stag. On their honeymoon, she has referred to mountains as places of delight, and she does so again. We see the selflessness in man and wife, both inviting each other instead of making demands on each other; both devoted to the pleasure of the other instead of self; both finding the true joy that can come only when we reach out to someone else rather than live in the self-imprisonment of self-absorption.

On the fateful night of their misunderstanding, we could see hints of selfishness in each of them. Shulamith was making demands on Solomon's priorities, while he was making demands on her patience and availability. Both were thinking of their own pleasure. It was almost a relief to see them stumble, because then we knew this was a human couple with a marriage set squarely in this world, not a fantasy one. We love the Bible because it is always about truth.

But then we watched the couple grow. It was their very stumbling that led to their leaps of maturity. This is how it goes in marriage. As single people, we have known how to live independently. As married people, we must learn to sacrifice that independence and the self-priority that goes with it.

Paul reminds us once again in 1 Corinthians 13:5: "[Love] does not seek its own."

We learn not to seek our own, to live instead as loving fellow servants, and thus find the truth at the heart of Jesus' paradoxes: the last shall be first, we must lose our souls to find them, and so on. In Matthew 16:24, Jesus invites us to deny ourselves, take up our crosses, and follow Him. Marriage is included in that process of self-denial. As with all things, it leads first to a cross, but ultimately to a crown.

If your marriage is in pain, remember that the reward is always still waiting ahead for you. Be strong and of good courage, and know that God will be with you. Keep following Him, beyond the cross, through all the difficulties, and you can reap the reward that comes to all those who persevere in His name. That means enjoying all the good things that come from a long marriage. Believe me—it's more than worth it, more than wonderful, more precious than gold.

### Taming the Foxes

You could argue that in the long run, marriage is more about the little moments than the big ones. Early in the book we talked about the "little foxes," those little irritations that lead to big trouble. But there are so many wonderful little moments in marriage, opportunities for something to go wrong, when instead we find we've gained the skill to make them go right. I'll give you an example from my life with Donna.

I love watching basketball. Due to its lengthy season and my tight schedule, however, I simply don't have the luxury of enjoying many games. My compromise is to try and carve out a little extra time during the NBA playoffs during the spring and early summer. My wife and I have an agreement. She knows that when playoff time comes, I'll have the family room TV set staked out. I don't watch a great deal of TV otherwise, and when I'm away from home, Donna will use that set.

On this particular occasion, my team had an important game and I was thoroughly into it. Donna was upstairs watching her own show on the upstairs set. I was on the edge of my seat, watching a tense fourth quarter. Suddenly, with no warning, a graphic appeared across the screen. "A recording," it informed me in ominous writing, "will begin in one minute."

"*What* recording?" I demanded of the screen. But the television ignored my question and, sixty seconds later, carried out its warning. The channel changed by itself, and I found myself watching some other show I didn't even recognize.

I'm sure you're techno-savvy and two steps ahead of me, since I'm still catching up with digital watches and microwave ovens. I have only the vaguest conception of what a DVR is, but Donna had just installed one. She had set it to record a regular show in case we were out some week and she missed it.

Naturally I was oblivious to all that. All I could do was wail in my loudest, least pastoral voice, "Oh, NO!"

Donna came running in a panic, wondering if aliens from Mars were descending upon San Diego. It didn't take long for her to see my face, my TV screen, and my evident problem. She attempted to quickly return me to the comforts of ESPN. The only problem was that she couldn't figure out how to stop the recording. It had never come up, and the DVR would not listen to her desperate pleas any more than me. This was a highly committed electronic component; it had its orders and was dedicated to carrying them out.

It took me only a couple of minutes to regain my composure and realize there would be a replay of the game. Then we looked at each other and began to chuckle over how ridiculous the whole scene was: the mysterious DVR, my lack of awareness of it, and her inability to save the day . . .

In a bad marriage, it could have been a bad moment. In a good marriage, all things work together for the good, because we've learned, by the grace and love of God, to *point* them in that direction. We know we are part of one another, and we are just as staunchly committed to one another as that DVR is to making me watch a show I don't care about.

It's a beautiful thing. I don't have to like Donna's show, and she doesn't have to become a basketball fan—although both of us would make those moves in a heartbeat if it felt important to the marriage. When any point of tension arises, we know how to recognize the little foxes and tame them before they get to the grapes.

### The Perfect Spouse

I wouldn't hold our marriage up as an example of perfection. We will have our moments, just like everyone else. But we are going and growing together on a journey we are very much enjoying. Love is no longer about what needs I want met, or what things I want done for me. It's not only more blessed to give than to receive, but in the end it's a lot more fun. It is truly important to me to please my wife, to be a part of her world, and to have her as a part of mine.

In *The Art of Understanding Yourself*, author Cecil Osborn tells about a couple receiving marriage counseling. In the presence of her husband, the woman told the counselor, "I'd like to have married a man who was very strong, yet very gentle. I'd like to have married a man who would have been strong enough to have put me in my place when I got out of line, but understanding and sensitive enough to know when I needed to have my own way. I'd like to have married a man who would be tolerant of my occasional outbursts and emotional tantrums, and wise enough to see that I need a good cry now and again. I would like to have married a man who would pat me and console me without bothering to argue with me."

On she went, describing the paragon of virtue that she felt she deserved as a husband. Meanwhile, the spouse in question simply sat and listened. At the end of the diatribe, he finally spoke: "You know, I think there was someone like that once, but if I recall correctly, they crucified Him between two thieves."[17]

If we're honest, we all want the perfect spouse, but we can no more find one nor become one. We're bound to fall short of each other's unrealistic expectations unless we bring a third party into the marriage. Yes, this third party was indeed crucified between two thieves, but we all know that was not the end of the story. He rose again in order to help us rise again. If death itself is no match for Him, how much more can He help us toward victory in marriage? What is there that Christ cannot accomplish if we're willing to invite Him into our households, into our kitchen, into our bedroom?

The kind of godly marriage that Solomon and Shulamith had is not humanly possible. On the other hand, it is supernaturally possible. The question for you, my friend, is what you will do with that fact—what you will do with all the truths we've discussed in this book. The beleaguered husband in the previous story was right: the only one capable of perfection was crucified between two thieves a long time ago. The good news is that there is more to the story. He rose again so that we can all do the same—not just when we die, but when we experience any other kind of death in life. A dead friendship can always live again. A dead career can be resurrected. The death of hope is never final, *including* when that hope has been lost for marriage.

Yes, the Resurrection of Christ applies to your marriage. It applies to every single factor of your life, as a matter of fact. If only we could comprehend the incredible, infinite meaning of that concept, how different this life would be. We would never give up hope in anything, least of all marriage, such a beautiful and essential gift of God.

If your marriage has been through torment, think of the torment of Christ on Good Friday. If you are tempted to take the easy way out, take courage in the fact that He didn't, even knowing what kind of suffering was ahead for Him. And if you find it hard to believe that something new and lovely can arise from the ashes of a dead marriage, ask God to help your unbelief. Meanwhile, act on that hope. Start treating your spouse as the most wonderful person in your life, and your marriage as the most important fact, other than your salvation. I believe your love can last a lifetime. Your Lord *knows* it is so.

Move forward in the faith of God, the love of Christ, and in devotion to your spouse.

# 13

## WHERE A KING MAKES HIS HOME

FROM: MY HEART'S DESIRE—LIVING EVERY
MOMENT IN THE WONDER OF WORSHIP

T he castle, it was said, was among the most elegant in the world. Its turrets dominated the medieval sky, and the bright banners of the kingdom could be seen for miles. The throne room was embellished by gifts from many lands, and the walls were trimmed in pure gold. Everything sparkled and shone—everything but the gloomy face of the king.

The old monarch truly loved his people, from miners to merchants to mothers. He enjoyed their humble ways and ready humor, and he longed to hear the tales of their daily adventures, however humble and homespun they may have been. But few of the common folk were ever seen near the palace. For one thing, they were busy with their daily chores; for another, the gleaming citadel made them painfully aware of their lowly peasantry. Royal things made them uncomfortable.

So the good citizens looked only rarely to the gleaming towers, and they ignored the trumpets that heralded the comings and goings of the king. In time, they built their cottages and estates at increasing distances from the castle. They ignored the king's eager invitations to come and visit, even to enjoy his hospitality at the royal table. The people loved their king, but they preferred to do so from a distance.

The king grew lonely and despondent. He felt like a loving parent whose children venture into the world, never to return. He preferred to be more a guardian to be loved than a monarch to be feared. And so he came to realize that if the people wouldn't come to him, he must go to them.

The king instructed his courtiers to stay behind, and he walked alone to the town square. Naturally enough, the merchants and children recognized him immediately, and a hush fell over them. As they watched nervously, the king stooped down and began to play a game with two of the children. Soon there was a crowd of children all around him, and the men and women began to draw nearer too.

As the hours passed, the people found themselves coming to feel more comfortable with their king than ever before. In the past, he had been something like a distant rumor; now he was in the very midst of them, laughing and telling wonderful stories. They could touch his magnificent bejeweled crown. They see the twinkle in his eye. All the people marveled at his wisdom, and many shared their problems with him; he always had solutions. Most of all, a great love grew between them—a love for his kindness, a love for his kinship, a love for his kingliness. When the sun finally set, a lively crowd surrounded the king. Someone said, "Your Majesty, remain among us. We never wish to leave your presence, for we never knew how kind and joyful and wise you were."

And the king smiled as he replied, "You need never leave, for this is our kingdom together. From the most ancient of traditions, I must make my home yonder, in a palace of splendor. But I will leave you with a special gift." And with that, the king produced, from the crimson folds of his robe, a small flute. He placed it gently in the hands of a young girl. "When you return to your homes," he said to the crowd, "you will each find waiting for you a flute, a harp, or some musical instrument with your own name engraved upon it. Whenever any one of you plays the simple melody I will teach you, I will hear and I will come. This is the Praise Song of the King, and it will bring me to you wherever you may be. Even if only one of you longs for my company, that one has the privilege of playing my melody and calling my name. Your king's greatest desire, as I hope you will never forget, is your companionship."

And at that moment, the little girl's curiosity got the better of her. She gently puffed her breath into the flute, and the sound that emerged stopped all conversation. It was the most exquisite music any of them had ever heard, and it opened whole worlds of wonder to their astonished imaginations. As they soon understood, the king's very heart and soul were wrapped within that melody. It was as if great clouds drifted suddenly from their eyes, and the people could clearly see their king for the first time. All they had shared before was merely child's play—now, from the flute of a child, came something both joyful and serious. The melody told who their king was, and therefore it told them who they were.

When the king finally left, each citizen hurried home to discover his or her musical instrument. That village, as you might expect, was changed forever. In golden boxes the people kept and cherished their instruments. They played them every day, and somehow the king had time for each of them. They came to understand that he was really much more than a king.

And as they played the ancient song, the instruments became more their own, more a part of them. The melody, they found, never became tiring or predictable, as other melodies do. It was ever deeper, ever more mysterious and wonderful, ever filled with new surprises.

Alone, one could play a beautiful song of the king in his or her own personal way. Together, the people could play their instruments and produce a symphony such as no human ear had ever heard. Either alone or together, they lived for the music, because somehow, through the world's deepest wonder, the king lived within the music. So the music lived on within them and filled their days.

Some say that the wonderful melody still drifts on the wind. Have you listened—can you hear it?

## NO PLACE LIKE HOME

I expect you've already worked out the meaning of my little story. In every sense, God, our King, has come to us because we could not—would not—come to Him. He has done so through what we call the incarnation of Jesus, of course: dressing Himself in humble, human flesh to dwell among us in Jesus. But the implications go much deeper and are expressed in a startling concept that predates even Bethlehem. Wrap your mind thoroughly around this idea: *God makes His home in our worship.* The implications of that are so incredible that I tremble to write about them. God has given us an instrument for knowing Him, an instrument every bit as wonderful as that special flute. He has given us *worship.*

We should keep the following verse engraved in large letters in the fronts of our sanctuaries, on the covers of our church bulletins, at the center of our hearts: "But thou art holy, O thou that inhabitest the praises of Israel" (Psalms 22:3, KJV). Do you see the amazing proclamation of that verse? God makes His throne in the worship and praise that we offer in His name. The word we find in Hebrew, translated *inhabit* or *enthrone*, means "to sit down, to remain, to settle." One translation phrases it this way: "The praises of Israel are your throne" (NCV).

As someone once described this truth:

Praise is where God lives. It is His permanent address. Praise is His home element. He is at home in praise. . . .

This settles one of the vast mysteries which accompanies praise. Why is it that when we praise the Lord things change so rapidly? Why does healing come on wings of praise? Why do human emotions undergo such transition when praise is the choice? How are we to account for those things which accompany praise? The simple answer is: While God is everywhere, He is not everywhere manifested. He is at home in praise and, being at home, He manifests Himself best as God! . . .

I spend much of my life in hotel and motel rooms across the world. I can get comfortable and enjoy almost any place. But I have a home to which I go often. It is there that you will find me in my natural element feeling "at home." . . . If you want to see God entirely "at home" and feeling comfortable, you may witness that happening in praise. God has an affinity for praise. He is enthroned and liberated to act mightily in praise.[1]

In his wonderful book *Reflections on the Psalms*, C. S. Lewis also writes about God's drawing near to His people through their praise and worship:

When I first began to draw near to belief in God . . . I found a stumbling block in the demand so clamorously made by all religious people that we should "praise" God; still more in the suggestion that God Himself demanded it. . . . I did not see that it is in the process of being worshipped that God communicates His presence to men. It is not of course the only way. But for many people at many times the "fair beauty of the Lord" is revealed chiefly or only while they worship Him together. Even in Judaism the essence of the sacrifice was not really that men gave bulls and goats to God, but that by their so doing God gave Himself to men.[2]

As you meet with God in the light of morning, as your thoughts turn to Him in the adrenaline rush of the day, as you move into the silent sanctuary on the Lord's Day—know that He takes His place upon the throne whenever you give Him your praise. Your bowed head, your humbled heart, and your attentive spirit open the door to heaven. It's a door that swings both ways, for we've already walked through it with John. But now God comes to us, no matter where we are. The wonder of worship is the wonder of His very real presence, and we feel something of what those villagers felt in the parable. It's music from another world, wonder that floods out all the darkness and the dust of death this life contains. We rediscover the innocence of children again as we praise and exalt God's name, for He opens Himself to us. It's the most awesome moment of life—more awesome than holding your first child in the delivery room, more awesome than meeting the person you're destined to marry, more awesome than seeing the earth from the window of the space shuttle. You've seen something more beautiful: the face of God Himself.

Try to create this picture in your mind. Imagine your Father relaxing into the cushions of His most comfortable easy chair with a sigh of satisfaction, luxuriating in the worship of His beloved child. That's what the Bible is telling us He does. *He inhabits the praises of his people.* He makes His home, His comfortable place of rest, in your heart and mine as we worship His name. When I'm away in lonely hotels, I can do what the citizens in that parable did. I can play the Praise Song of the King, and it brings Him to me. Or perhaps it takes me to Him.

This is all fine and good. But if worship is such a high priority—the one thing for which we have been created—how shall we then worship? What is that word all about, anyway? The word *worship* is almost like the word *love* in our society; it has been tossed around until it has been stripped of all meaning. It's a flute that has been coated by so much dust that it no longer seems to be capable of music; we're inclined to toss it on a dust heap. What a terrible mistake that would be! Instead, let's blow away the dust and take a fresh look at worship.

Let's find out what the Bible tells us about worship. Is sacrifice still necessary, such as they did in ancient times? What kind of music should we use? What are some good reasons for spending our time in worship? Is it really possible to worship God while we're at work or in a crowded shopping mall? What is meant by worshipping as an everyday lifestyle? How can worship help us in times of spiritual warfare? Each of these questions will be considered in this little book. Perhaps our discussion of worship will knock away a bit of that dust. Perhaps we'll put a shine on that old flute yet. But my greatest prayer is that you would summon your courage and place your lips to the flute. For if you do so, you'll hear the music. You'll feel the wonder. And you'll want to sing, "Joy to the world! The Lord is come!"

You'll be joyful because you'll feel His joy. And that will send the melody soaring even higher. You will be experiencing your very heart's desire—the wonder of worship.

# 14

# INTRODUCTION AND LIFE IS OBEDIENCE: EXPRESS IT!

## ECCLESIASTES 1:1–3

FROM: SEARCHING FOR HEAVEN ON EARTH—
HOW TO FIND WHAT REALLY MATTERS IN LIFE

# INTRODUCTION

I n the wide world of poetry, the name of John Berryman soared among the elite of his century. He seemed to have made every conquest a poet might crave. He was a beloved university professor. A Pulitzer Prize sat upon his shelf, given for *77 Dream Songs*, his boldly innovative collection of 1965. Widespread acclaim brought him fame, friends, and followers. He had seemingly found the pot of gold at the end of the rainbow.

But one frozen January day in 1972, he came to the final stanza. The poet walked across a bridge in Minnesota, waved to a stranger, and leaped to his death in the icy Mississippi River.

Why?

"At fifty-five, half famous and effective," he had written, "I still feel rotten about myself." And in one of his poems, Berryman wrote: "After all has been said, and all *has* been said, man is a huddle of need."[1]

Do you ever feel that way? Rotten about yourself? A *huddle of need?*

A recent survey asked 7,948 students at forty-eight colleges what they considered "very important" to them. The study, conducted by scientists from Johns Hopkins University, reported that 16 percent of the students answered "making a lot of money." We can't be too surprised. Even so, a whopping 75 percent said that their first goal was "finding a purpose and meaning to my life."

Psychologist Carl Jung, in his book *Modern Man in Search of a Soul*, wrote, "About a third of my cases are suffering from no clinically definable neurosis, but from the senselessness and emptiness of their lives. This can be described as the general neurosis of our time."[2] Jung wrote those words in the early part of the twentieth century, but with every passing year and decade their truth has become even more glaring.

Holocaust survivor Viktor Frankl produced an influential volume called *Man's Search for Meaning,* in which he wrote, "The existential vacuum is a widespread phenomenon of the twentieth century."[3]

That sense of a humanity-wide vacuum has followed us into the twenty-first century. Rick Warren's book *The Purpose-Driven Life* has been a *New York Times* bestseller because it isolates this need so well. Within every single one of us lies an intense desire to understand the *why* of our existence.

In his introduction, Warren describes a survey conducted by Dr. Hugh Moorhead, philosophy professor at Northeastern Illinois University. Moorhead wrote to 250 famous philosophers, scientists, writers, and intellectuals, asking a simple question: "What is the meaning of life?" Some offered their best guesses; others admitted they just made up a response; still others honestly admitted they were clueless. Several of the intellectuals even asked Moorhead to write back and tell them if *he* had discovered the purpose of life![4]

The conclusion is unsettling: in our time, the wise men are running low on wisdom.

Maybe this is why we look around at too many of our young people, expecting to see joy and humor and infectious energy, only to find instead substance abuse, promiscuity, and suicide.

Someone recently gave me a copy of an anonymous suicide note from a college student that said:

> To anyone in the world who cares: Who am I? Why am I living? Life has become stupid and purposeless. Nothing makes sense anymore. The questions I had when I came to college are still unanswered and now I am convinced there are no answers. There can only be pain and guilt and despair here in this world. My fear of death and the unknown is far less terrifying than the prospect of the unbearable frustration, futility, and hopelessness of continued existence.

## WISEST OF THE WISE

None of this is new. The times may be changing, but human nature is not. We can't feel a single shred of emotion that hasn't already been felt a million times over. The wisest of the wise have shared fully in our plaintive cry to the cosmos, including the wisest of them all—King Solomon. Successful though he was, luxuriously wealthy though he was, surrounded by great men and beautiful wives and concubines though he was, and exceedingly blessed by God though he was—Solomon still felt all that you and I feel today.

The Book of Ecclesiastes is an inner road map of his quest—a testament to his search for meaning. It stands unique within the Bible as a classic of real-world, everyday philosophy, seen through the eyes of the most powerful, influential, and educated man in the world at the time.

Solomon was the king of Israel. We find his story, both private and political, within eleven remarkable chapters in the book we call 1 Kings. At the time of his birth to David and Bathsheba, the Lord gave him a special name: *Jedidiah,* meaning "Beloved of the Lord." So it was from the very beginning that an air of greatness and destiny hung about this prince.

Imagine the incredible day of Solomon's ascension to Israel's throne, in the reflected glory of his father's wild popularity and unprecedented achievements. God asked the newly crowned Solomon to make a request (1 Kings 3:5).

Can you imagine being granted such a privilege? What would you have chosen, once you caught your breath and reflected upon the staggering possibilities? Solomon had the choice of a thousand lifetimes . . . and he chose the gift of wisdom.

The Lord was pleased. Most of His children, He observed, would have opted for lengthy years or unlimited riches. It took wisdom to ask for wisdom; Solomon understood that this one precious gift is the key that opens the door to every other rightful desire.

That wisdom was granted, and Solomon enjoyed a gilded life for many years. Every decision seemed to be a sound and perceptive one. His people loved him. And the greatest legacy of all, his crowning achievement, was building the Jerusalem temple—a wonderful dwelling place for God and His people. In seeing this project through, he fulfilled the dream of his earthly and heavenly fathers.

During his reign, the nation of Israel reached its golden age. It became the empire that had always been within its capability—a light unto the ancient world. Rulers from many countries, including the queen of Sheba, made pilgrimages to Jerusalem to pay homage to Solomon.

How wonderful if we could pronounce a "happily ever after" ending on Solomon's life and the golden age of Israel. It wasn't to be, for man or for nation. Solomon's vast wealth, his fame, and especially his sensual appetites tainted his special standing before God. Wealth, power, and pleasure can be dangerous even in the hands of the wisest; these things long not to be mastered, but to master. Solomon compromised himself before the Lord who had given him enough foresight to know better. The drifting came slowly, deceptively, but the further he moved from Lord and Creator, the greater became his emptiness, frustration, and confusion.

The course of Solomon's life—and perhaps something recognizably yours—can be traced in the three biblical books that were his legacy.

In the morning of his life came the Song of Solomon, a prose rhapsody of passionate romance.

In the noontime of his life came Proverbs, a book of heavenly rules for earthly living on the Main Streets of the world.

Finally, in the evening of his life came Ecclesiastes, a regretful retrospective. In the disillusioned autumn of his years, Solomon revisited the wreckage of a wasted life. The proverbial pithiness purged, he made one final stab at redemption: an attempt to block others from his own perilous downhill road to destruction.

"It's what we learn *after* we know it all that really counts," someone once said. If Ecclesiastes were a movie, the posters might read, "Solomon is back—*and this time it's personal.*"

Ecclesiastes is indeed a personal book. Solomon personally presided over a forty-year season of peace. Free of the consuming rigors of military command, he had time to think and write.

He had personally accumulated the wealth of an empire. The riches of the world were at his disposal, as well as the counsel of kings across the Mediterranean world.

Above all, Solomon had navigated life as the most intelligent and well-educated man of his time. He writes: "I communed with my heart, saying, 'Look, I have attained greatness, and have gained more wisdom than all who were before me in Jerusalem. My heart has understood great wisdom and knowledge.' And I set my heart to know wisdom" (Ecclesiastes 1:16–17).

The traditional name of this book, *Ecclesiastes,* and the author's title in verse 1, "Preacher," both come from the same Hebrew term: *qohelet.* This term described one who convened an assembly of wise men and served as its principal spokesman. Solomon chose this as his pen name for Ecclesiastes. Perhaps instead of the "Preacher," we might call Solomon the "Searcher" or the "Quester."

## EMPTY AT THE TOP

> *The words of the Preacher, the son of David, king in Jerusalem.*
> *"Vanity of vanities," says the Preacher;*
> *"Vanity of vanities, all is vanity."*
> *What profit has a man from all his labor*
> *In which he toils under the sun?*
> **—Ecclesiastes 1:1–3**

~

Solomon begins his book with his conclusion: "The words of the Preacher, the son of David, king in Jerusalem. 'Vanity of vanities,' says the Preacher; 'Vanity of vanities, all is vanity'" (Ecclesiastes 1:1–2).

Immediately we stumble across that word *vanity.* Let's make a closer acquaintance of this word, for it will cross our path more than thirty times in this book. Today we connect vanity with egotism—with that man or woman who is overly self-involved. Vanity is always based on an illusion.

A woman once told her pastor, "When I confess my sins, I confess the sin of vanity most of all. Every morning, I admire myself in the mirror for half an hour."

To this the pastor replied, "My dear, that isn't the sin of vanity. You're suffering from the sin of imagination."

As Solomon uses the word in his ancient Hebrew text, he refers to emptiness, to that which is transitory and has little meaning. In this case, vanity is akin to a vapor that lasts only a moment before quickly vanishing, leaving nothing behind. *The Message* paraphrases verse 2 this way: "Smoke, nothing but smoke. [That's what the Quester says.] There's nothing to anything—it's all smoke."

Talk about getting smoke in your eyes! Imagine getting to the top only to find that it's all smoke, illusion, vapor, nothingness, emptiness.

Jack Higgins, famous author of such bestsellers as *The Eagle Has Landed,* says the one thing he knows now that he wishes he'd known as a small boy is this: "When you get to the top, there's nothing there."

Solomon climbed the same ladder and made the same discovery. *There's nothing here; all is vanity.* His repetition of the word *vanity* was a Hebrew poetic device that intensified meaning. He was saying, "Life is utterly, absolutely, totally meaningless."

Jewish statesman Abba Eban tells of meeting Sir Edmund Hillary, the first man to climb Mount Everest. Eban asked Hillary precisely what he felt when he reached the peak. Hillary replied that there was an immediate rush of triumphal ecstasy—for a fleeting moment. It was quickly replaced by a sense of desolation. Where could he go from here? What mountains remained to climb?[5]

Interestingly, another Everest climber expressed a similar sentiment. In May 1996, journalist Jon Krakauer was part of an expedition that reached the top of Everest. Twelve of his companions were killed in the highly publicized descent, a story that Krakauer records in his chilling book *Into Thin Air.* But he begins his account by describing his feelings on May 10, 1996, as he reached the highest spot on earth:

Straddling the top of the world, one foot in China and the
other in Nepal, I cleared the ice from my oxygen mask,
hunched a shoulder against the wind and stared absently
down at the vastness of Tibet. . . . I'd been fantasizing about
this moment, and the release of emotion that would accompany it, for many months. But now that I was finally here,
actually standing on the summit of Everest, I just couldn't
summon the energy to care. . . . I snapped four quick photos .
. . then turned and headed down. My watch read 1:17 p.m. All
told, I'd spent less than five minutes on the roof of the world.[6]

Solomon spent forty years on the roof of history, only to feel the same
bland puzzle of anticlimax. Not only is it empty at the top, but it's empty at
the bottom—and everywhere in-between. Life, in and of itself, is a cluster
of electrons silently coursing through their appointed atomic revolutions;
cells dividing and redividing; nature recycling its rituals ad infinitum.
*Emptiness. Vanity.* As Peggy Lee used to sing, "Is that all there is?"

I think you know exactly what I'm talking about. What did you find
at the Everest of your own life? Perhaps you received the promotion, won
the lottery, made the dream vacation, got the book published—all for the
thorny crown of unexpected despondency. It is that horrifying emptiness,
not the first gray hair nor the unwelcomed birthday that is the real culprit
in draining our youthful adrenaline. It is the vacuum of success, not the
fullness of failure that deflates in the end.

Dreams come true, not free, and part of that price is realizing that alas,
one more time, that elusive joy has escaped our clutches. And deep within
the quiet of the soul, something suggests that one more time we have
looked in the wrong place. If heaven is to be found on earth, no mountain
could be high enough, no ocean could provide the necessary depth. The
search must continue somewhere else.

Come, then, and join the search. Climb with Solomon to the roof of the
world and take in the panoramic view. Then climb down again and walk
with him down the boulevards of life.

Our journey of discovery together is designed to require one brief month. Take one chapter at a time, one short reading per day. This is, after all, not a quick stroll but a crucial pilgrimage. You may never set out on a journey of greater import. You'll want to stop and smell a rose or two, take in a deeper truth, sit and reflect before moving on to the next short chapter and tall truth. Get to know Solomon—king, philosopher, philanderer, elder sage—as you've never known him.

Then, one month hence, we will rest like children, free and unburdened, with the weight of the world off our shoulders—for we will have found at last the object of every quest, the true North Star of every journey, the never-dimming light of our fondest hopes: heaven on earth.

# CONCLUSION

## LIFE IS OBEDIENCE: EXPRESS IT!

### ECCLESIASTES 12:13–14

Let us hear the conclusion of the whole matter:

> *Fear God and keep His commandments,*
> *For this is man's all.*
> *For God will bring every work into judgment,*
> *Including every secret thing,*
> *Whether good or evil.*
> (Ecclesiastes 12:13–14)

~

Old Solomon sits in his private chamber—the place where he studies and thinks the deep thoughts; the place where his path intersects with the path of the Shepherd who has herded him for so many years of obedience, grazing, growing, and wandering—and not a few wolf bites.

As Solomon ponders "the conclusion of the whole matter," he thinks not simply of the end of a book, nor the end of a king's life, but the beginning of wisdom in life before the King. All of it comes together here. Solomon thinks of childhood at the elbow of his beloved father, King

David. He thinks of that evening when he made his great request of God, the years of building and conquest and prosperity, the advisors, the too-many wives—all of it blurs together and he feels smaller than ever before the God of his fathers.

Having held the world's greatest jewels, built the world's greatest temple, and led the world's greatest nation, Solomon has sought the final treasure—no less than the meaning of life itself. He has hungered for the image of heaven on earth, the foretaste of heaven divine.

So much flashes before him: the world's great libraries, wise men from around the world, priests and princes and prophets, ships from exotic lands previously unknown. And all of it comes down to . . . *nothing*.

Never was there the brief hint of heaven on earth. But there was something Solomon's father taught him, something known to Abraham and Isaac and Jacob, to Joseph and all the brothers and their tribes, some simple little thing you might hear on the tongue of the poorest peddler down in the street. And somehow this brief word trumps all the wisdom and learning of the world.

And the word is this:

> *Fear God, and keep His commandments, for this is man's all.*
> (Ecclesiastes 12:13)

All indeed.

> *For God will bring every work into judgment, including every secret thing, whether good or evil.* (12:14)

You could have no riches, no power, no glory, none of life's ordinary pleasure, and if you knew that *one thing*—simple enough for any child—you would have the map to finding heaven on earth. Eternity is fixed in our hearts; light calls to light; deep calls to deep. Therefore we must travel or be forever wretched, miserable creatures.

*Fear God*: that's the point of departure. *Keep His commandments*: that's the path. Travel it seriously, eyes fixed ahead as you walk the narrow way, and you will indeed see glimpses of the Eternal City.

And thus Solomon comes to journey's end, a rest for his soul. It is as if the final installment of that gift he requested so many years ago has just been made. Surely this is the end point of all wisdom.

A single tear wells up in the eye of the world's wealthiest, wisest, and most powerful man. In his journal, he scribbles in blunt letters, jagged with a hand trembling from age and emotion: "fear God." To fear God means to be struck with awe in His all-consuming, holy presence; to stand always and forever in breathless exaltation of who He is and what He has done and how vastly and infinitely His greatness overshadows our brief, vaporous existence.

Just beneath that, Solomon scrawls, "keep his commandments!" Yes, Solomon nods, it is the only way. Find out what God wants done, and *go do it* regardless of the cost. All the rest is vanity, heartache, wandering blind.

In 1866, D. L. Moody was conducting a series of evangelistic meetings in Brockton, Massachusetts. Daniel B. Towner, director of the music department at Moody Bible Institute in Chicago, was leading the music for those meetings.

A young man rose to give his testimony of following Christ, and he included in his remarks these words: "I am not quite sure—but I am going to trust, and I am going to obey."

Mr. Towner was so touched by these words that he jotted them down and sent them to the Reverend J. H. Sammis, a Presbyterian minister and later a teacher at Moody Institute. Reverend Sammis expanded those words into the stanzas and chorus of the beloved hymn, "Trust and Obey." We could inscribe those words right beneath the ones Solomon has written:

> When we walk with the Lord in the light of His Word
> What a glory He sheds on our way!
> While we do His good will, He abides with us still,
> And with all who will trust and obey.
> Trust and obey for there's no other way

To be happy in Jesus, but to trust and obey.[1]

God created you with a place in your heart that only He can fill. He has set eternity in your heart. Life for you and for me is like a trip to the mall on Christmas Eve. There is color and music and mingled fragrances everywhere, all sensuous, all seductive, all competing for our attention—all the vanities and pursuits that come up empty. Solomon tried every one of them.

Then, in the back corner, we see the narrow door. It is quiet, plain, unmarked, and largely ignored as people rush by. But we know that our Savior has left this door ajar for us and that it leads us to the place where we will find all that our hearts have desired.

The door is open just a crack, as if in invitation, and we see a brilliant light trying to break through. We know instantly it is the light of another world. It is the light of heaven on earth.

The Good Shepherd said, "I have come that you might have life, and that you might have it more abundantly" (John 10:10). The door may be plain, but the world behind it is rich indeed. Rich and joyful, filled with pleasures. As a matter of fact, all the vain things that charmed us most in this earthly life—the pleasures and pursuits that felt and tasted so empty—are now as wonderful as they always should have been. The Shepherd makes the very sunshine itself feel brighter.

My friend, open that door. Begin the adventure that will be the greatest of your life and the joy that will be the richest. If you don't know my Lord Jesus Christ, I ask you to meet Him this very moment by praying:

~

*Lord, I realize now that my whole life has been a search for heaven on earth. I long to know, to taste, to feel the truth that is true, the love that is genuine, the Master who will never let me down. You died for me so many years ago on a painful cross, and I realize now that You took the payment for all my sins—every one of them. How I long to be relieved of their burden! Just as You rose from the dead, conquering death forever, I choose right now to accept eternal life—to know that death will have no hold on me. And I will pursue You down that path toward the Eternal City with every breath I breathe for the rest of this life until the day You and I meet face to face. Amen.*

# 15

## FIERY FAITH

From: THE HANDWRITING ON THE WALL—
SECRETS FROM THE PROPHECIES OF DANIEL

I n the late 1960s a man—a leader in terrorist activities and an advocate of the violent overthrow of the American government—escaped the police to become an exile in France. It was there that he claimed to see Jesus in the clouds and became a born-again believer. He returned to America prepared to face criminal charges and proclaim his conversion to the media and packed churches. Sometime later it was reported that he had joined the cult of Sun Myung Moon.

When a celebrity is saved, one of the first things that happens is an appearance on television, talk shows, and the banquet circuit. Before we know it, they have embarrassed us. We need to use the test of time before we elevate them as role models.

Nebuchadnezzar was a vocal witness of his faith in the Lord, but when we hear about him in the third chapter of Daniel, we're not too impressed. According to the Septuagint's (the oldest Greek version of the Old Testament) account of this passage, there were somewhere between sixteen and twenty years between the end of chapter two and the beginning of chapter three. So Nebuchadnezzar had plenty of time to rethink his impulsive commitment to the Lord and revive his own egomania.

## IMAGE IN THE DESERT

The king ordered his head masons, designers, and gold embossers to erect a statue in his image. He had become so impressed with the dream he had that he must have reasoned, *If I am the head of gold, why not be the whole body?* This statue was not like the ones we see pigeon-blessed in the middle of a public park; it was a colossal, grotesque, shining monstrosity. The Scripture says it was sixty cubits high and six cubits wide. That's ninety feet tall! It was also unbalanced (just as the king's mind). The ratio of the image was ten-to-one, which means that it was a skinny, skinny man. The average body ratio of a person today is five-to-one. All that gold, shimmering in the sun, could have been seen for miles away.

A guest list, consisting of the cream of Babylonian society, was prepared. "He then summoned the satraps, prefects, governors, advisers, treasurers, judges, magistrates and all the other provincial officials to come to the dedication of the image he had set up" (Dan. 3:2). Everyone accepted. It was an example of peer pressure at the highest level. The only one of the officials who was absent was Daniel, and he had probably been sent on a mission by the king. That seemingly insignificant detail has its purpose in God's ultimate plan.

It was no coincident that the designers of this bizarre statue made it sixty cubits high and six cubits wide. In Revelation 13:18, the number of the beast of the Antichrist was the number of man, 666. The Bible gives the number six to mankind; seven is the number for perfection. We fall short; we never come up to the standard.

The image is a good picture of mankind; it was made of wood overlaid with gold. That's the way our projects are: outwardly imperishable, but inwardly inferior. Man is always setting up his gigantic projects, but when you get down to the core of them, there's not much there.

The basic reason King Neb had this image set up in the desert is that he was doing his best to unite his kingdom religiously. He ruled over a vast empire, and he decided the way to unify his empire was to bring it together religiously and have everyone bow down before this image. In the end times this is what the Antichrist is going to do.

The second thing the king did was deify himself. When we study history we discover that the great egomaniacs who have wanted to conquer the world have been men who have tried to use religion for their own purposes. In the late 1930s, it was written:

> One cannot be a good German and at the same time deny God. But an avowal of faith in the eternal Germany is an avowal of faith in the eternal God. Whoever serves Adolf Hitler the Führer serves Germany, and whoever serves Germany serves God.

Later on, in 1942, this was written:

> There is a lot of talk in Germany about Hitler's Messianic characteristics. The thesis that Hitler is a miraculous being

sent by a Supreme Power, and that he is capable of mystic communion with the German masses is gaining greater currency. Consequently, the attack on Christian religion becomes more severe. In Germany, no attempt is made to stamp out the faith in the supernatural. The policy is more blasphemous. It is to replace Christ. Religion is now counterfeited rather than dismissed. This extraordinary tendency is perhaps without parallel during the last two thousand years. The Nazis are trying to create an anti-type of Christianity. They have made their leader their God.

We know that is historically true. Nebuchadnezzar was trying to unify the people around his image.

When this mass of humanity was gathered on the Plain of Dura, shading their eyes from the reflection of the beating desert sun on the golden image, the king gave orders to his paid preacher, a herald with a loud voice. As all false gods have their pulpiteers, the king had this fellow who told the crowd what he was paid to say. He announced that when the orchestra played, everybody had to hit the ground. Worship or burn were the options.

The orchestra was a weird bunch; they never would have made it to a philharmonic. Everything from a harp to bagpipes sounded the dissonant notes for worship. I believe this is one of the early indications in the Word of God of the prostitution of music. Almost every major cult and -ism, every false religion, has found some way to use music for its perverted purposes. It's a type of mind control. I believe with all of my heart that music belongs to God. It belongs to the angels. It belongs to God's people. The world will take what belongs to God and prostitute it for its own purposes.

The band played and the crowd, someone has estimated there were as many as three hundred thousand people from all of the vast empire, hit the dust. All of them, that is, but three. Can you image how they stuck out when thousands and thousands of people were on the ground and they were standing?

It reminds me of an experience my wife Donna and I had as newly-weds. We had a lot of good friends in college, and we used to do some interesting things to them when they were about to get married. One time, for instance, we managed to get the key to our friends' apartment while they were on their honeymoon, and we went in and took all the labels off the cans. For six months, every meal was an adventure. "Will it be dog food or peaches tonight?"

When we announced our wedding, we knew there would be some retribution. One thing I thought would be a target was our car. I had a 1961 red Chevy Impala convertible with a white roof. It was the pride and joy of our lives in those early days, and I knew somebody was going to try to get it. However, I thought I could outmaneuver them. I went to a shopping center near where we were to be married and parked it right in the middle of the parking lot. There must have been two thousands cars at that location. They would never find it, I thought.

That night after the wedding I went to retrieve our car, and there was my red-and-white Impala convertible all alone in the middle of the lot. The shopping center closed at 5 p.m.

I think the three Hebrew fellows stuck out in the crowd more than my lonely car.

## CONSPIRACY OF THE WISE MEN

Now the plot begins to thicken. The astrologers came out and bowed before Nebuchadnezzar, reminding him that he had ordered everyone to bow down. Perhaps King Neb had bad eyesight. How could he help but notice that there were three traitors who paid no attention to the order?

Solomon said, "Jealousy . . . burns like blazing fire, like a mighty flame" (Song of Songs 8:6), and the Chaldean crowd wanted to smell the seared flesh of Shadrach, Meshach, and Abednego.

Nebuchadnezzar was furious. He commanded the three Hebrews to be brought before him and repeated his order. This time he didn't assign his paid preacher to announce the worship moment; he gave it himself. He said, "When you three hear the orchestra play, you be ready to fall down and worship the image I made. But if you do not worship it, you will be thrown immediately into a blazing furnace. Then what god will be able to rescue you from my hand?" (Daniel 3:15).

The orchestra members had their instruments poised and waited for the baton to come down on the first beat. Thousands of eyes must have been boring into the backs of the three Hebrews as they stood before the king. In the minds of the doomed ones was the realization that there was really no option for them. They knew the Old Testament law that speaks clearly about idolatry. "You shall not make for yourself an idol in the form of anything in heaven above or on the earth beneath or in the waters below. You shall not bow down to them or worship them" (Exodus 20:4–5). The choice was between the king's command and God's Word.

Idolatry is not only the worship of false gods, but also the worship of the true God by images. John Calvin, the great theologian, said, "A true image of God is not to be found in all of the world, and hence, His glory is defiled and His truth is corrupted by the lie whenever He is set before our eyes in a visible form. Therefore, to devise any image of God is itself impious, because by the corruption of His majesty it is adulterated, and He is figured to be other than who He is."

A lot of idolatry goes on in our day, not just in the church, but also in the marketplace. God is not interested in being worshipped through something; He wants to be worshipped in spirit and in truth. Wearing a cross or a crucifix will not make a person a Christian, nor is it always honoring to the Lord. One of the current rock stars wears a cross and very little else when she performs.

The king was willing to give those fellows another chance if they would reconsider their disobedient attitude, but he made it clear that he would carry out the punishment if they refused. We can hear the sarcasm in his voice when he asks them, "What god will be able to rescue you?" How soon he has forgotten that it was that God who honored him with a wonderful dream that Daniel had been able to interpret. It was that God who made known the whole history of the world to him. That God created Nebuchadnezzar, protected him, clothed and fed him, and honored him with the rulership of the first world empire. He had forgotten that God, but in a few years he was going to experience the power of that God to bring him to his knees.

The history of the church has been written in blood. There will always be warfare between the powers of darkness and the powers of light, and there will always be pagan rulers who will cry out in sarcasm, *Who is that god?*

One of the greatest statements of faith in the Bible is the response of these three men. It thrills me to read it.

> Shadrach, Meshach and Abednego replied to the king, "O Nebuchadnezzar, we do not need to defend ourselves before you in this matter. If we are thrown into the blazing furnace, the God we serve is able to save us from it, and he will rescue us from your hand, O king. But even if he does not, we want you to know, O king, that we will not serve your gods or worship the image of gold you have set up."
>
> Daniel 3:16–18

They had a word from God and that's all they needed. The path of duty was plain; they didn't have to think about it or have a committee meeting. What an example!

This is what this world is crying for: men and women, boys and girls, who have conviction of heart and who do not change their convictions on the basis of their circumstances. These three men knew what God wanted them to do, and they weren't afraid of the consequences.

Athanasius was one of the early church fathers. We are indebted to him for the purity of the doctrine of the deity of Jesus Christ. The story is told that someone came to him and said, "Athanasius, don't you know that the emperor is against you, the bishops are against you, the church is against you, and the whole world is against you?" Athanasius answered, "Then I am against the whole world." A phrase was coined that became rather famous in the early church: *Athanasius against the whole world.*

Studdard Kennedy was a chaplain during World War II. He was often thrust into the frontlines of battle, ministering in places of danger to his life. One day as he was going through France, he wrote a letter to his son, who was about ten years old. This is what he wrote to his little boy:

> The first prayer I want my son to learn to say for me is not, "God, keep Daddy safe," but, "God make Daddy brave. And if he has hard things to do, make him strong to do them."
>
> Son, life and death don't matter. But right and wrong do. Daddy dead is Daddy still, but Daddy dishonored before God is something too awful for words. I suppose you would like to put in a bit about safety, too, and Mother would like that, I'm sure. Well, put it in afterwards, for it really doesn't matter nearly as much as doing what is right.

We don't know if Shadrach, Meshach, and Abednego had ever played fast and loose with what was right, but we do know that they had some pretty solid training in God's law.

When those three fellows responded to the king, he blew up. His pride was wounded, his will had been crossed, and he was so mad he exploded. King Neb is an interesting study. He was a man of superlatives: the biggest image, the most expensive gold, the most lavish party. He could put on a real show. When he pronounced judgment, it had to be the worst he could think of, and that was being burned alive in the furnace. But if that weren't enough, he said, "Throw in the coal! Make it seven times hotter! Turn on the heat!" Then he picked the strongest soldiers in his army to tie up the Hebrews so they couldn't move. The king was so furious that he was out of control.

It's curious that this furnace would be out in the middle of the desert, but it makes us wonder if the king hadn't planned ahead for what he would do if he was disobeyed. The furnace was a big pot-bellied thing with a large opening in the top. The victims were to be thrown in from above. When the soldiers pushed the Hebrews to the top of the furnace, the fire was so hot that the captors were turned to ashes before Shadrach, Meshach, and Abednego fell in. If that weren't enough to shock the partygoers, the next sight must have made their eyes pop.

The king's roller-coaster emotions were enough to give a man a heart attack.

> Then King Nebuchadnezzar was astonished; and he rose in haste *and* spoke, saying to his counselors, "Did we not cast three men bound into the midst of the fire?"
> They answered and said to the king, "True, O king."
> "Look!" he answered, "I see four men loose, walking in the midst of the fire; and they are not hurt, and the form of the fourth is like the Son of God."
>
> (Daniel 3:24–25)

It must have been with great caution, heart beating fast, and perspiration dripping from his face that the king approached the opening of the furnace and shouted, and "Shadrach, Meshach and Abednego, servants of the Most High God, come out!"

The three fellows walked out of the furnace, probably stepping over the charred remains of the guards, and stood before their accusers, calm and well-groomed. Their clothes and hair were untouched, and they didn't even smell of smoke.

King Neb, true to his impulsive and erratic nature, said, "Praise be to the God of Shadrach, Meshach and Abednego, who has sent his angel and rescued his servants! They trusted in him and defied the king's command and were willing to give up their lives rather than serve or worship any god except their own God" (Daniel 3:28).

With customary harshness, the king ordered that anyone who said anything against the God of the Hebrews was to be cut into pieces and their houses burned. Just as he had done with Daniel, he sent the uncompromising Hebrew trio from the firing line to the frontline.

## WHY WEREN'T THEY HURT?

Why does God save some and not others? Why does an innocent baby die and a murderer go free? We constantly wrestle with those questions. I do not have the answers; however, I believe God teaches through His book and through the stories of His children. When our Hebrew friends refused to bow to the statue, they expressed their absolute commitment to God. They didn't need to discuss it, have a conference call, or negotiate.

They also had absolute confidence in God. "We know God can deliver us from the fiery furnace." They also recognized that God's will might be different from their desire, but they didn't make their own obedience contingent upon God doing what would be pleasing to them. Here is where we fall far short of this standard. We pray, "Lord, just get me out of this mess, and I'll do whatever you wish." We make tearful promises to try to negotiate a contract with the Lord. But here were men who didn't try to rewrite the script. They just said, "Lord, we don't know how You are going to do it. We don't even know for sure what You're going to do, but we believe in You."

Stories of courage inspire us, but seldom do we see such absolute courage for God as was shown by the Hebrews. Whenever we have a hard assignment by God, there seems to be a list of reasons why we shouldn't do it. The three Hebrews didn't even have Daniel for support. He was out of town, probably on the king's business in another province. They were in a situation where they had great opportunity to move up into the hierarchy of the Babylonian kingdom. If they defied the king, obviously they wouldn't get promoted. They might have rationalized (and many of us are so good at that) by saying, "Lord, you need us in places of responsibility. Bowing down isn't such a big deal, is it?" If that had been their rationale, we never would have heard of them. They would have been part of the vast army of unknowns. History does not usually elevate acts of cowardice.

It has been said that when the executioner went behind Jerome of Prague, one of Christendom's early martyrs, to set fire to the pile where he was chained, Jerome said, "Come here and kindle the fire before my eyes, for if I had dreaded such a sight I would never have come to such a place when I had the free opportunity to escape." The fire was kindled in front of him, and he began to sing a hymn that was soon finished by the flames that consumed him. Absolute courage.

Martin Luther, when he was on his way to be excommunicated, appeared before King Charles V and an assemblage of princes and said:

> My cause shall be commended to the Lord, for He lives and reigns, and preserved the three Hebrew children in the furnace of the Babylonian king. If He is unwilling to preserve me, my life is a small thing compared with Christ. . . . Expect anything of me except flight or recantation. I will not flee, much less recant, so may the Lord Jesus strengthen me.

The Hebrews were absolutely conscious of the presence of God. When they were walking around in the fiery furnace, they were talking with the Lord. They knew the Lord before, and He was present with them. Isaiah prophesied (150 years before) "When you walk through the fire, you will not be burned; the flames will not set you ablaze" (Isa. 43:2). Incidentally, this passage does not validate a fire-walking experience today. Please don't try it.

I have found in my own life, and from what many people have told me, that when we are in the hottest furnace of our trials we are more conscious of the Lord's presence than at any other time in our lives. In the process of our personal fires, God takes care of our enemies too. The guards who threw them into the furnace went up in flames themselves.

The fire served to burn the cords with which they were bound and set them free. Many times when the fire is so hot for us that we think we are going to be consumed, we come out of it liberated from the things we worried about.

When King Neb saw the fourth form in the fire, he actually saw Christ hundreds of years before His virgin birth. What an astounding thought! Whenever His children are in the fire, He is there too. He was with Moses who saw Him in the burning bush, with the disciples in the midst of the storm at sea, and with Stephen as he was being stoned by an angry mob.

This story is a wonderful illustration of the willingness of God to involve Himself in the affairs of all people. It seems to me that He comes into our trials and troubles more than any other circumstance of life. He stands with the person who has lost a loved one, and if they are Christians they will say, "I have never felt the presence of the Lord like I have in these past days."

God uses our problem times to wake us up so that He might move into our lives. It seems like there are more problem areas today than there have been for the past decade. Maybe God has heated up the furnace in our lives just enough to get our attention. He doesn't promise to save us from the fire, but to be with us through the fire.

Through it all, God was exalted. First, the big, loudmouth king said, "Look, I'm going to throw you into this fiery furnace and see if your God can deliver you." But when he looked into the fire and saw God's presence, protection, and power, he praised the very God he had previously mocked.

People see God in us when we are in the fire. It's easy to be a Christian when everything is going great, but when the fire is hot, we are being watched.

I remember one time asking a couple how they came to know Christ, and they said, "We lived next door to a certain couple in our church, and it was at a time when all of the factories in our area were shutting down. People were being laid off every day and things were real tough. This particular Christian couple had been without work for over six months. All of their benefits had run out and they were just eking out an existence. We watched them as God literally took away everything they had. We saw them praising the Lord, having smiles on their faces and never complaining. One night after supper we were talking about them, and we said, 'Whatever they had, that's what we needed.' We went over to their house and they led us to Christ." They saw God in the fire.

The last thing that happened to Shadrach, Meshach, and Abednego is that their influence was enlarged. The king promoted them. When God tests us and we prove faithful, it is always for the purpose of enlarging our influence for Him.

The Bible says: "Be faithful, even to the point of death, and I will give you the crown of life" (Rev. 2:10).

"Now if we are children, then we are heirs—heirs of God and co-heirs with Christ, if indeed we share in his sufferings in order that we may also share in his glory" (Rom. 8:17).

John Chrysostom was one of the greatest of the Greek Church fathers. He lived in A.D. 347–407. As a very young Christian he was brought before the emperor, who said that if he would not give up Christ, he would be banished from the country.

Chrysostom said, "You cannot, for the whole world is my Father's land. You can't banish me."

The emperor said, "Then I will take away all your property."

"You cannot. My treasures are in heaven," was the reply.

"Then I'll take you to a place where there is not a friend to speak to."

Chrysostom replied, "You cannot. I have a friend who is closer than a brother. I shall have Jesus Christ, forever."

The emperor finally threatened, "Then I'll take away your life!"

The answer was, "You cannot. My life is hid with God in Christ."

And the emperor said, "What do you do with a man like that?"

Obviously, I do not know the words of that historical conversation, but this ought to be the way it is for all of us who are Christians. When we are tested in the fiery furnace, the world should say, "What do you do with a person like that?"

# 16

## WARNINGS
## IGNORED

From: ESCAPE THE COMING NIGHT—
AN ELECTRIFYING TOUR OF THE WORLD
AS IT RACES TOWARD ITS FINAL DAYS

C onvict Lake sparkled under the crisp winter sky of the Sierra Nevada. Surrounded by two-feet of snow banks, the ice above crystal clear waters invited daring souls with a siren song of beauty . . . and treachery.

Trained rescue people know a frozen mountain lake is the most illusive of natural phenomena. There is no such thing as "safe ice." It could be two to four feet dense in one place, but only a short distance away, pockets of warm springs bubbling under the surface might shrivel the thickness to a perilous few inches.

On a cloudless day in February, fifteen teenagers and two counselors from Camp O'Neal, a residential facility for troubled youth, were on a holiday outing at the lake. What began as an adventure ended in disaster.

Some of the boys stayed with Counselor Randy Porter on the breakwater by the marina, throwing rocks to break the shallow-water ice. Another group was about eight feet out on the ice, laughing and clowning around while Counselor Dave Meyers snapped pictures. At first no one noticed five boys who were headed toward the middle of the lake. When Randy spotted them, they were already far out from shore.

"Hey, you guys . . . get back here. It's dangerous out there!" His shouts fell on deaf ears.

Far out on the frozen lake, the boys heard a loud crack and looked down to see the ice fracturing beneath them. One boy shouted, "We shouldn't be doing this," and started back to shore. The other four boys forged ahead.

"I don't care if I die!" one boy shouted as he smashed the ice with his hiking boots.

Within seconds, the four boys fell into the freezing water as the loud crack of the ice fracture echoed through the canyon. Muffled screams coming from the middle of the lake could be heard on shore. Counselor Dave dropped his camera gear and began to race toward the sound of those frantic cries. With each step the ice gave way under his feet.

When Counselor Randy realized the danger, he immediately ordered the kids close to shore to get off the ice and instructed one of the wards to run to the ranger's residence for help. Then Randy headed out on the ice himself.

Dave reached the spot where the four boys had been hanging onto the edge of the ice, but only three were there. Shawn was gone. Without a wet suit, Dave's jeans and sweatshirt were frozen stiff, but he plunged into the ice-water and pushed Phil to the surface and coached him to crawl on his belly to the north shore, some two hundred feet away. Phil survived, but his buddy, Sellars, was unable to move, his body frozen to the surface of the ice. Dave and another boy, Ryan, struggled for life as hypothermia gripped their bodies.

On shore, Ranger Clay Cutter, caretaker for Convict Lake, had been called from his home by a hysterical boy. His wife, Teri, dialed 911 and reported to the emergency services dispatcher that four youths were "through the ice at Convict Lake." She told her three daughters, "Stay in the house," grabbed her binoculars, and headed to the lake that was consuming the lives of those caught in its freezing grip. She watched the entire event, including the valiant life-and-death battle her husband fought for the next forty-five minutes.

## MOUNTAIN RESCUE TEAM

In a mountain home twenty-five miles from Convict Lake, the beeper sounded for Reverend Russ Veenker, a man trained in underwater search and recovery and a skilled scuba diver. A few moments before two of his friends, Doug Englekirk and Doug Nidevar, expert athletes themselves, had stopped to visit the Veenker family and hearing the urgent call, asked, "Can we help?"

While Kandy Veenker rushed to the phone to alert other rescue team members, Russ paused for a quick prayer. "Lord . . . keep us safe." Prayer was SOP—Standard Operating Procedure—for Russ. He always prayed for the safety of the rescuers because many times they risked their own lives to save others. He knew that life-and-death situations were in God's hands.

"Get the rubber life raft and meet me at the lake," Russ instructed the two Dougs.

He gave Kandy a quick kiss and hug. "Love you." This was also SOP.

Kandy had great confidence in Russ's wilderness abilities and God's protection. But this time as he pulled out of the driveway, she felt oppressed by a vague presence of darkness. She began to pray more fervently.

## FROM FEAR TO PANIC

Ranger Clay Cutter and Counselor Randy Porter watched helplessly as one boy slipped away under the surface. As they were moving on their hands and knees toward the large ice hole where another boy and Counselor Dave Meyers were struggling to keep their heads above water, suddenly the entire edge of the hole cracked and gave way. Randy fell into the water just as Clay's frozen hand lost its grip on Sellars. Convict Lake had claimed two victims.

On shore, emergency units had arrived and begun a rescue effort. Paramedic Chris Baitx and Fire Captains Vidar Anderson and Ray Turner obtained an aluminum fishing boat and began to push over the ice toward the hole. However, the thin layer gave way from the weight, spilling Captain Turner overboard. Baitx and Anderson rescued him before he sank below the surface. While this drama was being played, far out on the ice a frantic voice was heard.

"Hurry up!" screamed Ranger Cutter.

Paramedic Baitx retrieved a ladder from the boat and, tying one end of a rope to himself and the other to the ladder, grabbed a pike pole and, pushing the ladder ahead of him like a sled, crawled over the ice toward the victims.

At the ice hole, Baitx saw Counselor Randy and one of the boys holding to the end of a rope and Counselor Dave floating on his back a short distance away. Baitx headed toward Dave, but the ladder he was using for support turned into a slick slide and plunged him into the water.

Meanwhile, Captain Anderson, using two ladders like giant snowshoes, was sliding across the surface of the ice in another rescue attempt.

Then Dave disappeared. One more fatality. How many more lives would be claimed before this nightmare ended?

# BEFORE IT'S TOO LATE

When Russ arrived on the scene he was not prepared for what he saw. There were a dozen or more fire volunteers standing on the breakwater looking at a couple of stick figures kneeling on the ice in the middle of the lake. They were Ranger Cutter and Captain Anderson, but no one on the shore could tell who they were.

Those on land were powerless. They could hear cries for help, but the voices were fading. When fire and rescue personnel are put in a situation they can't fix, it's like telling a small child to push a full-size cement truck around the block. Frustration turned to despair.

"How many out there?" Russ asked.

"We're not sure. We think three or four kids, a couple of counselors, Ranger Cutter, Captain Anderson, and Paramedic Baitx. . . . We don't have any communication with them."

Russ knew he had thirty to sixty minutes in thirty-four degree water with his wet suit on to go into the ice water hole and push as many victims as possible to the surface.

He started out onto the ice, but was confronted with stark reality. Spider fractures were breaking out around his feet with every step. *Lord, nobody should be out here.* He dropped on his belly and began to crawl along the rope that was being held on shore and attached to someone out on the ice. His wet suit constricted body movement; it was like running a mile with manacles on your ankles.

Suddenly there was a muffled sound of splashing and yelling—the rope under Russ was being pulled toward shore. Baitx was being dragged through the razor sharp ice as the skin on his body ripped into bloody shreds. Behind him were three, apparently alive, victims in the water.

*There are four of them, and only one of me,* Russ thought. Terror moved through his body like a lightning bolt, *Lord, help me!*

He was about twenty feet from Baitx. Russ turned toward shore and with all of his might shouted, "Stop pulling the rope!" When he looked around, he could no longer see Counselor Randy.

In quick succession, Captain Anderson succumbed to the icy depths, only six feet from Russ's outstretched hand. He could still hear Ranger Cutter yelling for help about one hundred feet away.

*Lord, this can't be happening!* Russ cried out under his breath. By now Paramedic Baitx was submerged under the ice, but Russ plunged below him and pushed him to the surface.

"It's okay, buddy. . . . This is Russ. I've got you. My wetsuit is buoyant."

Baitx moaned. He was still alive. However, the rope that was tied to his waist was also fastened to a fourteen foot fire ladder, which was pulling him down. Russ dove under water to see if he could free Baitx from the ladder, but discovered the rope was wrapped around the paramedic's legs like a tangled mesh of fishing line.

"Russ," Baitx murmured through purple lips. "I can't make it . . . tell my wife . . ."

"We'll make it . . . hang in there." Russ answered calmly, but fear gripped him.

As the possibility of survival waned, the two Dougs arrived, sliding through the broken ice with a life raft. Later Russ realized that it was no accident that the Lord sent those men at that moment to play a vital, life-saving role.

After unloosening the rope from Baitx's legs, they lifted him onto the raft and pushed to shore. Russ began to swim in the direction of the voice he had heard calling for help, but after a few strokes, he realized that nobody was there. All he could see was a jacket, a few gloves, and a couple of wool caps sitting on the surface.

Convict Lake had claimed its seventh victim, Ranger Clay Cutter.

## TRAUMA ON SHORE

Baitx was rushed to the emergency hospital by members of his own paramedic team. When his gurney was pushed through the double emergency door, a shocked and horrified nurse, Lori Baitx, looked down at the battered, nearly frozen body of her husband.

After the ambulance left the lake, the crowd on shore began to realize what had happened. "Where's Vidar? . . . Where's Clay? Did you see Randy or Dave out there? What about the boys?" The horror of reality set in. Teri Cutter was in shock. She had watched her husband fight for life until the very end.

Russ fell on his knees in the snow. He was too emotionally spent to stand. He heard his radio "cackling" in the background with the report, "We have seven confirmed fatalities . . . four, I think, were rescuers."

Because one man had the proper equipment, another man's life was saved. Tragically, because warnings were ignored on that fateful day, it was too late for the seven who plunged to their freezing death on the lake that was rightly named. It was, indeed, a brutal convict.

## WILL WE LISTEN?

The warnings are posted today. THIN ICE AHEAD. Our eternal destiny is determined by whether we heed the signs or ignore them. Rescuers may want to save us, but it could be too late.

The final days for all of the inhabitants of planet earth have been recorded for almost two thousand years. In our time, those signs are becoming closer and bolder.

The decade of the nineties has seen tremendous changes in the world. The high-decibel threats of communism have become less threatening as governments have toppled and new leaders have emerged. Many oppressed people have experienced a freedom they had never known.

*Time* Magazine had a cover story showing the heads of the world's two most powerful countries smiling at each other over the words, "Building a New World."

Although we may rejoice that old animosities are dissolving and experience new hope for peace in the world community, at the same time we suspect that we are being lulled into a false security.

Warnings have been posted about dangers ahead. We can either watch and listen or ignore them.

The signs of the time are on a fast track, pointing to the final days of Bible prophecy. It's true that many people shrug their shoulders and say, "Is this like the guy who said the end of the world would come on September 16, 1988? Come on now! I've heard this stuff before."

The apostle Peter said: "First, I want to remind you that in the last days there will come scoffers who will do every wrong they can think of, and laugh at the truth. This will be their line of argument: 'So Jesus promised to come back, did he? Then where is he? He'll never come! Why, as far back as anyone can remember everything has remained exactly as it was since the first day of creation'" (2 Peter 3:3–4, TLB).

There is a book in the Bible that scoffers should read. It contains warnings far more solemn than those directed at the young men on Convict Lake.

The Book of Revelation predicts the climax of the ages and the sequence of events leading up to the return of Jesus Christ. Furthermore, this book explains where every person will be for all eternity.

## WHO CAN PREDICT THE FUTURE?

When someone asks me, "When is your birthday?" I become wary. I don't believe they plan to send me a present. They probably want to know what sign I live under so they can tell me how to run my life. In spite of the nonsense of astrological predictions, most of the major newspapers in the country continue to carry these columns, and many people use these silly predictions to determine how they will plan their daily activities and future goals. Even people who are prominent in public life consult astrologers and psychics, searching for answers to life's complexities.

God predicts the future with inerrant accuracy. He knows the end from the beginning. However, He gives us the guide for the present. "Therefore do not worry about tomorrow, for tomorrow will worry about itself. Each day has enough trouble of its own" (Matthew 6:34).

We are not to worry about tomorrow, but He wants us to understand the future so we will know how to live *today*. His Book is filled with predictions that have already been fulfilled. Look at just a few of them.

# TRUE TO DATE

In the Old Testament there are more than 300 references to the coming Messiah that were fulfilled in Jesus Christ. In Genesis 3:15 we find the first reference to the fact that the Savior of the world would be born of "the seed of the woman" (KJV). This ancient promise predicts a struggle between Israel's Messiah and Satan, and it foretells the Messiah's eventual victory.

The prophet Isaiah tells that the Messiah will be born of a virgin. It was prophesied that He would be the Son of God and that He would trace His humanity to Abraham, father of the Jewish nation. He would come from the tribe of Judah and the house of David. Micah foretold that He would be born in Bethlehem and the psalmist wrote that He shall be called Lord. [1]

It was predicted that the coming Messiah would be a prophet, a judge, and a king. This Man whom the Jews were waiting for (and many are still seeking) would be more than an ordinary human being, for the Spirit of the Lord would give Him wisdom and knowledge beyond our comprehension.[2]

To me, prophecy is the most absorbing study in the Bible. The coming Messiah's ministry was described in such detail that no other person could have fulfilled the description.

# THE PERFECT RÉSUMÉ

Imagine a twentieth-century executive recruiter listing these requirements for a chief executive officer:

- An unqualified recommendation by a community leader (John the Baptist).
- His term of office to begin in Galilee.
- He must perform miracles.
- He must teach his management team by using illustrations.
- He should expose dishonest members of the firm and fire them.

- He must bring a new era of understanding and wisdom to a faltering company.

From all of the applicants, one man alone steps out of history and says, I'm your man." He fills every requirement so perfectly that the search team would be overwhelmed.

Some Old Testament prophets were instructed to give doleful predictions. More than seven hundred years before the birth of Christ, Isaiah said that He would be despised, wounded, bruised, and oppressed (Isaiah 53:3, 5, 7). The same old prophet said He would be crucified with thieves and rejected by His own people.

When we see the prophecies fulfilled in the life of Jesus, how can we doubt that He was the Messiah, the Christ, the Son of God? The cruel manner in which He would die, the grave where He would be buried, and His glorious resurrection were predicted by holy men, led by God to write His inspired Word.

After Jesus was resurrected, He appeared to His disciples over a period of forty days and told them many things. They must have listened with an intensity they had never experienced before, with a new urgency in their questions: "When will you establish the kingdom of Israel, Lord?" Jesus told them, as He had before, that they were not to know the time of His return and the establishment of His kingdom, but to watch for the signs of the times. As they were pondering this answer, He suddenly was lifted out of sight and disappeared into a cloud.

While the apostles stood with their mouths open, two men in white clothing came and gave the first post-Christian prophetic message: "'Men of Galilee,' they said, 'why do you stand here looking into the sky? This same Jesus, who has been taken from you into heaven, will come back in the same way you have seen him go into heaven'" (Acts 1:11).

When He left earth He was only in His thirties. Yet no other man in history has ever made such an impact on this planet.

He is coming again. More than three hundred times in the New Testament and one entire, exciting book describes in detail the time and chronological events leading up to His return.

# THE AUTHOR WITH THE KEY

The book that tells us the awesome events which will bring history to a finale is sometimes called "The Revelation of St. John the Divine," or "The Revelation of John." The correct title should be "The Revelation of Jesus Christ." John did not write an imaginative piece of spiritual fiction; he was chosen by Jesus to record the epic which would forever change the lives of those who read and understand it.

John, "the disciple whom Jesus loved," was special to Jesus. It wasn't that Jesus didn't love His other disciples, but there was a particular bond with this one. John and his brother, James, were called "Sons of Thunder" when they were young, but as he grew older, John became known for his gentleness; the thunder became a distant rumble.

John was bold, however, in telling everyone about Jesus. That severely offended Domitian, the Emperor of Rome from A.D. 81–96. This pompous fellow had assumed the title "Master and god," and he demanded that people take an oath to worship him. The apostle John refused to obey such a command, and for this crime he was sent to the isolated island of Patmos, a rocky, almost treeless wasteland, covered with volcanic hills and dented with caves. Domitian must have thought an old man like John, who was now in his nineties, could not survive long in such cruel exile.

Hovering in a barren grotto with criminals of every stripe, John probably approached his banishment as an opportunity to reach those wretched people with the love of Christ. However, he was given a greater mission: God told him of future events that would change the course of the world forever.

God sent an angel to communicate with John, and John tells us: "The revelation of Jesus Christ, which God gave him *to show his servants what must soon take place.* He made it known by sending his angel to his servant John, who testifies to everything he saw—that is, the word of God and the testimony of Jesus Christ" (Revelation 1:1–2, emphasis added).

# NO LONGER A MYSTERY

The word "revelation" means "the disclosure of that which was previously hidden or unknown." The Book of Revelation tells us that Jesus is coming again, how He is coming, and what condition the world will be in when He comes.

People frequently ask, "Why must Jesus come again?" The reasons are evident in the two phases of His return.

First, Jesus must return again to take His church to be with Him forever. The church is called the bride of Christ, and just as a bride eagerly awaits the day she will be united with the one she loves, so the church, made up of believers in Jesus, waits to be united with the Bridegroom. In heaven there will be the Marriage Supper of the Lamb, the symbolic joining of Christ, the Bridegroom, with the church as the bride, to be one forever in eternity.

Phase One in the second coming of Christ is called the Rapture. This is the great magnet process, when all true believers in Jesus Christ, sensitized to Him, will be drawn like a magnet to be with Him (1 Thessalonians 4:17).

Phase Two will take place at the end of a seven-year period after the Rapture, when Christ returns to reign over His earthly kingdom.

When Christ takes His own to heaven (those whose earthly bodies have died and those who are alive at that time), they will stand before the Judgment Seat of Christ. Some people have asked, "If there are so many to be judged, why doesn't Christ judge them immediately on their death, instead of letting all those millions of people pile up at the last minute?"

The answer is that we don't finish our work when we die. It lives on after us. What we have done on earth, if it amounts to anything, continues after we die physically. How could there be rewards and judgments when our earthly life is over? Our influence upon friends, family, the people we knew during our lifetimes, does not cease when our obituaries appear in the local paper.

I know of Kristin, a fourteen-year-old girl who died after a lingering and painful bout with cancer. One of her last concerns was for her friends who did not know Jesus Christ as she did. She asked her mother, "Who will tell them about Jesus after I'm gone?" Her testimony will live on, and its ripple effect will touch more lives than we will ever know until the kingdom comes.

Many people are still piling up points before appearing at the judgment seat in heaven. For instance, D. L. Moody went to be with the Lord in 1899, but his influence and the school he founded, Moody Bible Institute, have continued for decades.

## WHAT ON EARTH IS HAPPENING?

While Christians are appearing for their rewards, the people remaining on earth will be living in the worst time of final history. Although the Book of Revelation describes this time called the Tribulation, some of the great Christians of the past, like Martin Luther and John Calvin, virtually ignored this last book in the Bible. Perhaps they thought that some of the signs preceding the Second Coming were so obscure in their time that Revelation was a vast mystery to them. Now it is being understood and unraveled faster than the last pages of an Agatha Christie novel.

Christ will return not only to reward His own, but to judge the world. Between His first appearance and His second will be a time of trouble, and then the judgment of all those who rejected Him will occur. This will not be a judgment for believers, for they have already stood before the judgment seat. This will be a judgment with no parole, no lenient sentence, and no pleas of insanity.

Jesus will return for His church, then to judge the world, and finally to rule the world. More than five centuries before Christ was born, the Jewish prophet Daniel described this scene: "He was given authority, glory and sovereign power; all peoples, nations and men of every language worshiped him. His dominion is an everlasting dominion that will not pass away, and his kingdom is one that will never be destroyed" (Daniel 7:14).

When Jesus was on earth the first time He didn't rule over a small country. He wasn't mayor of a city, governor of a state, or president of

Palestine. But someday His kingdom will encompass not only the world, but the entire universe.

His disciples wanted to know what would be the sign of His coming and the end of the age (Matthew 24:3). Ever since that time people have been asking the same questions. The signs Jesus gave always pointed to establishing His kingdom on earth, not to the Rapture. But coming events cast their shadow before them, and these shadows are gathering around us now. Prophecy is not intended as a mental exercise for believers who are concerned about the intricacies of the Bible. God gives us prophecy so that we can learn how to live.

## WHAT CAN WE LEARN FROM PROPHECY?

Revelation reveals the sequence and magnitude of the future, but the New Testament tells us how prophecy can be a dynamic school for self-improvement. Here are a few courses offered:

- *Problem-Solving.* I don't know of a university that offers this course, but the Bible says that understanding the future will put our everyday problems into better perspective (Colossians 3:2).
- *Advanced Loving.* We will be more loving people, because our love will "increase and overflow for each other and for everyone else" as the impact of His coming soon penetrates our beings (1 Thessalonians 3:12–13).
- *Church Growth.* There's not a pastor of a large or small church who wouldn't be interested in this course. The best place to be as that important day approaches is in church worshiping or in the world serving (Hebrews 10:25).
- *Goal-Setting.* If we really believed He would come back today, we would change many of our habits. "Dear friends, now we are children of God, and what we will be has not yet been made known. But we know that when he appears, we shall be

like him, for we shall see him as he is. Everyone who has this hope in him purifies himself, just as he is pure" (1 John 3:2–3).

- *Cheerleading.* In the big games, the cheerleaders encourage the crowd. How about a course in encouragement? After Paul had written to the church at Thessalonica and the last events on the time chart had become clearer, he said to those believers, "encourage each other" (1 Thessalonians 4:18). We do not need to be doomsayers, but cheerleaders.

- *Life-Saving.* Even those who can't swim can take this course, for it is the most important one to be offered. Prophecy provides us an urgency to reach others for Jesus Christ, to "snatch others from the fire and save them" (Jude 23).

## VOICES FROM THE SHORE

When the danger from thin ice was seen on Convict Lake, warning shouts were heard on shore. Rescuers were not equipped with the proper gear and some perished, along with the boys they were trying to save.

For us, the proper equipment has been given to us in the Book. The escape route has been mapped out for almost two thousand years. As we approach the Third Millennium many people think time is growing short before Christ returns. In the past twenty years, since Bible prophecy captured the attention of the Jesus generation, history has been in high gear.

Are we listening today to the warnings from the mountain of evidence in front of us? The victims at Convict Lake showed us the foolishness of not being prepared.

# 17

---

# DO BUSINESS
# UNTIL CHRIST
# RETURNS

FROM: UNTIL CHRIST RETURNS—
LIVING FAITHFULLY TODAY WHILE
WE WAIT FOR OUR GLORIOUS TOMORROW

One of the criticisms often leveled at those who believe in the Rapture and imminent return of Jesus Christ is that such beliefs lead to a life of laziness and indolence.

After all, we *know* He is coming back. We know the end of the story. We've read the last chapter in the book. Why should we entangle ourselves in the messy affairs of this passing world? Why should we soil our garments in the rough-and-tumble of the "culture wars" and the struggle for a more just and moral society? Why don't we just hold hands, sing songs, read psalms, and wait for the inevitable?

I've heard this caricature painted again and again—mainly by those who believe our primary task as believers is to "reclaim our lost dominion" over the earth. These folks insist that evangelicals who believe in Christ's forthcoming return have copped out on responsibilities for this world and its governance.

A few weeks ago, I happened to tune in a nationally syndicated Christian talk show. At first, I couldn't believe my ears. The host of this program just tore into evangelical believers—especially those who believe in the Rapture. His attack was so full of venom and sarcasm it was almost more than I could bear.

His line of reasoning went something like this: "You pretrib jokesters think you're just gonna be helicoptered outta here, so you're willing to sit back and let the world slide into wreck and ruin because you *think* you aren't going to be here anyway. You're content to sit on your hands and wait for the Rapture. What a surprise you're in for!"

The "surprise" to which he refers pertains to his belief that believers must endure the Tribulation—that Christ will not spare His redeemed bride from the judgment and wrath that will fall upon our world.

I have (at least) three problems with this argument. First, I resent the condescending tone. While this radio host may sincerely believe in what he says, his delivery system needs a little work. The bitterness and poison on his tongue do no credit to his position—or to his Lord.

Second, I think he has created a straw man for an opponent. I really don't know of anyone who subscribes to this "sit on your hands till the

Rapture" stuff. I don't think I've ever met anyone who believes we ought to pull back from our involvements because of hope in His prompt coming.

Finally, our Lord Jesus certainly never left any such instructions. In fact, it's quite the opposite. I'm not a wagering man, but I would gladly take all the people I know who believe in the Rapture and put them up against any other group of believers in the world. Those who cling to "the blessed hope" have a deep sense of urgency about maximizing their life impact for Jesus Christ. Why? Because we realize the time may be short!

In a story told in the Book of Luke, Jesus used a phrase that keeps ringing in my ears. In my heart, I believe it ought to be the watchword for all believers who long for His coming: *"Do business till I come."*

I love that. The old King James has "Occupy till I come," but for me, The New King James makes it more specific: 'Do business till I come.' "

Here is how that line fit into His story:

"Therefore He said: 'A certain nobleman went into a far country to receive for himself a kingdom and to return. So he called ten of his servants, delivered to them ten minas, and said to them, "Do business till I come"'" (Luke 19:12–13).

A similar story is told in the book of Matthew. The latter parable dispels any notion of believers remaining idle while they wait for their Master's return. In this gripping story, Jesus gives us the key to our responsibilities as we wait for His coming:

"For the kingdom of heaven is like a man traveling to a far country, who called his own servants and delivered his goods to them. And to one he gave five talents, to another two, and to another one, to each according to his own ability; and immediately he went on a journey."

Do you notice the similarity to the first story? What Jesus describes must have been a fairly common situation.

> Then he who had received the five talents went and traded
> with them, and made another five talents. And likewise he
> who had received two gained two more also. But he who had
> received one went and dug in the ground, and hid his lord's
> money. After a long time the lord of those servants came

and settled accounts with them. So he who had received five talents came and brought five other talents, saying, "Lord, you delivered to me five talents; look, I have gained five more talents besides them." His lord said to him, "Well done, good and faithful servant; you were faithful over a few things, I will make you ruler over many things. Enter into the joy of your lord." He also who had received two talents came and said, "Lord, you delivered to me two talents; look, I have gained two more talents besides them." His lord said to him, "Well done, good and faithful servant; you have been faithful over a few things, I will make you ruler over many things. Enter into the joy of your lord." Then he who had received the one talent came and said, "Lord, I knew you to be a hard man, reaping where you have not sown, and gathering where you have not scattered seed. And I was afraid, and went and hid your talent in the ground. Look, there you have what is yours." But his lord answered and said to him, "You wicked and lazy servant, you knew that I reap where I have not sown, and gather where I have not scattered seed. Therefore you ought to have deposited my money with the bankers, and at my coming I would have received back my own with interest. Therefore take the talent from him, and give it to him who has ten talents. For to everyone who has, more will be given, and he will have abundance; but from him who does not have, even what he has will be taken away. And cast the unprofitable servant into the outer darkness. There will be weeping and gnashing of teeth."

(Matthew 25:14–30)

Now, you have to admit, Jesus tells good stories. Can't you imagine His disciples getting caught up in that parable as He sat with them on the sunny slopes of the Mount of Olives? The story falls in the sequence of Matthew 25 in an interesting way. Just prior to telling this story, Jesus told the parable of the ten virgins—ten young women who were not alert and did not ready themselves for the bridegroom's return. As a result, these virgins were turned away from the wedding party and the door was closed in their faces.

This earlier story underlines the importance of waiting for the Lord and always watching for His return. But the parable of the talents, which follows, teaches us what to do *while* we are waiting. The bottom line? We need to be *working*. We're not to be sitting around drinking diet soda and playing Bible Monopoly. We're to be involved, energized, doing business for our Lord.

The parable of the talents warns us against laziness and passivity in our outward vocations. It warns us to keep our hearts with all diligence. While the first parable emphasizes attitude, the second emphasizes action. Both parables encourage us to watch for His appearing and to faithfully labor in the work of God while we wait for that great day.

The point of the "talents" story is to show us what we're to be about while we anticipate and look forward to our Lord's return. First of all, notice . . .

## The Uncertain Return

A man traveling to a far country . . . called his own servants and delivered his goods to them. (Matthew 25:14)

In those days, long business journeys were inevitable. There were no airplanes, no trains, taxicabs, or rental cars. As a result, a business trip to another nation or distant city might mean weeks of travel. But what would the householder or business owner do about matters at home while he was gone? Commonly, he would give over responsibilities of his estate to trusted servants. Those servants were charged with handling affairs while the master pursued business elsewhere.

I can tell you this: If I lived in that era, I would be making fewer trips! Travel is complicated and disruptive enough dealing with high-speed transport. Not long ago I got on a plane in Cincinnati and the pilot told us, "We will be at the gate in San Diego at 10:24." He said that in Cincinnati. And when we rolled up to the gate in San Diego, it was exactly 10:24. I looked at my watch and thought to myself, *How do they do that?* But then we cooled our heels for ten minutes on the plane while the ground crew got the gates open. Go figure!

But modes of transportation were not so certain in New Testament days. When the lord of the household said, "I'm going to a far country," he had no idea when he would return—nor did his servants. Yet he expected those servants to be ready for his return every day. Every morning when those servants got up, the master expected them to be ready and available to give an account of their stewardship and their activities. What a powerful reminder that you and I are called to serve Jesus Christ in His absence, always looking for His return, even though we don't know when it will be!

Our Lord does expect us to watch for His return; yet as we watch, we are to keep working in His behalf.

Notice next that as he discharged the responsibility for the estate in his absence, he gave his servants some unequal responsibilities.

## THE UNEQUAL RESPONSIBILITIES

And to one he gave five talents, to another two, and to another one, to each according to his own ability; and immediately he went on a journey. (Matthew 25:15)

This interests me. Everywhere I go I hear people wondering why God did something for Jane or Joe that He didn't do for them. "It isn't fair," I'll hear them say. "Why do Jane or Joe have this privilege, or this opportunity, or this provision, when He hasn't done that for me?"

The hard truth is, we ought to be asking why God would ever do anything for any of us. As Jeremiah wrote, "Through the Lord's mercies we are not consumed, because His compassions fail not" (Lamentations 3:22). The only thing we "deserve" is His wrath. And if we have anything at all, if we are given any position of responsibility whatsoever, it is only because of God's great grace. Why in the world should we be measuring ourselves against anybody else's abilities?

I love Paul's gentle sarcasm when he wrote: "We do not dare to classify or compare ourselves with some who commend themselves. When they measure themselves by themselves and compare themselves with themselves, they are not wise" (2 Corinthians 10:12 NIV).

In the Matthew story, Jesus says, "And to one he gave five talents, to another two, and to another one." The "talents" spoken of here are not spiritual gifts or abilities, as the word implies in our culture today. A talent was simply a measure of money—a monetary term. (But we wouldn't be off the mark to apply the principle here to our gifts and abilities.)

So he gave one man five talents, another man two, and a third man just one. Please notice . . .

## 1. The Talents Were Dispensed According to the Judgment of the Lord

Why did the master in that story give differing amounts as he did? Jesus does not offer a reason. He simply did it because he was who he was. In the same way, God does what He does because He is Who He is. Who's going to question Him? Who's going to ask Him, "Why have You done this or that?"

Whenever God gives us an endowment or a responsibility, it is always according to His own judgment, His own determination. My friend, that thought ought to fill you with praise and adoration for almighty God for *whatever* you might have. Because whatever you've got, it's from His hand.

By the same token, however, you can improve upon what He gives you. I've told my sons that athletic abilities are God's gift; what you *do* with those abilities is your gift back to God. But the original gift is from Him, isn't it? That's what we read in 1 Corinthians 12:11: "All these are the work of one and the same Spirit, and he gives them to each one, just as he determines" (NIV).

Romans 12:6 speaks of our having "gifts differing according to the grace that is given to us."

"Who makes you differ from another?" asks the apostle in 1 Corinthians 4:7, "And what do you have that you did not receive? Now if you did receive it, why do you glory as if you had not received it?"

That's a good question, isn't it? If God gave it to you, why are you walking around all puffed up, thinking you somehow produced it for yourself? *God* gives us these gifts.

Here, then, is the story. The landowner goes away and gives to his servants different endowments. One gets five, one gets two, one gets one. Somebody says, "That doesn't seem fair." Don't be caught in that trap! Who are we to say that what God does or doesn't do is "fair"? God gives according to His own judgment, and His judgments are right. Notice a second truth about that dispersal.

### 2. *The Talents Were Dispensed According to the Capacity of the Steward*

The Bible tells us the talents were given "to each according to his own ability." The fact is, God knows who we are and what we can handle. And so, according to that which He knows we are capable of by the power of the Holy Spirit, He fills the vessel that needs to be filled.

Do you remember the business concept that surfaced some years ago called "the Peter principle"? The original wording by the author, L. Peter, went like this: "In a hierarchy, every employee tends to rise to his level of incompetence."[1] In other words, people tend to get promoted beyond their capabilities. They start off knowing what they're doing and have a good handle on their tasks. By the time they're through being promoted, however, they're in way over their heads! God doesn't do that. He never promotes anybody beyond his or her capacity.

This gifting is not only dispensed according to the will of God and according to the capacity of the individual steward, but it is also given to us so that we might be complete.

### 3. *The Talents Were Dispensed in Order to Fully Equip Each Man*

The five-talent person wasn't any more "complete" than the two-talent man or the one-talent man. Whatever we have from God—if He gave it to us and He knows it to be perfect and appropriate for us—we are complete in that gifting. Just as the master left his servants in charge of various portions of his estate, so God has given every one of us what we need to accomplish His purpose for our lives. We all have what God wants us to have!

Now you've got the picture. The landowner went away and gave his three servants some specific things to administrate. He rode off down the road on his donkey and disappeared into the distance. Now . . . what must those servants do? They must discipline themselves to continue acting and doing business just as if the master were still with them.

It isn't easy to stay accountable when the boss isn't looking over your shoulder, is it? It isn't easy to keep the routine when you don't have to get up at such and such a time or punch a time clock. In this case, the boss couldn't check in by phone or fax or e-mail. The servants are simply left to do their work; he has to trust them to act in his best interest. And each of these employees responded. Two responded one way one responded in another way.

## THE UNUSUAL RESPONSE

How, then, did each of the men respond to the trust placed in him by his master?

### 1. The Faithful Men Doubled Their Endowments

"Then he who had received the five talents went and traded with them, and made another five talents" (Matthew 25:16). Not bad! That's a 100 percent increase. That's "doing business," isn't it?

What about the next man?

"And likewise he who had received two gained two more also" (verse 17). He also doubled the master's money. That's good investment, good stewardship.

Which of them did better? Actually, they both did the same. They took what they had and increased it in the identical proportion. Which one had more? The one who had five—but he also had more to start with. Who had less? The one who had two—but he had less to start with. He took what he had, improved it, and made it something better than it was.

But what about the third man?

*2. The Unfaithful Man Hoarded His Endowment*

"But he who had received one went and dug in the ground, and hid his lord's money" (verse 18). This last employee didn't do anything with his endowment. He was so afraid of losing it, he probably took his shovel out to the corner of the estate in the dead of night and *buried* that solitary talent.

I can just see this old Fearful Charlie. Every morning when he was out walking the dog, he walked by that place where the money was buried—just to make sure it hadn't been disturbed. "Still safe and sound!" he told himself. "Boy oh boy, the boss is going to be so proud of me! I didn't spend one nickel of what he gave me. Put it all in the ground and covered it all up. When he gets back, I'm going to dig it up and hand it to him as he walks through the gate. He's going to be so happy."

But that man had the wrong approach. The faithful men doubled their endowments. The unfaithful man hoarded his endowment. Would his master truly be pleased? Everyone was about to find out.

## THE UNIQUE REWARD

> His lord said to him, "Well done, good and faithful servant;
> you were faithful over a few things, I will make you ruler over
> many things. Enter into the joy of your lord." (Matthew 25:21)

I have taught this parable over and over again, and you can't get by these three things. There was a *commendation,* a *promotion,* and an *invitation.*

The two servants who had doubled their master's money were called before him. He commended them for doing business while he was away—for taking their initial investments and multiplying them. As a result, each received a significant promotion. "Well done, good and faithful servant.

I have given you a little to manage. Now you are going to have much to manage."

Has the thought ever gripped you, my friend, that the way you pursue the Lord's business in this world today determines the kind of administration you will have in the coming kingdom? Do you ever ponder that? Perhaps in the Millennium, you will be the mayor of Chicago or Los Angeles. I don't know what your task will be. But I do know that the way you exercise your responsibility *now* will have a direct impact on what responsibility you will be given *then*.

To me, that thought is one of the greatest keys to stewardship in the Word of God. I've heard people say over and over again, "If you give to the Lord, He'll give back to you. You give with your little shovel, and He gives back with His big shovel. You can't outgive God." That is true. I believe that. Yet I think the principal reason people who give to the Lord end up receiving more is because God sees they are capable of managing what He has put into their hands! He takes note of their faithfulness, enlarges their capacity, and enlarges their responsibilities. That's how it works.

So, my friend, if you want to have more—in this life or the next—you had better manage what He has already given you as faithfully as you possibly can. The people God trusts with more are those who have proved faithful with little.

## THE UNTHINKABLE REBUKE

You may find yourself identifying a bit with the fear expressed by the one-talent man. In Matthew 25:24 he said, "Lord, I knew you to be a hard man."

A hard man? I would say he proved to be a most generous and equitable man. But this third servant really didn't know his master. That was his first problem. That might be your problem too. If you don't know the Lord, if you don't know what kind of a Master He is, you will never trust Him.

The man goes on to say, "I knew you to be a hard man, reaping where you have not sown, and gathering where you have not scattered seed. And I was afraid."

In other words, "I didn't trust you, lord." If you don't trust your Lord, it's a simple fact that you will not invest your time and energy and involvement in serving Him. This man failed because he did not know and, therefore, did not trust his master.

> But his lord answered and said to him, "You wicked and lazy servant, you knew that I reap where I have not sown, and gather where I have not scattered seed. Therefore you ought to have deposited my money with the bankers, and at my coming I would have received back my own with interest. Therefore take the talent from him, and give it to him who has ten talents." (verses 26–28)

The result of his failure? He was condemned. And why was he condemned? He hadn't wasted his master's goods, like the unjust steward in Luke 16. Nor had he spent all he had in riotous living, as the young man in Luke 15. He was not ten thousand talents in debt, like the unmerciful servant in Matthew 18. He hadn't done any of those things. The point was not that he had done something wrong. The point was that *he hadn't done anything.*

That's where so many of God's people find themselves in the kingdom today. It's not that they're doing bad things and undercutting the work of God. It is just that they're not doing much of anything at all. We talk about this all the time in our church family at Shadow Mountain Community Church. We call it our "employment problem." Eighty percent of the people are cheering on 20 percent of the exhausted workers. "All right! Go for it! Three cheers! Get it done!"

I believe if we allow the truth of this parable to really grip our hearts, we would all be "fully employed," doing what we could until our Lord and Master returns and calls us to account. This is not a time to sit on our hands. This is a time for us to get busy for almighty God as never before! This is a time for using every gift and ability He has so graciously given us to advance His Word and His will in our world.

"Well," you say, "that's easy for you. You're a preacher and an author. You know what you're supposed to be doing. But I *don't* know what I'm supposed to be doing."

My reply would be, "What has God put in your hand? What has He given you? What are your opportunities?" If you are a Christian, you (yes, you!) have a special gifting from God the Holy Spirit. Those gifts usually follow along lines you can identify in your own life. You may have the gift of helps. Or the gift of mercy. Or the gift of teaching and exhortation. Or the gift of administration. I know that God gave me the gift of teaching, and listen, *I do everything I can to multiply that gift, to manage that gift, and to use it with all of my heart.* If I don't do those things, I am an unfaithful, unprofitable servant, and the Lord will call me to account for that someday.

I really appreciate the J. B. Phillips paraphrase of Romans 12:6–8. Listen to this stirring list of imperatives!

> Through the grace of God we have different gifts. If our gift is preaching, let us preach to the limit of our vision. If it is serving others let us concentrate on our service; if it is teaching let us give all we have to our teaching; and if our gift be the stimulating of the faith of others let us set ourselves to it. Let the man who is called to give, give freely; let the man in authority work with enthusiasm; and let the man who feels sympathy for his fellows in distress help them cheerfully.

Whatever God has gifted you to do, my friend, do it! Manage that gift, make it work, grow it, develop it, practice it, and in God's wonderful grace, make it multiply. What God has given to you as an ability, give back to Him as an improved ability by managing it with all of your heart. That is what this parable is all about.

You say, "All right, Jeremiah, how am I supposed to be gainfully employed? Specifically, what am I supposed to do?" As I said, you pursue the areas in which God has uniquely equipped you to serve. But just in case you still don't know where to begin, I would like to add three more biblical imperatives that apply to every one of us, no matter what our gifting.

## THREE PLACES TO START

Wondering where to put your oar in the Lord's work? Let me give you three places to launch. If you are doing these three things in the power of the Spirit, you cannot—I repeat, *cannot*—go wrong. And I also firmly believe that as you plunge into the Lord's work, He will direct and guide you more specifically into unique areas of service for His name and His glory.

### 1. We Are to Be Busy Equipping Believers

And becoming equipped ourselves, in the process! When you know Jesus Christ may return at any moment, it changes the way you live. As one of my friends put it, "If you knew that at any moment the Lord Jesus were going to step through the clouds, right into your life, would it change anything?" Of course it would!

In his first letter, the elderly apostle John penned these words: "Beloved, now we are children of God; and it has not yet been revealed what we shall be, but we know that when He is revealed, we shall be like Him, for we shall see Him as He is. *And everyone who has this hope in Him purifies himself, just as He is pure*" (1 John 3:2–3, *emphasis added*).

The upcoming return of Jesus Christ ought to increase our godliness and righteousness before almighty God.

Notice the same truth in some selected verses from 2 Peter 3:

> Therefore, since all these things will be dissolved, what manner of persons ought you to be in holy conduct and godliness, looking for and hastening the coming of the day of God, because of which the heavens will be dissolved, being on fire, and the elements will melt with fervent heat? . . . Therefore, beloved, looking forward to these things, be diligent to be found by Him in peace, without spot and blameless; and

account that the longsuffering of our Lord is salvation—as also our beloved brother Paul, according to the wisdom given to him, has written to you. (verses 11–12, 14–15)

Peter is saying that the Lord Jesus could come at any moment. And I am finding in my own heart that if I really believe that, if I really understand that, if I truly concentrate on that, it changes the way I live. In an earlier chapter we poked a little fun at the old attitudes of "not wanting to be caught in a movie house" when the Lord returns. But we don't want to make fun of that attitude to the point where we lose the emphasis of *living carefully* in light of His coming. It *does* matter what He finds us doing when He steps through the clouds. Someone has speculated that one of the reasons God will have to wipe tears from our eyes in His presence (Revelation 21:4) is because of our grief and shame over how He will find us when He comes.

Here is a second emphasis. Not only are we to be equipping believers . . .

## 2. We Are to Be Busy Evangelizing the Lost

In Acts chapter 1, the disciples were gathered around the risen Lord, just before He ascended into heaven before their eyes. What priorities did He leave with them at that final farewell?

Therefore, when they had come together, they asked Him, saying, "Lord, will You at this time restore the kingdom to Israel?" [Sound familiar? When, Lord, when?] And He said to them, "It is not for you to know times or seasons which the Father has put in His own authority. But you shall receive power when the Holy Spirit has come upon you; and you shall be witnesses to Me in Jerusalem, and in all Judea and Samaria, and to the end of the earth." Now when He had spoken these things, while they watched, He was taken up, and a cloud received Him out of their sight. (Acts 1:6–9)

Knowing the precise time of His coming is not important. But what is important is declaring His name and His salvation, near and far. Within your family and within your city. To your own neighborhood. To the whole world. Jesus says, "Don't be asking Me about times and seasons. Get busy and do the work."

Many of us have been caught up in speculations about computer bugs and about what the turning of the millennium might mean to our nation and world. And that's okay; I'm not opposed to the cautions and preparations. But in the process, let's not lose our Lord's strong emphasis. The precise timing of this event and that event are simply not important. What really counts is taking as many people to heaven with us as we possibly can.

Let me ask you a question. Do you have anyone in your immediate or extended family who has not yet come to know Christ as Savior? That ought to be one of the first things you put on your prayer list. Do you pray for that individual?

You say, "Well, Jeremiah, why wouldn't I?" I'll tell you why you might not. Because you and I get so busy, so involved, so preoccupied, so wrapped up and strung out by so many good and worthy activities that we put prayer on a low-priority shelf. Pretty soon weeks go by, months go by, and you suddenly realize you can't even remember the last time you prayed for your unsaved loved one.

There's a third priority.

### 3. We Are to Be Busy Encouraging the Church

You may possess the spiritual gift of encouragement, but if you don't, you should practice encouraging others anyway! Hebrews says this clearly in chapter 10: "And let us consider how we may spur one another on toward love and good deeds. Let us not give up meeting together, as some are in the habit of doing, but let us encourage one another—and all the more as you see the Day approaching" (verses 24–25 NIV).

Earlier in that same book, the author exhorts us to "encourage one another daily, as long as it is called Today, so that none of you may be hardened by sin's deceitfulness" (Hebrews 3:13 NIV).

My friend, if you are convinced in your heart that Jesus Christ could return at any moment, you ought to be a champion encourager! Do it with words. Do it with phone calls. Do it with e-mails. Do it with hugs and words and prayer and flowers and gifts and smiles and heartfelt applause. Just do it! He is coming soon!

So what do we have on our plates as we anticipate His imminent return?

*Building up fellow believers.*

*Reaching the lost.*

*Encouraging one another with all our hearts.*

Does that give you enough "work" to start with? Will that keep you busy for a while? If any of you run out of something to do in those three categories, drop me a line at Turning Point Ministries, and I might have another idea or two!

## WORK WHILE YOU WAIT

Believing in the imminent return of Jesus is not simply a matter of "waiting," as important as that may be. It is rather a matter of *working*. Working hard. Working faithfully. Working in the power and joy and filling of the Holy Spirit. And when you work in such a way, you never know what God may be up to! You never know where your next kingdom assignment might be.

Someone asked me what I would like to be doing when the Lord comes back. That's easy. I would like to be standing behind my pulpit before my flock, declaring and explaining and applying the Word of God. For me, there's nothing better. There is no greater joy.

What would you like to be doing when He returns? Where would you like to be when the trumpet sounds, when the archangel shouts, and when in the twinkling of an eye we are changed and race into the clouds to meet Him?

What has He given you to do?

Do that.

Do business until He comes.

# 18

---

# When Changing
# Your Mind
# Could Save
# Your Life

---

From: I Never Thought I'd See the Day!

*Not infrequently these days, I will hear someone express a variation on this theme: a longing to return to the "good old days." They are thinking wistfully about a time that was happier and less stressful, simpler and less complicated.*

Have you noticed that no one who longs for the good old days seems to know exactly when those days were? They were the days that came before today—days lodged vaguely somewhere in the past. The implication is, of course, that life has never been as complicated and perilous as it is today.

When someone my age refers to the good old days, it's usually a reference to the 1950s. That's the decade of my childhood, and if I can trust my memory, it was indeed different from the decade we have just completed. World War II was over, the economy was on a roll, military personnel were back home starting new families (the baby boomers were conceived in the fifties), a conservative political and cultural wind was blowing, and life was good. At least, it was a lot better than life in wartime.

Then came the 1960s, when young people rebelled against the status quo and the Vietnam War, then the seventies when the nation tried to figure out what the sixties meant, and then the eighties—the so-called Decade of Greed. By the time the 1990s arrived—the Digital Decade— the good old days appeared as a faint image in the rearview mirror of life. Then came the first decade of the twenty-first century, when society started pulling down long-standing pillars upon which our nation was built. That's when many people became alarmed and started polishing that mirror to the past, trying to recapture something they felt they had lost. The changes of the last two or three decades came so fast and furious that we began to long for a simpler, quieter, more predictable time in which to live.

The past is not always as rosy as our memories make it. I believe much of the nostalgia for the good old days stems from selective memory. Our minds tend to latch on to the good memories and filter out the rest. In reality, the fifties were not exactly a carefree decade.

It only seemed that way at first because World War II had ended. The 1940s had been a decade of a "hot war," but the 1950s were the decade of the Cold War. People tend to forget that during the 1950s, the United States and the former Soviet Union aimed enough nuclear missiles at each other to completely destroy both nations. It was the decade of nuclear-attack drills in American schools and fallout shelters in American back-yards. Americans went to bed at night wondering if they would wake up to a nuclear holocaust.

My point is this: There is no such thing as the good old days! Because life seems to get more and more complicated with every passing year, we all think it would be nice to reverse the passage of time and revert to the goodness we had yesterday. And never has that been truer than now.

In 2007 I had no idea I would write four books over the next four years dealing with the crises in our world. But neither did I (nor anyone else) foresee the massive economic tsunami that swept over the shores of nations around the world. The title of my 2008 book—*What in the World Is Going On?*—said it all. Never in our lifetimes had people felt more con-fused and uncertain over the chaos they were witnessing. Never had they seen America experience such upheaval—the ripple effects are still being felt today. And many, including myself, believe that the worst is yet to come, as I explained in my 2010 book, *The Coming Economic Armageddon*.

The economic upheaval beginning in 2008 was, in my view, symptom-atic of greater and even more dangerous changes that had occurred in the previous several decades. Financial and economic activities that led to the collapse of 2008 were in many cases deceitful and immoral—indicative of a society that had lost its moral and spiritual compass. Any nation that is drowning in debt, at war around the world, and in danger of losing her status as an example to other nations clearly has serious problems at home.

In the preceding nine chapters, I have explained some of the evidences of American disintegration that cause me great concern—things whose day I never thought I would see. This does not mean I am a pessimist; I am not. But I am a realist. You have waded through lots of statistics and historical narrative in this book by which I have documented the alarming reality of our situation as a nation. My goal has been to hold up a mirror and say, "Here's where we are—and it is not where many of us would like to be."

Though there are still plenty of secular humanists who believe man is either capable of solving his own problems or capable of surviving whatever collapse our problems produce, I am not one of them. In that respect, I am a pessimist. I am pessimistic about man's ability, independent from his Creator-God, to solve the problems he creates—especially problems of enormous scale such as those our nation and the world face today.

I am, however, an optimist about God. And it is toward Him that we must turn our attention in this final chapter. But first I must sharpen the definition of *optimism* on the whetstone of biblical realism. By optimism in God, I do not mean that I expect God to swoop down and erase our massive debts; put an end to threats of terrorism; cause a spiritual revival to sweep the nation that impacts schools, government, and commerce; and return America to the good old days. I don't think that's biblically realistic, and it's not a lack of faith that causes me to say so.

Rather, as I read my Bible I find compelling reasons to believe that the human race is on a collision course with calamity—that things are going to get worse before they get better, which will not happen until the return of Jesus Christ to earth. I believe the Bible teaches that in the last days of this age, only the return of Christ will keep humanity from destroying itself.

So what is there to be optimistic about? I am optimistic about God's ability to keep you and me from being conformed to the chaos around us. I am optimistic about God's ability to transform us—to raise us higher as the world sinks lower.

Regardless of what happens in the future, I need that protection from conformity and that power to be transformed. And I need it *today*! Even if the intensity of the storms around us doesn't increase in my lifetime or yours, they are bad enough today to make me know that I need protection and power to endure. I do not know God's timetable for America or the world. The return of Christ could be further away than I think it is, and this period of crisis that threatens us now may temporarily smooth itself out. Indeed, I hope it does. I do not wish ill upon my nation or the world.

But the truth is, even in the best of times—even in the good old days—this world is not our friend. It has been usurped by Satan, and we need to defend ourselves against being conformed to it. We need to be constantly in the transformative process of becoming more like Jesus Christ regardless of what is happening around us.

This protection from conformity and power to be transformed is the only way to find peace and joy in this life. If we allow our well-being to depend on external circumstances—our financial security, our comfort, the satisfaction of material or sensual desire, or our health, we consign ourselves to lives of anxiety over events we cannot control. We are dependent on a world that cannot offer the ultimate security and meaning we desire. The only solution is to follow a different path from that of the disintegrating world around us.

I know this is true because the apostle Paul wrote about this very protection from conformation and power for transformation nineteen hundred years ago in his letter to the Christians in Rome. Those believers were living under the hateful eye of emperors such as the demoniacal Nero, who made sport of persecuting them. And to those beleaguered believers who were no doubt already sacrificing much, Paul gave what must have sounded like the strangest advice: In order not to be conformed, and in order to be transformed, you must sacrifice yourselves.

Sacrifice yourselves? They must have wondered what in the world Paul meant. To anyone living in the first-century Mediterranean world, sacrifice was an ever-present reality. The slit throats, draining carcasses, and burning flesh of sacrificial animals were common in every city with a pagan temple. Every loyal Mediterranean Jew who made his or her way to Jerusalem for the annual celebrations to Yahweh was also familiar with the bloody ritual of sacrifice. The only redeeming aspect of sacrifice was that worshippers were glad it was the animal they contributed lying on the altar, and not themselves.

Yet Paul's words in Romans 12:1–2 changed all that. Paul told them (and he tells us) that protection against conformity and power to be transformed can happen only if we sacrifice ourselves:

> I beseech you therefore, brethren, by the mercies of God, that
> you present your bodies a living sacrifice, holy, acceptable to
> God, which is your reasonable service. And do not be con-
> formed to this world, but be transformed by the renewing of
> your mind, that you may prove what is that good and accept-
> able and perfect will of God.

As we will see in this chapter, these two verses give us all the answers we need to be optimistic, at peace, and even filled with joy as we face the problems I've addressed in the previous nine chapters.

Those chapters were lectures on the state of our nation and the world; I want this chapter to be a conversation. Those chapters were filled with challenging facts and realities; in this chapter you will find encouragement. Those chapters brought us face-to-face with what man does; I now want you to see what God can do. And specifically, what God can do in *you* if you will heed the apostle Paul's admonition to sacrifice yourself for Him.

## A NEW KIND OF SACRIFICE

Let's begin by defining the most arresting word in the passage: *sacrifice*. Romans 12:1 tells us to "present your bodies a living sacrifice." The idea of sacrifice is not readily embraced in our modern society.

To illustrate, think about the economic downturn that began in 2008. It came to light with the collapse of the housing market—the subprime housing debacle. Unscrupulous lenders provided mortgages to unqualified borrowers who could not afford the payments. Loans were so easy to get that greedy investors bought property sight unseen for the sole purpose of "flipping" it at a profit in the soaring real estate market. Investment banks bundled these worthless mortgages and sold them to investors. Other banks issued insurance policies guaranteeing the worth of the bundled mortgages. It was a greed-based house of cards built on bad credit, and it came crashing down on the country. People lost their homes and their jobs, companies laid off workers, and—like throwing gasoline on a fire— our government began printing money to stimulate the economy. The U.S.

Treasury began selling bonds to the U.S. Federal Reserve bank, which paid for them with newly printed dollars—the classic case of "robbing Peter to pay Paul."

It all started because no one was willing to sacrifice—to say no to the allure of a bigger, newer home they couldn't afford; to say no to the fees generated by writing mortgages for unqualified borrowers; to say no to the fees from selling bundled mortgages; to say no to the fees from insuring those bundled mortgages. Because no one was willing to sacrifice immediate desires for the sake of long-term integrity, we ended up where we are today.

We have been trained by our culture not to believe in sacrifice—to believe instead that we can have it all. And this carries over to our spiritual lives. As Christians, we have a healthy regard for the sacrifice Jesus Christ made for us two thousand years ago by willingly laying down His life. But we think of sacrifice as "won and done"— since He won that victory by sacrificing Himself, it's not something we are called to do.

So when the twenty-first-century Church reads Paul admonishing her to "present your bodies a living sacrifice" to God, it doesn't sit too well—if for no other reason than because we're Americans. It doesn't fit the kind of life we all enjoy. We have everything we need either at our fingertips or at the nearby shopping mall, where we can get it instantly just by sliding a plastic card. We're not used to having to sacrifice for much of anything.

If *sacrifice* is such a foreign word in this land of instant abundance, maybe we'd better talk a little about just what that word really means. *Sacrifice* always means one of two things:

- Somebody has to pay.
- Somebody has to die.

If you are the one being called to sacrifice yourself—depending on the sacrifice called for—either you have to pay or you have to die.

Let's say you and your spouse bought tickets to a play, and on the way to the theater you come upon a serious accident that just happened. There are injuries, and you have had a little emergency medical training. So you stop, call 911, and render aid while awaiting the EMTs. Before it's over your good suit is dirty, you're hot and sweaty, and you've missed half the play. So you have no choice but to return home.

You have sacrificed in the sense that you had to pay. Helping another person cost you something. You paid in resources you possessed—time and skill—and you also paid the price of missing the play. You sacrificed.

Paying is one kind of sacrifice; now let's look at the other kind.

Charles Dickens's novel *A Tale of Two Cities* is set in the bloodiest days of the French Revolution when aristocrats—even innocent ones—are executed under the guillotine by the ruling mob. The hero, Sydney Carton, saves Charles Darnay, a truly noble aristocrat, by slipping into the prison where Darnay is held, drugging him, exchanging clothing, and having him slipped out of the prison. The next day Sydney Carton is executed under the guillotine. His sacrifice called for him to die.

These two stories illustrate the realistic definition of the word *sacrifice*. We pay with time, talent, or treasure, or we pay with our very lives.

Those two forms of sacrifice are easily understood, but Paul shocked his Roman readers by introducing to them (and to us) an altogether new idea—the idea of a "living sacrifice."

To be a living sacrifice actually combines the two common meanings of *sacrifice*. The term includes the word *living*, yet we are called on to die. That's what it means to become a Christian. We die to the people we were when we lived by the power of the sinful nature we inherited from Adam. The old self is laid upon the altar and "killed." In its place, we receive the indwelling of the Holy Spirit, by which we live a new kind of life.

Living that new life involves the other definition of *sacrifice*. Since we "died" to our old selves, we are now new creatures, no longer living under the selfish power of the sinful nature. As new creatures we live a new kind of life, one directed by the power of the Holy Spirit and God's Word. That new life will be one of giving—of sacrificing our resources, our self-centered wants, our time, for the sake of the kingdom of God.

This radical concept of self-sacrifice, which is the first idea introduced in Romans 12:1–2, is a prerequisite to the second idea: the renewing of our minds. And it is the renewal of our minds that will keep us from being conformed to the world in which we live. We cannot separate the idea of sacrifice from the concept of renewal: *No one's mind will be renewed whose body has not first been given as a living sacrifice to God.*

As we can see, these two verses in Romans 12 give us a three-step process: (1) We sacrifice ourselves to God. This empties us of self so that God's Holy Spirit can step in and (2) transform us by renewing our minds. (3) This transformation will enable us to keep from being conformed to the deadly values of the world.

## A Radical Decision

Needless to say, the decision to sacrifice one's self is a radical one. Dickens's Sydney Carton surely had to spend considerable time in thought before he decided to give his life for another person. Giving one's life is a pretty big deal. The martyrs for Christ who died in Roman arenas, at the stake, or under the sword could have avoided their fate simply by renouncing Christ. But they made the radical decision that their commitment to God was worth far more than their lives.

The call of Paul in Romans 12:1 to sacrifice ourselves demands this kind of radical decision. We are called to give up something—to turn our backs on our former lives and put ourselves in the hands of God, who does not guarantee that we will retain the comfort, lifestyle, or ease we've been used to having. It's a call for a radical decision.

In verse 1 when Paul calls for this decision, the first clue that he is about to say something important is the presence of the word *therefore*. We have to know what that word is "there for" in order to understand what follows. "Therefore" always connects what immediately precedes it with what immediately follows. So what did Paul say prior to Romans 12:1 that led him to call for this radical decision?

## This Radical Decision Is Crucial

In chapters 9 through 11 of Romans, Paul develops a sweeping view of God's redemptive plan for Jews and Gentiles. In those three chapters, which immediately precede the word *therefore* in 12:1, the word *mercy* occurs nine times. It occurs not a single time in chapters 1 through 8. So something of critical importance is being presented in chapters 9 through 11 that has to do with mercy. Quite simply, it is that both Jews and Gentiles are saved by the mercy of God, "that He might make known the riches of His glory on the vessels of mercy, which He had prepared beforehand for glory" (Romans 9:23).

And what is mercy? It is the withholding of deserved punishment or retribution.

> *Mercy is not getting something bad we deserve.*
> *Grace is getting something good we don't deserve.*

The Roman Christians to whom Paul wrote (and we as well) were "vessels of mercy" on whom God chose to bestow the grace and favor of salvation. We deserved judgment because of our sin, yet God chose to have mercy upon us and save us by giving His Son to die the death we deserved.

In verse 1 of chapter 12, Paul shows the connection between God's mercy and our self-sacrifice: "I beseech you therefore, brethren, by the mercies of God, that you present your bodies a living sacrifice." In other words, in view of the mercy God has offered you, here is what you need to do in response: Sacrifice yourself to Him. Kill your old sin-infested self and open yourself to this new life He offers by His loving mercy.

That requires a decision on our part, and it's a crucial one. Will we open ourselves to the new life and mercy God offers? Or will we refuse to make the sacrifice and turn our backs on it?

The primary point of C. S. Lewis's book *The Great Divorce* is that God's mercy is free, and we must make the crucial decision to either accept it or reject it. He does not *send* anyone to eternal punishment or eternal reward. Each goes to his final destination by his own choice. Lewis's story shows that all people are offered heaven, but many choose to reject it, preferring to retain instead some pleasure, some comfort, some pet activity. They choose to sacrifice nothing. They will not make the crucial decision to accept God's mercy.

## This Radical Decision Is Comprehensive

Paul asks us to present our *bodies* as a living sacrifice—not our time or talent or treasure or some other compartment of our lives, but our bodies. That's Paul's way of saying, "Present your whole self to God—all that you are and have." Paul refers to the body eleven times in Romans as a reference to the totality of who we are as persons.

We get a clear picture of what Paul means by "present your body" when we compare Romans 12:1 with a similar term used in Romans 6:13. Here Paul exhorts Christians not to "present your members as instruments of unrighteousness to sin, but present yourselves to God as being alive from the dead, and your members as instruments of righteousness to God." "Members" refers to body parts, a euphemism for one's whole self. Taking these two verses together, we can see that rather than presenting our whole selves to sin, we are to present our whole selves to God as living sacrifices.

We who live in modern societies are used to dividing our lives into a multitude of compartments. But making religion one of the subdivisions of our lives will not work at all. To have any meaning, our relationship to God must form the foundation of every facet of our lives. It must permeate every relationship, every decision, every action. That means we sacrifice our own wills in all these areas. God calls us to give everything to Him as a living sacrifice. It is a comprehensive decision.

## This Radical Decision Is Costly

When a Jew selected a spotless animal from his flock to offer as a sacrifice to the Lord, there was one thing he knew for sure: He would not return home with that animal. The very definition of the word *sacrifice* means giving up something forever. Even if we sacrifice our time or talent or financial resources, what we give is gone forever. We will never get it back. Therefore, the idea of presenting ourselves to God as living sacrifices requires us to think carefully about the costs involved.

Jesus did not pull any punches when He told the crowds of the cost involved in following Him. He warned that it might cost them the love of their families; it might even cost them their lives. Because the price could be so great, He warned them not to be like a builder who doesn't count the cost of his project before beginning, or like a king who goes to battle without being sure his army is strong enough to win the victory (Luke 14:25–33). A serious commitment to Christ requires putting oneself on the sacrificial altar. And as Jesus told His disciples, He does not want quitters: "No one, having put his hand to the plow, and looking back, is fit for the kingdom of God" (Luke 9:62).

Someone once said, "The problem with living sacrifices is that they keep crawling off the altar!" That's what a quitter does, and that's why we must count the cost before presenting ourselves to God as living sacrifices. We do not know what lies ahead in our lives, the life of our nation, or the life of our world. Our faith might be tested in ways it has never before been tested. The time to count the cost and make the decision is now, before those difficult times come.

A father I know raised three daughters, all of whom married godly Christian men. When his girls began dating, the father talked to them about sexual pressure and making the right decisions: "If you wait until the moment of temptation to decide whether to stop or proceed, you've waited too long. Your aroused feelings will overpower your resolve. So, it is important that you make chastity your personal commitment before you contemplate dating any boy. A decision made in advance will be solidly in place before you need it, and it will hold you back from entering into even the first stages of 'harmless' sensual behavior."

Girls who make this decision will pay a price. Some boys will never call them for a second date. They will "miss out" on the experiences their girlfriend peers boast about at slumber parties. But what they will gain outweighs what they lose like a pot of gold outweighs a feather.

If we don't count the cost in advance and make that costly decision to follow Christ, we may find ourselves capitulating to the pressures of this world almost at the moment they arise. Without making that costly decision, we will become conformed to the world instead of transformed.

## THIS RADICAL DECISION IS CREATIVE

When we make the decision to sacrifice ourselves, we are telling God that we are willing to be His personal representatives on earth, to be open to His will and to do it. But I am often asked, especially by young people, how to find the will of God for one's life. I tell them the same thing my father told me as a young man: "David, get the car moving. It's a lot easier to steer a moving car than one that's sitting still." In other words, you already know enough of the will of God to get you started in serving the Lord. The Bible is filled with it. These are things everyone is enjoined to do and not do—don't lie, don't steal, don't cheat, love your neighbor as yourself, love God—the commandments and related instructions on living a godly life.

Yet each of us has a unique role to play in reflecting the nature of God. That's why God created each of us with unique abilities. This means that within the "generic" will of God, He has a specific will for you. How you find that plan is simply to follow my father's advice: "Get the car moving." We fulfill God's will for every Christian by giving, studying, encouraging others, serving where needs exist, worshipping, and keeping ourselves unstained by the world. And in the midst of that service, God will begin to reveal new, creative directions for you personally. Make the decision to do what you know of His will, and the creative parts that apply to your particular life will begin to flow.

## THIS RADICAL DECISION IS CREDIBLE

Paul says that presenting yourself to God as a living sacrifice is "your reasonable service." What? You call giving up all you have and maybe even your life *reasonable*? Well, yes, considering the sacrifice Christ made for us, I'd say that what He asks in return is quite reasonable.

One thing I love about the phrase "a reasonable service" is that Paul does not discount the involvement of the mind in the process of becoming a living sacrifice. Such a commitment is reasonable. The Greek word for reasonable is *logikos*, the root of our English word *logical*. In other words, it is reasonable, logical, credible. It makes perfect sense that in light of God's mercy toward us we would present ourselves to Him as living sacrifices.

The opposite also follows logically: It is unreasonable for a Christian *not* to present his or her whole life to God as a living sacrifice. Indeed, not living wholly and sacrificially for God calls into question whether one really understands or has experienced the mercy of God at all. How could anyone receive God's mercy—that is, *not* receive God's judgment for sin—and not want to live wholly for the God who has granted that mercy?

## A RATIONAL DETERMINATION

*Sacrifice* is not a pretty word. It means losing something valuable—one's time, energy, resources, wants, or even one's life. Why should we make such a sacrifice? What makes it worthwhile? What is the benefit? Sacrificing one's self is too big a step to take without having a very good reason to do it. We touched briefly on the reason early in the chapter—we sacrifice ourselves in response to the mercy God offers us and to have our lives transformed. Now we want to flesh out that reason more fully.

When we lay ourselves on the altar, we open ourselves to the new life God gives us through the Holy Spirit. This means we have new power, new direction, a new goal, a new standard of behavior, a new standard for relationships. The old standard was conformity to this world, but the new standard is to "be transformed by the renewing of your mind." It is our sacrifice—our death to the old sinful self—that submits us to God so we can undergo this transformation.

This transformation, though accomplished by the power of God, does not occur automatically. God does not violate our free will, which is why a personal decision is involved. After making the radical decision to present yourself to God as a living sacrifice, you are now qualified and prepared to make a rational determination—to not be conformed to the world but to be transformed by the renewing of your mind. First, total sacrifice; then, total transformation.

This transformation is vital, for it determines your response to everything we've addressed in this book. It enables you to live through whatever comes without fear or anxiety—more than that, it enables you to live joyfully. Fail to make this transformation, and you will find yourself vulnerable in the nine arenas of life I have discussed in this book. You will be weakened and unable to stand against the conforming powers of this world. Slowly but surely you will find yourself . . .

- questioning the very existence of God;
- victimized by Satan in spiritual warfare;
- fearful of identifying publicly with Jesus Christ;
- questioning the necessity for entering into, or remaining in, marriage;
- lowering your moral standards;
- spending less and less time reading and studying the Bible;
- becoming disinterested in and uncommitted to your local church;
- growing fearful and confused about the rise of rogue nations like Iran;
- putting America at risk by growing complacent about the future of the Jews.

The reversals I documented in the preceding chapters are realities I never thought I would see in my life as a Christian in America. Yet these changes are fully upon us and growing more prevalent with each passing year. Only persons who make a rational determination to *not* be conformed to these trends will survive with spiritual and personal integrity intact. That is exactly the twofold determination Paul presents: "Do not be conformed to this world, but be transformed by the renewing of your mind" (Romans 12:2). That's the choice—to be either conformed or transformed. Let's look at what these two options mean.

## Do Not Be Conformed

A little study in Greek will help us here:

- "Be conformed" is from a compound Greek word, *suschematizo*, which combines *sun* (with, together with) and *schema* (figure, shape, appearance). "To be conformed," then, means "to become together with (like) another figure or shape." In the New Testament, *suschematizo* appears only in Romans 12:2 and 1 Peter 1:14, where the word refers to conformity to the world (Romans) and conformity to the lusts of the world and flesh (1 Peter).
- In both Romans and 1 Peter, the word appears in the passive voice. That means pressure to conform comes from a source outside ourselves. We do not "conform"; we are "conformed" by outside pressure.

Paul commands the believers in Rome not to allow the world to conform them to its agenda, values, culture, norms, priorities, or expectations. The force pushing at us from the culture to "be conformed" is powerful and unrelenting, like the massive flood of water pouring over Niagara Falls. Water is thundering over the edge of that waterfall at this very moment. It will be thundering tonight, tomorrow, next week, next month, and next year. It is loud and powerful and unstoppable. No individual in his own strength can do a single thing to stop the force of that natural flood.

That is why Paul used the passive voice. It would do no good to tell us not to conform, as if we could resist this force by our own power. He tells us instead not to be conformed, which indicates that in spite of our own inability to resist, there is a way to avoid being swept away by this unrelenting force. More about that in a moment.

Perhaps the most vivid translation of Romans 12:2 is in the paraphrase by the late English bishop J. B. Phillips, *The New Testament in Modern English*: "Don't let the world around you squeeze you into its own mould." That is a perfect picture of the pressure that the world applies constantly to every person on the planet—including Christians.

Eugene Peterson's paraphrase from *The Message* gives us another helpful slant: "Don't become so well-adjusted to your culture that you fit into it without even thinking." I find the phrase "without even thinking" extremely helpful. The pressure is so constant, so ongoing, so pervasive that it becomes part of the environment and we no longer notice it. I've heard that the malodorous reek of old tanners' shops was so strong it would make visitors sick. But the tanners who worked within the shops did not notice the smell at all. They had grown accustomed to the odor and thought nothing about it.

How many of us are guilty of fitting in better in the kingdom of this world than in the kingdom of God because we have stopped thinking about the difference?

## BUT BE TRANSFORMED

If, as we have noted, we do not have the power to resist the world's unrelenting pressure to conform us to its mind-set, how can we respond to Paul's admonition not to be conformed? He provides the answer in the very next phrase of Romans 12:2: "but be transformed." To get the full picture of what that means, let's go back to Greek grammar school for a moment:

- "Be transformed" is translated from the word *metamorphoo*, which is a compound made up of *meta* (together with, accompanied by) and *morphoo* (to form). Literally, it means "be formed with"; or in our English, "transformed." From this compound word comes our word *metamorphosis*, which, as we all learned in school, is the name of the process whereby a caterpillar turns into a butterfly.
- In its four uses in the New Testament, *metamorphoo* is always rendered in the passive voice. That means no one transforms himself, but he is transformed by a process initiated by a power outside himself.

In this verse God has given us two commands. Obeying the second command gives us the power to obey the first:

- DO NOT be conformed by the power of the world around you. That power comes from Satan.
- DO submit to the process of transformation. The power to do that comes from God and His Word.

Before we go on, let's pause and connect the links we have forged so far. Our overarching need is to learn how we can live positive, optimistic lives concerning our future while living in a disintegrating society that threatens to take us down with it. The first step is to give ourselves over to God by sacrificing our lives to Him. This submission to Him makes us available for His power and His Word to come into our lives and transform us into a new kind of creature with a new way of thinking. This transformation enables us to resist the growing tide of culture and live by a higher standard that promises peace and joy in spite of all the turmoil about us.

Now we have one more step to make the process complete. What are the means by which this transformation is accomplished?

## A RIGOROUS DISCIPLINE

In the phrase following Paul's admonition to be transformed, he tells us how this is to be done: "Be transformed by the renewing of your mind" (Romans 12:2). Just what does it mean to renew one's mind?

A friend of mine in North Carolina was once driving through the mountains in search of an old farmhouse to purchase and renovate. He came around a bend in the road and there it was, standing in a beautiful field directly in front of him. Actually, it was nothing but two tall, stately brick chimneys standing like sentinels keeping guard over the patch of charred ashes on the ground between them. What had once been a large, probably beautiful two-story farmhouse had been reduced to ashes. Indeed, for the *This Old House* crowd, that was certainly the ultimate fixer-upper! It's like saying you're going to patch up an old shirt when there's nothing left of it but a button.

When Paul speaks of the renewing of our minds, he doesn't mean this kind of renovation. He doesn't mean that God is willing to leave certain solid parts standing and rebuild from there. If your mind was that old fixer-upper house in North Carolina, those two chimneys would have to be knocked down and the charred foundation scraped away. Why? Because what the apostle Paul wrote of himself is true of all of us: "I know that in me (that is, in my flesh) nothing good dwells" (Romans 7:18)—not even in the chimneys and foundations.

God is not interested in renewing most of your mind—not even 99 percent of your mind. He wants to renew it all. He wants to pull down every remnant of your pre-Christian "house" and fill your mind with His agenda, values, culture, norms, priorities, and expectations. If He leaves intact any remnant at all of the old mind, that one little part, like a bad apple, can infect the rest. He wants to renew our minds completely through the renewing work of the Word of God as employed by the Holy Spirit.

## TWO AGENTS: THE HOLY SPIRIT AND THE WORD OF GOD

The apostle Paul obviously liked the picture of the believer's mind being renewed by the Holy Spirit. Look how often he repeated it:

- 2 Corinthians 4:16: "The inward man is being renewed day by day."
- Ephesians 4:23: "Be renewed in the spirit of your mind."
- Colossians 3:10: "Put on the new man who is renewed in knowledge according to the image of Him who created him."
- Titus 3:5: "He saved us, through the washing of regeneration and renewing of the Holy Spirit."

And in 2 Corinthians 10:5, Paul speaks of "bringing every thought into captivity to the obedience of Christ."

All these terms—"the mind" . . . "the inward man" . . . "renewed in knowledge" . . . "renewing of the Holy Spirit" . . . "taking thoughts captive"—refer to the same jewel of truth that Paul holds up to the light so we can see it from a number of different angles. It is clear that our transformation—which is our defense against worldly conformation—takes place as our minds are renewed by the Holy Spirit; as our minds are filled with new knowledge and new truth about life and this world. To use Paul's metaphor from Ephesians 6:17, we fight off the forces of conformity by using the "sword of the Spirit, which is the word of God."

When I underwent cancer treatment in the 1990s, part of the protocol in preparation for a stem cell transplant was a process called *pheresis*. First, I was given a drug to increase my white blood cell count. Then my blood was removed through one arm, run through a machine that separated out the white blood cells, and returned to my body through the other arm. That's a bit like what happens when the Holy Spirit floods your mind with the Word of God. There is a replacing, a renewing, that takes place as truth replaces the lies and distortions that filled your mind before.

A well-known Christian psychiatrist, the late Dr. John White, described the renewing result the Word of God had in his life:

> Bible study has torn my life apart and remade it. That is to say that God, through his Word, has done so . . . If I could write poetry about it I would. If I could sing through paper, I would flood your soul with the glorious melodies that express what I have found. I cannot exaggerate for there are no expressions majestic enough to tell of the glory I have seen, or of the wonder of finding that I, a neurotic, unstable, middle-aged man have my feet firmly planted in eternity and breathe the air of heaven. And all this has come to me through a careful study of Scripture.[1]

There are many areas in which the world pressures us to conform to its perspective—especially when it comes to fear and anxiety about what life on Planet Earth might be like in the not-too-distant future. Prolonged fear and anxiety are sins. The only way to avoid them is to follow the path of the psalmist: "Your word I have hidden in my heart, that I might not sin against You" (Psalm 119:11).

What we learn from God's Word and submission to Him does not change anything about our external circumstances. The world may still deteriorate; we may be persecuted or otherwise suffer. But what will change is our minds, and that makes all the difference. The apostle Paul was one of the most abused, persecuted, and oft-imprisoned men who ever lived. Yet he was also one of the most joyful. His joy came from his renewed mind and its strong connection to God.

## Two Actions: External and Internal

Did you know it's possible for a person to listen to biblical preaching and teaching, and even read the Bible himself, yet have it make very little difference in his life? I say that being fully aware that God's Word never returns void (Isaiah 55:11) and that it is alive, penetrating into our deepest thoughts (Hebrews 4:12).

My point is this: It takes more than just the mechanical exposure to the Bible to accomplish the renewing of the mind. It takes a receptive heart that is eager to receive the Word—a mind that desires to be renewed. Jesus and His half brother James both touched on this reality. Jesus compared the heart to soil in varying degrees of cultivation. Only the heart that is made ready to receive the Word will produce fruit (Matthew 13:1–23). James must have remembered Jesus' illustration when he expanded the metaphor, saying that only the implanted word "is able to save your souls" (James 1:21).

So the external dimension of renewing the mind is exposure to the Word of God, which is necessary but does not alone guarantee success. What is required is the internal dimension, which is a cultivated heart and mind that *want* to be renewed. This doesn't happen automatically. Remember the image of the water thundering over Niagara Falls with millions of tons of pressure? That's the pressure that's working against you, urging you to maintain the status quo; urging you not to do anything radical or rigorous in your life; forcing you to be squeezed into the mold of this world.

Renewing the mind is your only defense against this force, and so it's not surprising that it pushes hard—propelled by Satan himself—against the process of renewal. It takes daily discipline of the kind described by famous basketball coach Bobby Knight: "Discipline is doing what needs to be done, doing it when it needs to be done, doing it the best it can be done, and doing it that way every time you do it."

If collegiate basketball players can exercise discipline to gain a "perishable crown," how much more should we be willing to exercise discipline in order to gain an "imperishable crown" (1 Corinthians 9:25)? Just as the never-ending force of water over a cliff eventually wears away the face of the fall, so the never-ending pressure of the world will wear down our spiritual defenses and cause us to conform—if we are not involved daily in the discipline of renewing our minds with the Word of God.

## TWO ATTITUDES: SERIOUS AND SUBMISSIVE

Someone once said to me, "The problem with the Christian life is that it is so *daily*." I laughed at that expression; I knew exactly what my friend meant. Does the world ever stop its relentless attempts to squeeze you into its mold? No. We never get a break. The Christian life is "so daily" because the world's attempts to conform us are so daily. Which is why the renewing of our minds must be just as daily. In the original language, the word "be transformed" in Romans 12:2 is in the present tense. In another reference to renewal Paul says, "The inward man is being renewed day by day" (2 Corinthians 4:16).

Again he uses a present-tense verb, showing that renewal is a continuing, ever-present, never-ending reality that requires our ongoing "day-by-day" diligence.

Being transformed by the renewing of the mind is serious business, as anything that never ends must be. But it is also a submissive business. Remember that the Greek term "be transformed" is rendered in the passive voice. This is not something we do. We are the old, burned-out house that submits to the process of renewal. It is the Holy Spirit who does the work in us. We each submit to His rebuilding and renewing work by offering up a heart and a mind that are receptive to the Spirit's chief tool, the Word of God. In other words, by offering ourselves as living sacrifices.

## A REAL DEMONSTRATION

How can we know whether we're being conformed to the world or being transformed by a renewed mind? Paul gives us the evidence: "You may prove what is that good and acceptable and perfect will of God" (Romans 12:2).

The nine categories of cultural and international decline I have written about in this book are areas in which God has a will for His people. He wants us to be committed to marriage, to the Bible, to the lordship of Christ, to understanding the rise of rogue powers on the world stage, to supporting His chosen people, the Jews, and so on.

Now I urge you to demonstrate the "good and acceptable and perfect will of God" in each of these areas by the way you live your own life. If you are not sure what that will of God is in one or more of these areas, you can discover it by giving the Holy Spirit free access to reveal the Word of God to you. You can move from being confused and complacent about these critical areas to being committed and consecrated in each. By this way of thinking and living, you can know that you are being transformed by the renewing of your mind.

A Christian who is thus transformed will *learn* the will of God, *live* the will of God, and *love* the will of God. That person will not fear the chaos and collapse he sees around him. He will stand like an immovable beacon of light, life, and hope to all who are tired of being squeezed into the mold of this world.

I wish I could announce to you that the decline I have noted in these nine areas is going to undergo a major reversal by such and such a date. But I cannot. No one knows the future. America is at a delicate tipping point in her national life, and only God knows which way she will tip. As I have stated earlier, I do not believe the world will get a permanent reprieve from chaos and confusion until the return of the Lord Jesus Christ. So whether or not we get a temporary reprieve from our nation's downward course, the Church of Jesus Christ has to prepare herself for the long-term indications of Scripture.

There is no middle ground in which to stand. Jesus Himself said, "He who is not with Me is against me, and he who does not gather with Me scatters" (Luke 11:23). Either a person will be transformed by the renewing of his mind or he will be conformed to the beliefs of this world system—a system that is continually degenerating and will pass into oblivion. The apostle John wrote, "The world is passing away, and the lust of it; but he who does the will of God abides forever" (1 John 2:17). How do we know the "good and acceptable and perfect will of God"? By being transformed by the renewing of our minds as the Holy Spirit fills us with the Word of God.

Romans 12:1–2 and this chapter are both about making a choice between two words: *conformed* or *transformed*—conformed to this world or transformed into the image of Christ to do the will of God. May you and I decide, determine, and discipline ourselves to make the right choice: to be living demonstrations, day after day, of His will.

# 19

## Vanished Without a Trace

From: What in the World Is Going On?—
10 Prophetic Clues You Cannot
Afford to Ignore

One of the more popular CBS TV shows is the fictional drama *Without a Trace*. It is set in New York City's special FBI missing persons unit. Each episode is devoted to finding one missing person, and, usually, one of the agents assigned to the case develops a strong emotional interest that carries the story along. In reality, the FBI has no dedicated missing persons unit; investigations into disappearances are assigned to agents on a case-by-case basis. At the end of each episode, however, the show does touch on reality by providing public service information to help the FBI locate real-life missing persons.

Another TV show built on the theme of missing persons was the Fox Broadcasting drama *Vanished*. The plotline centered on a Georgia senator whose wife apparently vanished into thin air. That series failed to attract enough viewers to survive the season, provoking anger among those who had become hooked when the thirteen aired episodes never resolved the mystery.

And mystery is exactly what the word *vanished* implies. Headlines about people who vanish rivet our attention: "Relatives Wait for Word of Vanished Sailors"; "Man Vanishes After Concert"; "Search Continues for Woman Who Vanished"; "Police Say Man Vanished Without a Trace." We read such headlines with eerie wonder: *What could have happened to the missing person? How could he have simply been there one moment and not the next?*

According to the Bible, a time is coming when this very thing will happen on a massive, global scale. A day is coming when a billion people will suddenly vanish from the face of the earth without a trace! And when that event occurs, calling in the FBI will be of no use. A TV series based on the mystery would never have a conclusion, for these vanished people will never again be seen until the Lord Himself returns. What will this worldwide phenomenon be like? That is a question in the minds of many who—through popular novels, sermons, or religious writings—have heard of this event but don't understand it. They know that Christians call it the Rapture, yet they have little idea what it means or what in the world is going on that could bring it about. In this chapter I will seek to resolve this common confusion.

# THE GREAT DISAPPEARANCE

Some of us are familiar with massive evacuations, which leave large areas empty and desolate, as if their inhabitants had simply vanished. As I mentioned in a previous chapter, I pastor a church located in the fire zone of Southern California. In October 2007, we witnessed the largest evacuation of homes in California history, and the largest evacuation for fire in United States history. Emergency personnel evacuated 350,000 homes, displacing 1 million Californians as sixteen simultaneous fires swept through our community.[1]

Imagine a person who missed the call to evacuate, waking up after everyone was gone and stumbling through the acrid smoke and empty streets, confused and amazed, wondering why he had been left behind. That person's reaction would be nothing compared to the shock of those who witness the coming worldwide evacuation.

The Bible tells us that on that day, millions of people will disappear from the face of the earth in less than a millisecond. And the purpose of that evacuation is similar to that of the emergency evacuation of Southern Californians: to avoid horrific devastation. This evacuation will remove God's people from the disastrous effects of coming earthquakes, fire, and global chaos. As Bruce Bickel and Stan Jantz explain, the evacuation itself will create considerable chaos and destruction:

> Jumbo jets plummet to earth as they no longer have a pilot at the controls. Driverless buses, trains, subways, and cars will cause unimaginable disaster. Classrooms will suddenly be without teachers . . . Doctors and nurses seem to abandon their patients in the middle of surgical operations, and patients will vanish from operating tables. Children disappear from their beds. People run through the streets looking for missing family members who were there just moments ago. Panic grips every household, city and country.[2]

Attempting to put realism into this event for my first youth group as a fledgling pastor, I utilized the idea of an imaginary newspaper covering the recent Rapture. The lead article read:

> At 12:05 last night a telephone operator reported three frantic calls regarding missing relatives. Within fifteen minutes all communications were jammed with similar inquiries. A spot check around the nation found the same situation in every city. Sobbing husbands sought information about the mysterious disappearance of wives. One husband reported, "I turned on the light to ask my wife if she remembered to set the clock, but she was gone. Her bedclothes were there, her watch was on the floor . . . she had vanished!" An alarmed woman calling from Brooklyn tearfully reported, "My husband just returned from the late shift . . . I kissed him . . . he just disappeared in my arms."

These two descriptions of the coming disappearance are quite disturbing. Considering the devastation, loss, grief, and confusion the event will cause, it may seem strange that it is called the Rapture. According to my online dictionary, the word *rapture* means "an expression or manifestation of ecstasy or passion," and "being carried away by overwhelming emotion."[3] Everyone wants that kind of euphoric delight, which is why marketing experts have made *rapture* a popular term in today's culture.

There's a perfume called Rapture, and also a well-known New York City-based rock band. Many novels and movies carry the word *rapture* in their titles. A concert-promoting agency calls itself Planet Rapture. One sporting goods company even sells a set of golf clubs called Rapture! The world is looking for rapture, so marketers offer it everywhere.

So why would Christians use *Rapture*, of all terms, to denote a chaotic event when a billion people will suddenly disappear from the earth? The word *Rapture* is the Latin version of a phrase the Bible uses to describe the catching away of all Christians before the end times.

The focus is on looking at the event not from the viewpoint of those who remain, but from that of those who are evacuated. All true Christians will be caught up from the earth and raptured into the presence of the Lord before the seven-year period of evil, the Tribulation, breaks throughout the earth. This will fulfill the promise He made to His disciples in John 14:1–3:

> Let not your heart be troubled; you believe in God, believe also in Me. In My Father's house are many mansions; if it were not so, I would have told you. I go to prepare a place for you. And if I go and prepare a place for you, I will come again and receive you to Myself; that where I am, there you may be also.

Followers of Christ who are raptured will be spared the trauma of death and the coming disasters that will occur when the Tribulation breaks out upon the earth. That is indeed a cause for true rapture on the part of those who love the Lord and long to be with Him.

One morning recently I spoke about the Rapture during a series of messages on prophecy. Later I was told that on the way out of church, a girl expressed confusion to her mother about something I had said. "Dr. Jeremiah keeps talking about all the signs that are developing concerning the Lord's return. And then in the next breath he says that nothing needs to happen before Jesus comes back to take us home to be with Him. I don't understand!" It seemed to this girl that I had contradicted myself. First, I seemed to say that certain prophesied signs would occur before the coming of Christ; then I seemed to say that nothing needed to occur before Jesus comes to claim His own. The girl's honest confusion deserves to be addressed because I believe she speaks for many who are similarly puzzled about events relating to the Rapture.

Most of the misunderstanding comes from confusing two events: the Rapture and the Second Coming. When we talk about the signs that signal the return of Christ, we speak not of the Rapture but of the Lord's ultimate return to the earth with all His saints. According to the book of Revelation, this coming of Christ occurs after the Rapture and differs from it in at least two ways: First, the Rapture will be a "stealth event" in which Christ will be witnessed by believers only. His second coming, on the other hand, will be a public event. Everyone will see Him. "Behold, He is coming with clouds, and every eye will see Him, even they who pierced Him. And all the tribes of the earth will mourn because of Him" (Revelation 1:7; see also Zechariah 14:1, 3–5; Revelation 19:11–21).

Second, all believers are raptured. He will immediately take them back into heaven with Him. But when Christ returns to earth seven years later in the Second Coming, He is coming to stay. This return, usually referred to as "the Second Advent," will take place at the end of the Tribulation period and usher in the Millennium—a thousand-year reign of Christ on this earth. So, first, the Rapture will occur seven years before the Second Advent. At that time Christ will take us to be with Him in heaven, immediately before the seven-year tribulation period. Then second, we will return to earth with Him at His Second Advent.

There is another important difference. There are no events that must take place before the Rapture occurs. It's all a matter of God's perfect timing. When I preached that signs are developing concerning the Lord's return, I referred to events that must yet occur before the return of Christ in the Second Advent.

The prophecies I spoke of concern the Second Advent, but that does not mean that the Rapture doesn't figure into prophecy. Future events cast shadows that are precursors to their coming. Since the Rapture takes place seven years before the Second Advent, the signs that point to the Second Advent cast shadows that clue us in to the imminent Rapture. The fact that the Rapture precedes the Second Advent makes the signs portending the Advent all the more immediate and ominous. For those who are left behind, the Rapture will give irrefutable confirmation of end-time events, seven years before they come to pass.

The New Testament indicates that the Rapture of those who have put their trust in Christ is the next major event on the prophetic calendar. In other words, the Rapture awaits us on the horizon—it could happen at any moment. This is the clear message of the Bible, and it is a truth I have taught consistently for more than thirty years.

## UNRAVELING THE RAPTURE

The apostle Paul was the first to reveal the details of the Rapture. He wrote of it in his first letter to the Corinthians, but it was in his first letter to the church in Thessalonica that he presented his most concise teaching on the subject.

Like many today, the Christians in that city were confused about the events that would take place in the future. They, too, wondered what in the world was going on. While they believed that Jesus was coming back someday, they could not figure out what would happen to their Christian parents and loved ones who had already died. So Paul wrote to instruct them concerning God's plan for both the living and the dead in the Rapture. In this writing, he explained in detail exactly what the Rapture is all about.

> But I do not want you to be ignorant, brethren, concerning those who have fallen asleep, lest you sorrow as others who have no hope. For if we believe that Jesus died and rose again, even so God will bring with Him those who sleep in Jesus.
>
> For this we say to you by the word of the Lord, that we who are alive and remain until the coming of the Lord will by no means precede those who are asleep. For the Lord Himself will descend from heaven with a shout, with the voice of an archangel, and with the trumpet of God. And the dead in Christ will rise first. Then we who are alive and remain shall be caught up together with them in the clouds to meet the Lord in the air. And thus we shall always be with the Lord. Therefore comfort one another with these words.
>
> (1 Thessalonians 4:13–18)

This passage tells us all we need to know about the Rapture. Let's look more deeply into what Paul said, point by point. First, he wrote: "But I do not want you to be ignorant, brethren, concerning those who have fallen asleep, lest you sorrow as others who have no hope" (1 Thessalonians 4:13).

In this statement, the apostle addressed the ignorance of the Thessalonians concerning the state of those who had died believing in Christ. The word he used to describe that state has great significance for every believer today. Paul said that they had fallen asleep. For the word translated *asleep*, he used the Greek word *koimao*, which has as one of its meanings, "to sleep in death." The same word is used to describe the deaths of Lazarus, Stephen, David, and Jesus Christ (*emphasis added in the following examples*):

Lazarus: "These things He said, and after that He said to them, 'Our friend Lazarus *sleeps*, but I go that I may wake him up.'" (John 11:11)

Stephen: "Then he [Stephen] knelt down and cried out with a loud voice, 'Lord, do not charge them with this sin.' And when he had said this, he *fell asleep*." (Acts 7:60)

David: "For David, after he had served his own generation by the will of God, *fell asleep*, was buried with his fathers, and saw corruption." (Acts 13:36)

Jesus Christ: "But now Christ is risen from the dead, and has become the firstfruits of those who have *fallen asleep*." (1 Corinthians 15:20)

This concept of death is emphasized in the wonderful word early Christians adopted for the burying places of their loved ones. It was the Greek word *koimeterion*, which means "a rest house for strangers, a sleeping place." It is the word from which we get our English word *cemetery*. In Paul's day, this word was used for inns or what we would call a hotel or motel. We check in at a Hilton Hotel or a Ramada Inn, expecting to spend the night in sleep before we wake up in the morning refreshed and raring to go. That is exactly the thought Paul expressed in words such as *koimao* and *koimeterion*. When Christians die, it's as if they are slumbering peacefully in a place of rest, ready to be awakened at the return of the Lord. The words have great import, for they convey the Christian concept of death, not as a tragic finality, but as a temporary sleep.

In the next part of the Thessalonian passage, we find Paul affirming their hopes that their loved ones will live again. He did this by tying that hope to the Resurrection and the Rapture: "lest you sorrow as others who have no hope. For if we believe that Jesus died and rose again, even so God will bring with Him those who sleep in Jesus" (1 Thessalonians 4:13*c*–14).

Here Paul tells the Thessalonians (and us) that God's plan for our future gives us such a new perspective on death that when someone we love dies, we are not overcome with sorrow and despair, for on that day when those who are alive in Christ are raptured, those who died in Christ will be raised to be with Him.

Paul reasoned that Christians can believe this promise of resurrection because it is backed up by the resurrection of Christ Himself. The logic is simple: if we believe that Jesus died and rose again, is it hard to believe His promise that He can perform the same miracle for us and those we love?

Paul did not forbid us to grieve; it is natural to feel sorrow when a loved one passes away, even when that loved one is a Christian. We miss the person terribly, and as Tennyson put it, we long for "the touch of a vanished hand and the sound of a voice that is still."[4] Jesus Himself wept by the tomb of Lazarus. But because of our Lord's promise of resurrection, we are not to grieve the way non-Christians do—as people to whom death is the ultimate tragedy—for they have no grounds for hope.

Tim LaHaye is the coauthor of the famous *Left Behind* series, which at last count had sold more than sixty-five million books. He became fascinated with the doctrine of the Rapture as a nine-year-old boy at his father's grave. He wrote:

> My love for second-coming teachings, particularly the Rapture of the church, was sparked as I stood at my father's grave at the age of nine. His sudden death of a heart attack left me devastated. My pastor, who also was my uncle, pointed his finger toward heaven and proclaimed, "This is not the last of Frank LaHaye. Because of his personal faith in Christ, one day he will be resurrected by the shout of the Lord; we will be translated to meet him and our other loved ones in the clouds and be with them and our Lord forever." That promise from Scripture was the only hope for my broken heart that day. And that same promise has comforted millions of others through the years.[5]

As Dr. LaHaye said, the promise of the Rapture has comforted millions, and it is right that it should, for it is a promise we can depend on to be utterly sound.

# THE CHRONOLOGICAL PROGRAM OF THE RAPTURE

As Paul continued in his letter to the Thessalonians, he wrote: "For this we say to you by the word of the Lord" (1 Thessalonians 4:15a).

Here Paul affirms that what he is about to say is by divine authority. He is authorized to say it "by the word of the Lord." This bold assertion suggests that what followed was not to be taken lightly because it was a revelation given directly to the apostle by God himself. In 1 Corinthians, Paul referred to the Rapture as a "mystery" (15:51). And the biblical definition of a mystery is "a truth that has not been revealed before."

Having established his authority to reveal what had formerly been a mystery, Paul went on to explain the first of the sequence of events that make up the Rapture.

### There Will Be an Order of Priority

Paul then told the Thessalonians, "We who are alive and remain until the coming of the Lord will by no means precede those who are asleep" (1 Thessalonians 4:15b). Here Paul was saying that not only will those who have died in Christ be present at the return of the Lord, but they will actually have a place of priority. He said that those who are alive at the Rapture will not be taken up to Christ ahead of "those who are asleep," which means all believers who have died prior to the Rapture.

There is a linguistic root we need to examine here. The Greek word *phthano* in this verse means "come before, precede." When the Greek was translated into the English of the King James era, the word "prevent" was used because it then carried the meaning "to go or arrive before." Over many years, *prevent* has come to mean "to keep from happening." The emphatic point of this verse is that we will "by no means precede those who are asleep" in Christ. Those who have died believing in Christ will take precedence over us in the Rapture.

*There Will Be a Return*

Paul continued by saying, "For the Lord Himself will descend from heaven with a shout, with the voice of an archangel, and with the trumpet of God" (1 Thessalonians 4:16*a*).

As you read these words, the Lord Jesus Christ is seated in the heavens at the right hand of the Almighty Father. But when the right moment comes, He will initiate the Rapture by literally and physically rising from the throne, stepping into the corridors of light, and actually descending into the atmosphere of planet Earth from which He rose into the heavens over the Mount of Olives two thousand years ago. It is not the angels or the Holy Spirit but the Lord Himself who is coming to draw believers into the heavens in the Rapture.

The details of this passage paint an amazingly complete sensory picture of the Rapture. Paul even gave the sounds that will be heard—a shout, the voice of an archangel, and the trumpet of God. The purpose and relationship of these three sounds have generated considerable discussion. Some have claimed that the shout is for the church, the archangel's voice is for the Jews, and the trumpet is for all Gentile believers. But these claims are mistaken. The three allusions to sounds are not to be taken as coordinate but rather as subordinate. Paul was not describing three separate sounds; he was describing only one sound in three different ways.

This sound will be like a shout, ringing with command authority like the voice of an archangel. It will also be like the blare of a trumpet in its volume and clarity. And the sound will be exclusively directed—heard only by those who have placed their trust in Christ. When Jesus raised Lazarus from the dead, he shouted "Lazarus, come forth!" (John 11:43). I've heard Bible students speculate as to what might have happened had Jesus forgotten to mention Lazarus's name. Would all the dead within the range of His voice have emerged from their graves? At the Rapture that is exactly what will happen. His shout of "Come forth!" will not name a single individual, but it will be heard by every believer in every grave around the world. All those tombs will empty, and the resurrected believers will fly skyward.

This arising from the grave was the hope that Winston Churchill movingly expressed in the planning of his own funeral. Following the prayer by the archbishop of Canterbury and the singing of "God Save the Queen," a trumpeter perched in the highest reaches of the dome of St. Paul's Cathedral sounded "The Last Post" (or "Taps" as we know it). As the last sorrowful note faded, "high in another gallery, sounded the stronger blaring 'Reveille.'"[6] The call to sleep was followed by a call to arise.

## There Will Be a Resurrection

As Paul continued his writing to the Thessalonians, he asserted that the expectation expressed by believers such as Churchill is not vain. The coming resurrection is a reality. Paul wrote, "And the dead in Christ will rise first" (1 Thessalonians 4:16b). As he indicates here, the call to resurrection at the Rapture will not summon all the dead, but believers only. A time will come much later when *all* the dead will be raised to stand before the white throne in judgment. But at this first call, our believing loved ones who have already died will arise to take first place in the program of the Rapture.

## There Will Be a Rapture

Paul explained the next event in the Rapture sequence: "Then we who are alive and remain shall be caught up" (1 Thessalonians 4:17a). The words *caught up* are translated from a Greek word that has as one of its meanings "to snatch out or away speedily." This word emphasizes the sudden nature of the Rapture. Paul described this suddenness in his letter to the Corinthians: ". . . in a moment, in the twinkling of an eye, at the last trumpet. For the trumpet will sound, and the dead will be raised incorruptible, and we shall be changed" (1 Corinthians 15:52).

In a split second the Lord will call all believers to Himself to share in His glory; not one will remain behind. It is hard to imagine just what that will be like, but I read a paragraph recently that created this vivid picture:

> Millions of people from all parts of the earth feel a tingling sensation pulsating throughout their bodies. They are all suddenly energized. Those with physical deformities are healed. The blind suddenly see. Wrinkles disappear on the elderly as their youth is restored. As these people marvel at their physical transformation, they are lifted skyward. Those in buildings pass right through the ceiling and roof without pain or damage. Their flesh and bones seem to dematerialize, defying all known laws of physics and biology. As they travel heavenward, some of them see and greet those who have risen from their graves. After a brief mystical union . . . they all vanish from sight.[7]

Lest such pictures as this lead us to think the Rapture is a fanciful, futuristic dream, we find such experiences validated historically. Throughout the Bible, we have records of several people who had actual experiences very similar to the Rapture:

Enoch: "By faith Enoch was taken away so that he did not see death, 'and was not found, because God had taken him'; for before he was taken he had this testimony, that he pleased God." (Hebrews 11:5)

Elijah: "Then it happened, as they continued on and talked, that suddenly a chariot of fire appeared with horses of fire, and separated the two of them; and Elijah went up by a whirlwind into heaven." (2 Kings 2:11)

Paul: "I know a man in Christ who fourteen years ago—whether in the body I do not know, or whether out of the body I do not know, God knows—such a one, was *caught up* to the third heaven. And I know such a man—whether in the body or out of the body I do not know, God knows—how he was *caught up* into Paradise and heard inexpressible words, which it is not lawful for a man to utter." (2 Corinthians 12:2–4, *emphasis added*)

I find it significant that twice in this passage Paul used the words *caught up*, which are translated from the word meaning "rapture" in the Greek language.

> Jesus Christ: "And while they looked steadfastly toward heaven as He went up, behold, two men stood by them in white apparel, who also said, 'Men of Galilee, why do you stand gazing up into heaven? This same Jesus, who was taken up from you into heaven, will so come in like manner as you saw Him go into heaven.'" (Acts 1:10–11)

These records affirm the utter reality of the Rapture by providing us with prototypes of sorts to show that God can accomplish this coming event He promises to His people.

### There Will Be a Reunion

Paul continued his explanation of the Rapture: "Then we who are alive and remain shall be caught up together with them [the believing dead who have arisen] in the clouds to meet the Lord in the air. And thus we shall always be with the Lord" (1 Thessalonians 4:17). Note that Paul began here with the word *then*, which is an adverb indicating sequence. It connects the previous events of the Rapture that we have already considered with this final event in a definite order of sequential reunions as follows:

1. Dead bodies reunited with their spirits
2. Resurrected believers reunited with living believers
3. Resurrected believers and raptured believers meet the Lord

As Paul pointed out, the ultimate consequence of this reunion with the Lord is that there will be no subsequent parting. After His return, our union and communion with Him will be uninterrupted and eternal. This glorious fact alone shows us why the word *rapture* is an altogether appropriate term for this event.

## THE COMFORTING PURPOSE OF THE RAPTURE

After completing his description of the Rapture to the Thessalonians, Paul wrapped up the passage with this practical admonition: "Therefore comfort one another with these words" (1 Thessalonians 4:18).

Here the apostle was telling both the Thessalonians and believers today that it's not enough simply to passively understand what was just explained about the Rapture, Christian death, and the Resurrection. Our understanding should spur us toward a certain action—to "comfort one another." And in the preceding verses he gave exactly the kind of information that makes true comfort possible. When believers suffer the loss of family members or dearly loved friends, we have in Paul's descriptions of Christian death and resurrection all that is needed to comfort each other in these losses. Christian death is not permanent; it is merely a sleep. A time is coming when we and our loved ones will be reunited in a rapturous meeting, when Christ Himself calls us out of this world or out of our graves to be with Him forever in an ecstatic relationship of eternal love. Nineteenth-century Bible teacher A. T. Pierson made this interesting observation about these things:

> It is a remarkable fact that in the New Testament, so far as I remember, it is never once said, after Christ's resurrection, that a disciple died—that is, without some qualification: Stephen *fell asleep*. David, after he had served his own generation by the will of God *fell asleep and was laid with his father*. Peter says, "Knowing that I must shortly *put off this my tabernacle* as the Lord showed me." Paul says, *"the time of my departure is at hand."* (The figure here is taken from a vessel that, as she leaves a dock, throws the cables off the fastenings, and opens her sails to the wind to depart for the haven) . . . The only time

where the word "dead" is used, it is with qualification: "the *dead in Christ*," "the *dead which die in the Lord*."[8]

As Pierson implies, Christ abolished death so completely that even the term *death* is no longer appropriate for believers. That is why Paul wrote that we should comfort one another with reminders that for Christians, what we call death is nothing more than a temporary sleep before we are called into our uninterrupted relationship with Christ forever.

Today as never before, we are beginning to see the signs of our Lord's impending return. Some of these signs we have already covered—the rebirth of Israel as a nation, the growing crises over oil, the reformation of Europe in accordance with Daniel's prophecy, and the growth of militant, radical Islam. All these developments point toward that day when our Lord will come to rapture His followers out of this world.

I believe it is the Rapture that will trigger the cataclysmic upheavals that will ravage the earth for the seven years that follow it. The Tribulation will come about by the law of natural consequences. According to Jesus, Christians are the salt and light of the world (Matthew 5:13–14). Salt prevents decay; light proclaims truth. When all the Christians in the entire world are removed from the earth in one day, all the salt and all the light will suddenly be gone. The result is predictable. You may think the world today is degenerating into rampant greed and immorality, and indeed it is. But as bad as things are becoming, we can hardly overstate the horror that will occur when society loses the tempering influence of Christians.

As the Bible teaches, every believer in Christ is indwelt by the Holy Spirit. This means the Holy Spirit ministers to today's world through followers of Christ. When all Christians are removed from the earth, the restraining ministry of the Holy Spirit will be completely absent. No salt! No light! No indwelling Spirit of God! The result will be horrific. Jesus himself described what will happen next: "For then there will be great tribulation, such as has not been since the beginning of the world until this time, no, nor ever shall be. And unless those days were shortened, no flesh would be saved" (Matthew 24:21–22).

As these dire words are being fulfilled during the Tribulation period, we who are followers of Christ will have already been raptured to heaven. This is another source of great comfort for Christians. No promise has been more precious to believers than the one made to the church of Philadelphia in Revelation: "Because you have kept My command to persevere, I also will keep you from the hour of trial which shall come upon the whole world, to test those who dwell on the earth" (Revelation 3:10).

Please note that our Lord's promise is not merely to keep us *in* the hour of trial, but rather *from* the hour of trial. As Paul wrote, "God did not appoint us to wrath, but to obtain salvation through our Lord Jesus Christ" (1 Thessalonians 5:9). The promise is that we who are believers will not experience the horrors of the Tribulation, and this is an enormous source of comfort.

## HOW SHALL WE THEN LIVE?

We have been given two directives as to how we should live as we anticipate Christ's return. We should be looking for Him and living for Him.

### We Should Be Looking for the Lord

Paul warned us in three of his letters to be alert and watchful for the Lord's return:

> *Looking for the blessed hope and glorious appearing of our great God and Savior Jesus Christ.* (Titus 2:13)
> *For our citizenship is in heaven, from which we also eagerly wait for the Savior, the Lord Jesus Christ.* (Philippians 3:20)
> *And to wait for His Son from heaven, whom He raised from the dead, even Jesus who delivers us from the wrath to come.*
> (1 Thessalonians 1:10)

Wayne Grudem suggests that the degree to which we are actually longing for Christ's return is a measure of our spiritual condition. As he explains:

> The more Christians are caught up in enjoying the good things of this life, and the more they neglect genuine Christian fellowship and their personal relationship with Christ, the less they will long for His return. On the other hand, many Christians who are experiencing suffering or persecution, or who are more elderly and infirm, and those whose daily walk with Christ is vital and deep, will have a more intense longing for His return.[9]

As Dr. Grudem suggests, the idea is not merely to watch for Jesus' coming as we might watch for a storm in a black cloud, but rather to anticipate it as something we look forward to and long for.

*We Should Be Living for the Lord*

The three great apostles, Paul, Peter, and John, all had something to say about how we should live in the face of Christ's impending return:

> For the grace of God that brings salvation has appeared to all men, teaching us that, denying ungodliness and worldly lusts, we should live soberly, righteously, and godly in the present age, looking for the blessed hope and glorious appearing of our great God and Savior Jesus Christ, who gave Himself for us, that He might redeem us from every lawless deed and purify for Himself His own special people, zealous for good works. (Titus 2:11–14)
>
> Therefore, since all these things will be dissolved, what manner of persons ought you to be in holy conduct and godliness. (2 Peter 3:11)

> Beloved, now are we children of God; and it has not yet been revealed what we shall be, but we know that when He is revealed, we shall be like Him, for we shall see Him as He is. And everyone who has this hope in Him purifies himself, just as He is pure. (1 John 3:2–3)

You would think it obvious that since signs tell us that Christ is coming soon, people would take extra care to live as God would have them live—lives of purity and holiness. If you know that guests are coming soon to your home but you don't know exactly when they will arrive, you will keep your house swept, picked up, and dusted in anticipation. You don't want them ringing your doorbell with your dishes piled in the sink, beds unmade, and mud prints tracking the carpet. The admonitions of Paul, Peter, and John to stay ready by living pure and holy lives are hardly more than just plain common sense. But common sense does not always prevail in the lives of fallen humans, and that is why these apostles felt it worthwhile to admonish us to live as if Jesus could come at any moment. The fact is He can.

Two years after the wildfires of 2003, San Diego regional authorities installed Reverse 9-1-1. The early warning system was first used to warn residents of the approaching wildfires of 2007. Some home owners, however, did not receive a call or had phone systems that screened out the warning call as an unrecognized number. Others received the call but chose to ignore it. Some of those who did not hear the warning did not vacate their homes and, as a result, lost their lives.[10]

God has sounded the warnings loudly and clearly. They have come through His prophets in the Old Testament, through New Testament writers, and even through Jesus Himself. The firestorm is coming in the form of the seven years of tribulation, when no Christian influence will temper the evil that will plunge the earth into a cauldron of misery and devastation. But you can avoid the destruction and be evacuated. You can enter your name on the list of those who will hear the trumpet call of the Rapture by turning to Christ and beginning to live the pure and holy life that characterizes those who will enter heaven. As the apostle John wrote:

"But there shall by no means enter it [the heavenly city of God] anything that defiles, or causes an abomination or a lie, but only those who are written in the Lamb's Book of Life" (Revelation 21:27).

If your name is not in that book, when the Rapture occurs you will be left behind to experience horrors worse than anything the world has yet seen. I hope you will not wait another day; turn to Jesus Christ now, before it is too late, and become one of those who will hear His call on that great and terrible day.

# 20

---

# KEEP YOUR HEAD
# IN THE GAME
# AND YOUR HOPE
# IN GOD

---

FROM: THE COMING ECONOMIC ARMAGEDDON—
WHAT BIBLE PROPHECY WARNS ABOUT
THE NEW GLOBAL ECONOMY

G atlinburg, Tennessee, is a family friendly tourist town that serves as the gateway to the Great Smoky Mountains National Park. It is known for its rustic hotels, quaint shops, and popular restaurants, all surrounded by green-clad hilltops and Smoky Mountain peaks. Few people take time to trace the back roads around Gatlinburg; but those who turn onto Campbell Lead Road, just off the bypass from Pigeon Forge, drive by a remarkable house sprawled at the end of a sloping, winding drive. It's a 16,512-square-foot superchalet nestled on the side of a mountain. The three-story living room offers lofty windows and fabulous views of the Smoky Mountain beauty. It is a massive home—and empty.

It belonged to Dennis Bolze, a middle-aged stock trader who apparently bilked clients out of millions of dollars in an elaborate Ponzi scheme. Some say he's the hillbilly version of Bernie Madoff. Having been forced into bankruptcy, Bolze very well may be swapping his chalet for a jail cell. The real losses, however, are those of his victims. One victim, Virginia Borham, a recently widowed woman who worked for years as a secretary in Europe, lost the bulk of her life savings.

"I don't know what my future is going to be now," said Ms. Borham, "because I have only enough income to pay my rent. Literally, I am living on the charity of friends."[1] Like many others, Virginia Borham thought her investments were sure and her money was safe; and now it's gone.

The loss of one's personal financial stability can and does happen for many reasons other than being cheated or making bad investments. Money seems to have a way of getting away from us. The Bible says, "Cast but a glance at riches, and they are gone, for they will surely sprout wings and fly off to the sky like an eagle" (Proverbs 23:5 NIV). We've always known that money has wings, but only lately have we begun to comprehend its wingspan. Our financial security can vanish in an instant. As we have explored in this book, events occurring today portend a bleak economic outlook for this nation and, indeed, for the world. All of us are sure to be affected, and many of us have already felt the pinch.

If you have stood helplessly by and watched your savings and investments shrink to the point that you must scale back your retirement plans, you're in good company. Millions of people have recently suffered losses in pension accounts, retirement funds, and investment income. Many have suffered loss of wealth trying to help children, family, and friends in these distressing times. Others have drained their savings during prolonged bouts of unemployment or because of catastrophic illness and crippling medical bills.

In this last chapter I want to turn away from the bleak picture of the global economic future and speak directly to you about what you can do now to prepare and either avoid or ease the stress to your own finances. We cannot escape what is happening in the world. As I have said, we are now seeing the looming shadow being cast by biblically predicted catastrophic events, and we cannot avoid living under that shadow. We may experience difficulties due to the global economic and political disintegration, but we know that we are in God's hands. Not only can we trust Him for our future well-being; He has also given us sound financial principles that can rule our economic lives in a way that stabilizes our personal finances and gets us through tough times.

So, in spite of the coming global economic Armageddon, we Christians need not despair. We have good reason for hope. That hope is what I want to show you in this chapter. I am not so presumptuous as to offer you specific financial advice. I simply want to give you sound, proven, workable principles from the Bible that can see you through the coming economic shadows now creeping across the world.

## THE BIBLICAL APPROACH TO MONEY

The Bible doesn't see money and riches exactly as we do. In fact, Scripture shows that God's perspective on wealth is the opposite from that of most of us. He's not overly concerned about our building massive wealth here on earth, but He's highly concerned that we build a solid foundation for our spiritual future. No surprise there; we've heard that from the pulpit all our lives. But it's easy to get caught up in the societal race for wealth and tend to forget the perspective of Scripture.

In many places the Bible warns that money is as transient as a butterfly. Proverbs 27:24 says that "riches are not forever." Through His prophet

Haggai, the Lord told the backslidden Israelites that they were earning wages only to put the money into a bag with holes (see Haggai 1:6). Paul warns us not to trust in wealth, which is uncertain (see 1 Timothy 6:17), and Jesus said, "Do not lay up for yourselves treasures on earth, where moth and rust destroy and where thieves break in and steal" (Matthew 6:19). He wasn't forbidding us to be prudent savers or to plan for the future. He was simply saying our permanent wealth is eternal, but the dollar, the pound, and the euro are not.

In his book *Just Walk Across the Room: Simple Steps Pointing People to Faith*, Bill Hybels tells about an experience that underscored the difference between the temporary and the permanent:

> I was sitting in a meeting one time when the speaker suddenly unfurled a roll of stickers in his hand. "There is something we must all understand," he said as he walked across the front of the room. Periodically, he would stop and put a red sticker on a tiny replica of a house, and a red sticker on a Hot Wheels car, and a red sticker on a dollhouse-sized desk that represented our vocational lives.
>
> "You may not be able to tell from where you're sitting, but each red sticker has a single word on it," he said. "The word is 'temporary.' And these things I'm putting them on are all temporary. They will fade away, turning cartwheels like leaves in the wind when this world ends.
>
> "If you are living for these things, then you are living a life of temporary pleasure, temporary satisfaction, and temporary fulfillment." He continued walking around the room, now silent as he labeled everything in sight with red stickers. I watched his hands declare the fate of the best this world has to offer as those stickers made their way to the goods in front of us. Temporary. Temporary. Temporary.
>
> "There is only *one* thing in this room that is not temporary," he continued. "There is only one thing that you can take with you into the next world."

He called someone up to join him on the stage, and he placed a blue sticker on her lapel. "When you get to the end of your life and take in your last breath," he said, "what do you want your life to have been about?" . . .

No earthly commodity is going to make it from this world into the next. Not land, not homes, not bank accounts, not titles, not achievements. Only *souls*. Friends, Jesus Christ taught that every human being would be resurrected to spend an eternity in community with God in heaven or in isolation from God in hell. And because Jesus understood these eternal realities and believed them to the core of His being, He focused His attention on the only entity that would extend into the next reality: people.

I don't know what the final assessment of my earthly life will be once I am gone. But I know this much: my quest while I am here is to seek people out and point them toward faith in God. I've tried enough approaches in my five decades of living to know that to invest yourself in anything other than people is to settle for the pursuit of a lesser vision—that ugly ensnaring trap of the temporal.[2]

Solomon, the wisest man who ever lived, seems to agree with Hybels. In his memoirs, the often-neglected book of Ecclesiastes, King Solomon had much to say about money, even devoting an entire chapter to the dispensing of his monetary wisdom. He began by saying five things about money and greed:

- The more we have, the more we want (see Ecclesiastes 5:10).
- The more we have, the more we spend (see Ecclesiastes 5:11).
- The more we have, the more we worry (see Ecclesiastes 5:12).
- The more we have, the more we lose (see Ecclesiastes 5:13–14).
- The more we have, the more we leave behind (see Ecclesiastes 5:14–17).

Then Solomon went on to say two things about money and God:

- First, the power to earn money comes from God. "Here is what I have seen: It is good and fitting for one to eat and drink, and to enjoy the good of all his labor in which he toils under the sun all the days of his life *which God gives him* ; for it is his heritage" (Ecclesiastes 5:18, *emphasis added*).
- Second, the power to enjoy money also comes from God. "As for every man to whom God has given riches and wealth, and given him power to eat of it, to receive his heritage and rejoice in his labor—*this is the gift of God*. For he will not dwell unduly on the days of his life, because God keeps him busy with the joy of his heart" (Ecclesiastes 5:19–20, *emphasis added*).

Solomon's insights about money echo God's instructions to the people of Israel as they were about to enter the Promised Land: "And you shall remember the Lord your God, for it is He who gives you power to get wealth, that He may establish His covenant which He swore to your fathers, as it is this day" (Deuteronomy 8:18).

Based on this perspective that money, its uses, and the benefits of it are gifts from God, let me suggest a four-point formula for financial survival during these days of economic confusion.

## KEEP YOUR HEAD IN THE GAME

My youngest son, Daniel, was the quarterback on his high school football team. During one of the games in his junior year, he took a vicious hit from the opposing linebacker, which resulted in a concussion. At the time, we did not know it was a concussion, and so the coach let him go back into the game.

During the final quarter of the contest, Daniel threw for a touchdown and ran for another, but afterward he did not remember any of it. His teammates told me later that he could not remember the plays to call in the huddle, so they would just go to the line of scrimmage and improvise.

Daniel told me that he could not remember anything that happened after his head injury, but he kept on playing, and only his teammates knew that anything was wrong.

Daniel's experience reminds me of the way many people are functioning financially today. Outwardly, they are playing the game. But if you get close enough to them, you realize they have no idea what the game is all about. They have no plays to call, and while they might bumble into doing some things right, they are living every moment in jeopardy of taking a hit that will put them on the sidelines, perhaps for the rest of their lives.

You've probably heard friends say, "I don't even listen to the news anymore. It's all so depressing; I just ignore it." Or, "What's the use of trying to keep up with the mess we're in? There's nothing I can do about any of it, so I have just decided to ignore it all and go on with my life." These are two actual quotes from people I have talked to in recent days, and I think they represent the attitudes of a huge segment of our population.

This attitude is a major mistake, and it demonstrates an irresponsible approach to financial management that can result in disaster. In his book *The New Economic Disorder*, Larry Bates wrote:

> We are creatures of comfort and as such have grown accustomed to our comfort zones. We will never be moved to anything unless our comfort zones are invaded. I can tell you that, if you lack understanding and knowledge of the times, your comfort zones are about to be wrecked. Our standard of living, incredible compared to the rest of the world, and our ease of life have literally disconnected from reality.[3]

Yes, we have enjoyed our comfort zones, and many have talked themselves into believing that life will go on being comfortable to the end. But recently the discomfort level has suddenly skyrocketed, and some have decided that the game is basically over. Now they are going through the motions of living with no idea where life is taking them. While we can understand their frustration and sense of futility, it is hard to mesh these attitudes with the information we find in the Word of God. He has included several key verses in His Book for such a time as this: "It is high time to awake out of sleep" (Romans 13:11). "Therefore let us not sleep, as others do, but let us watch and be sober" (1 Thessalonians 5:6).

Like the Old Testament sons of Issachar, we need to develop an "understanding of the times," so that like them, we will know what we ought to do (1 Chronicles 12:32). On one occasion, Jesus reprimanded the Pharisees and the Sadducees, saying, "You know how to discern the face of the sky, but you cannot discern the signs of the times" (Matthew 16:3).

As we have shown in this book, we are living in very fragile times. The truth is, these are unprecedented times. We are charting new territory almost every day. In fact, things are changing so quickly that some of the chapters in this book have been updated five or six times. Far from giving us cause to turn off the news in despair, the rapid changes in our times actually increase our urgent need for diligence in staying aware of what is going on.

When I began to see the great fluctuations and changes in national and global economics, I jumped into the game and began to learn all I could about the financial world. I am far from being an expert; there is much about economics that I will never comprehend. But what I have done is this: I have gotten my head into the game! I have become a student, and I am the better for it.

In his book *What Your Money Means and How to Use It Well*, author Frank J. Hanna talks about the four things he does in his business and in his private life to handle not only finances, but anything else in the way it should be handled:

1. Find out the truth about how things are now.
2. Discover the truth about how they're supposed to be.
3. Figure out how to change things from how they are now to how they're supposed to be.
4. Make myself want to change them enough that I'll do what's necessary to bring about that change.[4]

Every important decision in life starts with finding the truth. When you know the truth, you have someplace to go. Without the truth, there can be no meaningful journey, simply because progress is impossible unless there is a fixed point toward which you can progress. So first of all, let's agree that we need to know the truth about sound finance. That means keeping our heads in the financial game and becoming students of economics.

There was a time or two other than when my son was playing football with a concussion that his coach felt his focus was not as sharp as it could be. I remember hearing the coach yell, "Daniel, get your head in the game!" I know I am not your coach, but I feel the need to "yell" if you will allow it: When it comes to your financial future, you desperately need to get your head in the game!

If you have not already begun that process, I hope you will do so now. I hope this book has opened your eyes to a few things about the future and the national and international economy that you did not know. But don't stop the learning process with this book. There are other books to read, knowledgeable people to consult, and helpful seminars to attend. In this generation of instant information, knowledge about any subject is only a click away. All it takes to access it is simply the desire to get your head in the game.

And whatever you do, don't forget the best resource of all: the Bible. Although it was never intended to be a book about finances, you will discover many timeless and helpful principles salted away in the pages of this great Book. I will share a few of them with you later in this chapter.

## Keep Your House in Order

You and I can do nothing about the problems we see in the world economic order. I think that sense of helplessness is the reason so many people despair and turn off the news. But we are not helpless. There are things we can do to insulate ourselves significantly against the worst of any economic disaster that may come. We cannot control world economics, but we can do much to control our own. In this section I will offer you a few pointers in that direction.

### Take a Personal Inventory

As I said above, until you know the real truth about any situation, you cannot know for sure what to do. Affecting the future starts with knowing the truth.

One of the most important things Donna and I have done as a couple during these last few months has been to take a financial inventory of our lives. With the help of professional planners, we began the process of finding out exactly where we are financially. This has been a good experience for us, but it has not been without some surprises. Frankly, we have been so busy with our lives and our ministries that we have not always kept our heads in the game as we should have.

We are on target to change all of that, and I encourage you to do the same. You may resist this exercise out of the fear of what you will discover. But almost no financial situation is totally without hope. If there are real problem areas in your financial picture, it's much better to know of them than to leave them buried like land mines, waiting to destroy you. You will never change what you do not acknowledge.

### Minimize Your Indebtedness

Years ago the late Lewis Grizzard wrote a newspaper column in which he told of a former coworker who received a letter from one of his creditors:

> "They're mad at me about the fact that I missed a payment," said the coworker. "The way I pay my bills is I put them all in a hat. Then I reach into the hat without looking and pull out a bill. I keep doing that until I'm out of money. There are always a few bills left in the hat, but at least everybody I owe has a chance of being paid out of the hat. I wrote the people back and told them if they sent me another nasty letter I wouldn't even put them in the hat anymore." [5]

Apparently there are a lot of folks today who are leaving unpaid bills in the hat. The total U.S. consumer debt, which includes credit card and non-credit card debt (but not mortgage debt), reached $2.45 trillion as of March 2010.[6]

The Bible does not forbid indebtedness, but it warns about its misuse. For instance, Proverbs points out that the borrower is in danger of becoming a servant to the lender (see Proverbs 22:7). Six times Proverbs warns against cosigning on another's notes (see Proverbs 6:1–2; 11:15; 17:18; 20:16; 22:26; 27:13).

One of the best ministries we have at the church that I pastor is called Crown Financial Ministries. Those who have graduated from this eleven-week, in-depth study have reduced their personal debt by an average of 38 percent, increased their savings by 27 percent, and increased their giving by 72 percent! For those of you struggling to balance your budget, pay your bills, or establish a plan for your finances, I highly recommend that you visit the Crown Financial Web site and start turning your debt around today.[7]

### Manage Your Money

Some of my friends who know I have been working on this book have asked if I have any investment advice for them. My answer is no. For me to attempt such a thing would be foolish and arrogant. That's a scary question even in times of financial stability, let alone in today's market chaos.

While I would not advise anyone on investments, I have discovered that when I stay focused on what the Bible actually says, I can give some pretty good general advice on the placement and use of money we possess. The following Scriptures speak for themselves and need no amplification from me. This list is by no means exhaustive, but it illustrates the powerful things the Bible has to say about money and finances. These truths come from the 126 financial principles found in the New Testament and more than 2,350 Bible verses that speak to the subject of finances and material possessions.

1. The Desire Principle:

- "It's obvious, isn't it? The place where your treasure is, is the place you will most want to be, and end up being. . . . You can't worship two gods at once. Loving one god, you'll end up hating the other. Adoration of one feeds contempt for the other. You can't worship God and Money both" (Matthew 6:19–21, 24 The Message).

2. The Discernment Principle:

- "Remove falsehood and lies far from me; give me neither poverty nor riches—feed me with the food allotted to me; lest I be full and deny You, and say, 'Who is the Lord?' Or lest I be poor and steal, and profane the name of my God" (Proverbs 30:8–9).

3. The Discussion Principle:

- "Listen to counsel and receive instruction" (Proverbs 19:20).

- "In the multitude of counselors there is safety" (Proverbs 11:14; also see 24:6).

4. The Discipline Principle:

- "A faithful man will abound with blessings, but he who hastens to be rich will not go unpunished. . . . A man with an evil eye hastens after riches, and does not consider that poverty will come upon him" (Proverbs 28:20, 22).

5. The Depreciation Principle: "Do not lay up for yourselves treasures on earth, where moth and rust destroy and where thieves break in and steal; but lay up for yourselves treasures in heaven, where

neither moth nor rust destroys and where thieves do not break in and steal" (Matthew 6:19–20).

6. The Due Diligence Principle:

- "For which of you, intending to build a tower, does not sit down first and count the cost, whether he has enough to finish it—lest, after he has laid the foundation, and is not able to finish, all who see it begin to mock him" (Luke 14:28–29).

7. The Diversification Principle:

- "Give a serving to seven, and also to eight, for you do not know what evil will be on the earth" (Ecclesiastes 11:2).

8. The Descendant Principle:

- "A good man leaves an inheritance to his children's children, but the wealth of the sinner is stored up for the righteous" (Proverbs 13:22).

- "But if anyone does not provide for his own, and especially for those of his household, he has denied the faith and is worse than an unbeliever" (1 Timothy 5:8).

- "For the children ought not to lay up for the parents, but the parents for the children" (2 Corinthians 12:14).

9. The Devotion Principle:

- "Honor the Lord with your possessions, and with the first-fruits of all your increase; so your barns will be filled with plenty, and your vats will overflow with new wine" (Proverbs 3:9–10).

- "So let each one give as he purposes in his heart, not grudgingly or of necessity; for God loves a cheerful giver" (2 Corinthians 9:7).

Follow the advice given in this sampling of wise and practical principles from the Bible and your finances will stay afloat in the worst of economic storms.

## KEEP YOUR HEART IN YOUR FAITH

For the last several months, I have been spending a great deal of time in the Old Testament Book of Daniel. Not only is this one of the most important prophetic books of the Bible, it also records the courageous experiences of Daniel and his Jewish friends during the years of their captivity.

While little of what we read of Daniel's life pertains directly to economics, his unwavering conviction and dedication to the truth of God forms an underlying foundation of trusting one's security in all matters to the only power that is ultimately dependable in seeing us through any kind of crisis. As the shadows of the end times begin to encroach, not only upon our finances but upon all facets of our lives, I find the example of Daniel extremely inspiring. And I want to share with you some of what I've learned from him.

These were difficult years for Daniel. God was revealing to His prophet information about the future that was overwhelming, just as much of what we've shown in this book about the world's imminent future is overwhelming. As he began to internalize what God was telling him, Daniel broke down emotionally. The descriptive terms that tell of Daniel's agonized responses remind me of things I have heard people say during these days of frightening financial fallout:

> I, Daniel, was grieved in my spirit within my body, and the visions of my head troubled me. . . . My thoughts greatly troubled me, and my countenance changed. . . . And [I] fainted

and was sick for days. . . . [I] was mourning three full weeks. I ate no pleasant food, no meat or wine came into my mouth, nor did I anoint myself at all. . . . And no strength remained in me; for my vigor was turned to frailty in me, and I retained no strength. . . . I turned my face toward the ground and became speechless. . . . Because of the vision my sorrows have overwhelmed me. (Daniel 7:15, 28; 8:27; 10:2–3, 8, 15–16)

Daniel had faith in God, but he was not prepared for the dark visions of the future that God gave him. He temporarily lost heart. These words from the seventh through the tenth chapters of Daniel clearly show the anguished pressure he was feeling as he began to get his heart back into his faith. These were very difficult days, and there was no way to get through them but to go through them.

Does that sound familiar? If our responses to the ominous economic and political news of today produce similar anguish, it simply shows our need to get our hearts into our faith.

The Book of Daniel is a great read for Christians of our generation whose faith may tend to be shaken by current news headlines. It reveals the kind of life we should aspire to live when we are under pressure. In each of the twelve chapters of Daniel's prophecy, we find incidents that show us how to keep our hearts in our faith when we might be overwhelmed by the powers that seem to be aligned against us. Here are just a few of them.

In the first chapter we learn that Daniel was among a group of young Jews from noble families who were brought to Babylon by King Nebuchadnezzar. At the outset, Daniel had to decide whether to go along just to get along or to stand up for what he believed. The record shows that Daniel "purposed in his heart that he would not defile himself with the portion of the king's delicacies, nor with the wine which he drank" (Daniel 1:8). Daniel risked his life for his convictions, and God blessed him for it.

In chapter 3, Daniel's three friends refused to bow down to Nebuchadnezzar's idol, and the king threatened to burn them alive. We reviewed their response in an earlier chapter, but it is worth repeating simply to be inspired yet again by their conviction and courage:

> O Nebuchadnezzar, we have no need to answer you in this matter. If that is the case, our God whom we serve is able to deliver us from the burning fiery furnace, and He will deliver us from your hand, O king. But if not, let it be known to you, O king, that we do not serve your gods, nor will we worship the gold image which you have set up. (Daniel 3:16–18)

In chapter 4, Daniel interpreted one of King Nebuchadnezzar's dreams. The interpretation exposed the ruthless wickedness of the king and foretold God's judgment upon him. At the conclusion of his interpretation, Daniel confronted the king with these words: "Therefore, O king, let my advice be acceptable to you; break off your sins by being righteous, and your iniquities by showing mercy to the poor" (Daniel 4:27). Imagine standing before the most powerful man on earth and telling him that he is a sinner and needs to repent!

In chapter 5, Daniel confronts Nebuchadnezzar's grandson Belshazzar. In the first part of the chapter, the story of Nebuchadnezzar's judgment is repeated and Daniel says to Belshazzar, "But you his son, Belshazzar, have not humbled your heart, although you knew all this. And you have lifted yourself up against the Lord of heaven. . . .

And you have praised the gods of silver and gold . . . and the God who holds your breath in His hand and owns all your ways, you have not glorified" (Daniel 5:22–23).

Before that very evening was over, Daniel revealed the judgment concealed in the mysterious handwriting on the banquet room wall: Belshazzar's kingdom was to be divided between the Medes and the Persians, and "Belshazzar, king of the Chaldeans, was slain" (Daniel 5:30).

In chapter 6 we are told that Daniel refused to obey the royal statute that said no prayer or petition was to be offered to "any god or man for thirty days" (verse 7) except to Darius, king of the Medes. Instead of complying, Daniel went to his own house and prayed to the God of heaven: "Now when Daniel knew that the writing was signed, he went home. And in his upper room, with his windows open toward Jerusalem, he knelt down on his knees three times that day, and prayed and gave thanks before his God, as was his custom since early days" (6:10).

Some writers have described Daniel's conduct as an act of defiance against the king. It was not that at all. Daniel simply went home and did what he had always done. In other words, he did not let the pronouncement of the king or the plot of his enemies change the course of his life. He would not be bullied into denying his God.

Because of his faithfulness to God, Daniel was thrown into a den of hungry lions. But, as Daniel reported later, "My God sent His angel and shut the lions' mouths, so that they have not hurt me, because I was found innocent before Him; and also, O king, I have done no wrong before you" (6:22).

This incident reveals a real challenge for us today. Whether we are pressured into bowing to political correctness, multiculturalism, or ecumenicalism, we cannot allow ourselves to be pushed off course. We must continue to keep our hearts in our faith and be God's people, holding up His standard and obeying His will no matter what the consequences. Increasingly today the political powers apply financial pressure to those who resist their efforts to enforce political correctness. Our businesses may be boycotted, or we may be threatened with being fired from our jobs. Financial pressure has a way of softening our resolve. If we are not vigilant, we begin to make small concessions to societal pressure, compromising God's truth in order to align ourselves with cultural norms in an effort to strengthen our sense of immediate security. That's where the example of Daniel can really help us.

In chapter 8, Daniel was given an astonishing vision of the Antichrist so frightful that he "fainted and was sick for days." But read what the Bible says he did next: "Afterward I arose and went about the king's business" (verse 27). This may not be as dramatic as some of the events we have already cited, but it is perhaps the most important of all. Daniel was trusted with great insight into the future, but he did not allow this lofty calling to take him away from his daily responsibilities. He arose and went about the king's business.

This is a great rallying cry for these days of financial hardship and economic and political confusion. We must not give up in despair and helplessness. We must not, as some have foolishly done, sell our homes, abandon our lives, and camp on a mountaintop waiting for the Lord to come. Like Daniel, we need to get the facts, and then get up and get about the King's business—the business of doing the will of God.

Chapter 11 of Daniel foretells the story of Antiochus IV Epiphanes and his brutal assault against Israel. In the middle of the narrative describing this attack, we read these wonderful words: "But the people who know their God shall be strong, and carry out great exploits. And those of the people who understand shall instruct many" (verses 32–33).

In one of the most horrendous moments in Israel's long history of suffering, the people who knew their God stood their ground. In every generation and in every situation, God has His people. When we put our hearts into our faith, we join this courageous band of brothers and sisters. Standing together we give courage and strength to one another, ensuring companionship and support as the world moves toward the inevitable chaos of the end times.

In the magazine *Evangel*, J. K. Gressett writes about a man named Samuel S. Scull who settled on a farm in the Arizona desert with his wife and children:

> One night a fierce storm struck with rain, hail, and high wind. At daybreak, feeling sick and fearing what he might find, Samuel went out to survey the loss.
>
> The hail had beaten the garden and truck patch into the ground; the house was partially unroofed, the henhouse had blown away, and dead chickens were scattered about. Destruction and devastation were everywhere.
>
> While standing dazed, evaluating the mess and wondering about the future, he heard a stirring in the lumber pile that was the remains of the henhouse. A rooster was climbing up

through the debris, and he didn't stop climbing until he had mounted the highest board in the pile. That old rooster was dripping wet, and most of his feathers were blown away. But as the sun came over the eastern horizon, he flapped his bony wings and proudly crowed.

That old wet, bare rooster could still crow when he saw the morning sun. And like that rooster, our world may be falling apart, we may have lost everything, but if we trust in God, we'll be able to see the light of God's goodness, pick ourselves out of the rubble, and sing the Lord's praise.[8]

Though the world may seem to be crashing down around us, it really changes neither our basic duty nor our ultimate security. We know the truth. We know who we are and to whom we belong. We are God's people, living under His grace and assured by His promises that whatever happens, we are in His strong and dependable hands. Lions' dens, fiery furnaces, storms that crash our world down around our heads don't matter. Our task is still the same: greet the approaching sunrise with joy. The sun will come up. It always does for those who love the Lord.

## Keep Your Hope in God

Not long ago, I saw a bumper sticker that carried this profound message:

*KNOW GOD—KNOW HOPE*

*NO GOD—NO HOPE*

These simple words summarize the final message of this chapter and this book. If you are looking for the kind of hope you need for difficult days, you will find that hope only in God.

During the difficult days of World War II, a young Jewish girl in the Warsaw ghetto of Poland managed to escape over the wall and hide in a cave. Tragically, she died in that cave shortly before the Allied army broke into the ghetto to liberate the prisoners. But before she died, she scratched on the wall some powerful words that sound like a creed:

*I believe in the sun, even when it is not shining.*
*I believe in love, even when I cannot feel it.*
*I believe in God, even when He is silent.*

This young girl endured dark days and great trauma in her life, but she maintained hope in the face of apparent hopelessness. Her last statement about God comes very close to describing what many today have been experiencing. Through faith and hope, we can know God is there even though the growing shadow cast by coming events may obscure a clear vision of Him.

It may be that as you have read what I have written in this book, you are wondering whether there is any hope. Perhaps you find yourself feeling like Job, who asked, "Where then is my hope? As for my hope, who can see it?" (Job 17:15). To be sure, there may be many causes for discouragement. But there are far more reasons for hope. Every generation since Adam has faced calamity. Within its epochs, the Bible records a long history of wars, plagues, famines, corruption, depravity, and suffering. Yet God is still in control. He has a plan, and His Bible is a book of hope. When we walk in fellowship with God, we find ourselves lifted by the irresistible updraft of biblical hope.

If we maintain this hope, nothing can destroy our real security or our joy. The psalmist wrote, "Why are you cast down, O my soul? And why are you disquieted within me? Hope in God, for I shall yet praise Him for the help of His countenance" (Psalm 42:5).

Commenting on this passage, Dr. Martyn Lloyd-Jones said,

> The first thing we have to learn is what the Psalmist learned—
> we must take ourselves in hand. This man was not content just
> to lie down and commiserate with himself. He does some-
> thing about it. He takes himself in hand—he talks to himself. .
> . . I say that we must talk to ourselves instead of allowing "our-
> selves" to talk to us! . . . Have you realized that most of your
> unhappiness in life is due to the fact that you are listening to
> yourself instead of talking to yourself?[9]

The good doctor is right. We must learn to preach to ourselves. We must learn to encourage ourselves in the Lord. We must learn to search out and claim God's promises for our present needs and future fears. We must ask the Holy Spirit to make these verses so real in our minds that the hope we draw from them will lift our spirits like giant balloons of spiritual helium.

In many places the Bible makes it clear that even in the darkest hours, we have good reason for hope. The psalmist said, "I will hope continually, and will praise You yet more and more" (Psalm 71:14).

Solomon said, "The hope of the righteous will be gladness" (Proverbs 10:28).

Jeremiah wrote, "Blessed is the man who trusts in the Lord , and whose hope is the Lord . For he shall be like a tree planted by the waters, which spreads out its roots by the river" (Jeremiah 17:7–8).

And in the book of Lamentations, "This I recall to my mind, therefore I have hope. . . . His compassions fail not. They are new every morning; great is Your faithfulness. 'The Lord is my portion,' says my soul, 'Therefore I hope in Him!' . . . It is good that one should hope and wait quietly" (3:21–26).

Paul calls God "the God of hope" (Romans 15:13) and assures us that "hope does not disappoint, because the love of God has been poured out in our hearts by the Holy Spirit who was given to us" (Romans 5:5).

The writer of Hebrews gives us a great visual of the kind of hope we have in God when he writes: "This hope we have as an anchor of the soul, both sure and steadfast, and which enters the Presence behind the veil, where the forerunner has entered for us, even Jesus, having become High Priest forever according to the order of Melchizedek" (6:19–20).

According to Isaiah 40:3, those who hope in the Lord shall renew their strength and mount up with wings like eagles. In a world in which we're beset by burdens big and small, we have these strong gusts of hope, catching our wings and sending us soaring heavenward as God's hopeful, joyous people.

Alexander Solzhenitsyn was a man who knew how to hang on to hope. He became an icon of perseverance through his suffering as a political prisoner in Russia where he was forced to work twelve hours a day at hard labor while existing on a starvation diet. The story is told of a time when he became gravely ill. Although the doctors predicted his death was imminent, his captors did not spare him from his daily forced labor.

One afternoon he stopped working, even though he knew the guards would beat him severely. He just could not go on any longer. At that precise moment another prisoner, a fellow Christian, approached him. With his cane the man drew a cross in the sand. Instantly, Solzhenitsyn felt all the hope of God flood his soul. In the midst of his despair, that emblem of hope where Christ fought and won the victory over sin gave Solzhenitsyn the courage to endure that difficult day and the grueling months of imprisonment that were before him.[10]

The next time you feel hopeless, take your finger and draw a cross in the sand. Or take your pen and draw one on paper and remember what it means. It means that there was a day when hopelessness encountered a Person on a cross. And three days later, the Lord Jesus banished all hopelessness by rising from the dead, offering true hope to all who would believe and receive it. When we hang on to hope, we can go through anything.

As Christians, we should never place our hope in the systems of this world. The real hope that Christ gave us does not depend on the shifting sand of politics and economics. If you long to have this hope for life after death, you will find it in Jesus Christ and in Him alone.

Archbishop Desmond Tutu, the leading figure in the fight to end apartheid in South Africa, suffered greatly at the hands of the racists in his country. When an interviewer asked if he was hopeful about the future of South Africa, he replied, "I am always hopeful, for a Christian is a prisoner of hope." [11]

Financial pressures have one great benefit. They push us to new levels of faith, forcing us to be utterly dependent on God. And that dependence is solidly justified, for the Bible is filled with promises that God will meet the needs of His children. No matter how dark the horizon may seem, we who trust in the Lord need not fear at all. Psalm 23 says that if the Lord is our Shepherd, we shall not lack. Jesus counseled us to study birds and flowers, for the God who cares for them will care for us (see Matthew 6:25–34). The psalmist said, "I have been young, and now am old; yet I have not seen the righteous forsaken, nor his descendants begging bread" (Psalm 37:25).

Paul told his readers, "My God shall supply all your need according to His riches in glory by Christ Jesus" (Philippians 4:19). And in another letter, "God is able to make all grace abound toward you, that you, always having all sufficiency in all things, may have an abundance for every good work" (2 Corinthians 9:8).

We can only lose hope if we take our eyes off the God of Hope. In his book *Disappointment with God*, author Philip Yancey tells a story that perfectly summarizes this principle and provides a fitting ending to this book:

> Once a friend of mine went swimming in a large lake at dusk. As he was paddling at a leisurely pace about a hundred yards offshore, a freak evening fog rolled in across the water. Suddenly he could see nothing: no horizon, no landmarks, no objects or lights on shore. Because the fog diffused all light, he could not even make out the direction of the setting sun.
>
> For thirty minutes he splashed around in panic. He would start off in one direction, lose confidence, and turn ninety degrees to the right. Or left—it made no difference which way he turned. He could feel his heart racing uncontrollably. He would stop and float, trying to conserve energy, and force himself to breathe slower. Then he would blindly strike out again.
>
> At last he heard a faint voice from shore. He pointed his body toward the sounds and followed them to safety.
>
> All of us can relate to this story. Recently it seems as if we have been forced to live life in an increasingly dense fog. All the familiar surroundings that we once knew are shrouded and clouded, and we do not know which way to go. If we are honest, we are often scared and sometimes desperate, longing for some direction from God.
>
> But if we will just stay quiet and trust in Him, we will hear the sounds from the shore and we will know which way to go.[12]

# NOTES

**CHAPTER 1:** *THE JOY OF ENCOURAGEMENT*—"THE ENCOURAGEMENT ZONE"

1. Anonymous Author.
2. George Bernard Shaw, quoted in the *The Portable Curmudgeon*, ed. Jon Winokur (New York: New American Library, 1987), 191.
3. F. Herwaldt, "The Ideal Relationship and Other Myths About Marriage," *Christianity Today*, April 9, 1982, 20-21.
4. F. S. Pittman, "Beyond Betrayal: Life After Infidelity," *Psychology Today*, May/June 1993, 32-38.
5. Dwight Hervey *Small, Design for Christian Marriage* (Westwood, NJ: Fleming H. Revell, 1959) 32.
6. Dr. Robert B. Taylor, "Behind the Surge in Broken Marriages," *U.S. News and World Report*, (22 January 1979), 53.
7. *The Holy Bible: The New King James Version* ©1984 by Thomas Nelson, Notes, 11.
8. Ken Canfield, "The Father's Greatest Gift," *New Man*, 54.
9. R. Kent Hughes, *Disciplines of a Godly Man* (Wheaton, IL: Crossway Books, 1991), 35-36.
10. Dwight Hervey Small, *Design for Christian Marriage* (Westwood, NJ: Fleming H. Revell, 1959), 35.
11. Richard Selzer, *Mortal Lessons: Notes in the Art of Surgery* (New York: Simon and Schuster, 1976), 45-46.
12. Jerry D. Twentier, *The Positive Power of Praising People* (Nashville: Thomas Nelson Publishers, 1993), 190-191.

**CHAPTER 2:** *PRAYER—THE GREAT ADVENTURE* – "A PERSONAL MAP TO BURIED TREASURE"

1. Gordon MacDonald, *Ordering Your Private World* (Chicago: Moody Press, 1984), 141.
2. Bill Hybels, *Too Busy Not To Pray* (Downers Grove, IL: InterVarsity Press, 1988), 103-104.
3. Gordon MacDonald, *The Life God Blesses* (Nashville: Thomas Nelson Publishers, 1994) 41.
4. Harry J. Cargas and Roger J. Radley, *Keeping a Spiritual Journal* (Garden City, NY: Doubleday, 1981). 8
5. Donald S. Whitney, *Spiritual Disciples for the Christian Life* (Colorado Springs: NavPress, 1991), 195.
6. Ronald King, *How to Keep a Spiritual Journal* (Minneapolis: Augsburg Press, 1993), 19.
7. Gordon MacDonald, *Ordering Your Private World*, 141.
8. Elisabeth Elliot, ed. *The Journals of Jim Elliot* (Old Tappan, NJ: Fleming H. Revell, 1978), 58.
9. Arthur Gordon, *A Touch of Wonder* (Old Tappan, NJ: Fleming H. Revell, 1974), 165, quoted by Ronald Klug, *How to Keep a Spiritual Journal* (Minneapolis: Augsburg Press, 1993), 23.
10. Steven Covey, *First Things First* (New York: Simon & Schuster) 64-65.
11. MacDonald, 202.
12. Hybels, 47.
13. Morton Kelsey, *The Other Side of Silence*, quoted by Luci Shaw in Life Path (Portland, OR: Multnomah Press, 1991) 32.
14. MacDonald, 142.
15. Luci Shaw, Life Path—*Personal and Spiritual Growth Through Journal Writing* (Portland, OR: Multnomah Press, 1991) 34.
16. Ibid., 51.
17. Ibid., 201.
18. Ibid., 201.
19. Ibid., 205

**CHAPTER 3:** *GOD IN YOU*—"THE BEST EVIDENCE OF THE SPIRIT"

1. W. A. Criswell, *Ephesians: An Exposition* (Grand Rapids, MI: Zondervan Publishing House, 1974), 165.
2. Alan L. McGinnis, *The Power of Optimism* (San Francisco: Harper and Rose, 1990), 15-17.

**CHAPTER 4:** *CAPTURED BY GRACE*—"THE CONVERTING POWER OF GRACE"

1. Henri J. M. Nouwen, *The Return of the Prodigal: A Story of Homecoming* (New York: Doubleday, 1992).
2. Kenneth E. Bailey, *The Cross and the Prodigal* (Downers Grove, IL: InterVarsity, 2005), 52-53.
3. Ibid., 67.
4. Ibid.

**CHAPTER 5:** *WHAT TO DO WHEN YOU DON'T KNOW WHAT TO DO*—: "INTEGRITY—WHEN THE MIRROR DOESN'T LIE"

1. Howard G. Hendricks and William D. Hendricks, *Living by the Book* (Chicago: Moody Press, 1991), 10.
2. *USA Today*, 1 February 1990.
3. Donald S. Whitney, *Spiritual Disciplines for the Christian Life* (Colorado Springs: NavPress, 1991), 34.
4. Spiros Zodhiates, *The Work of Faith* (Grand Rapids: Zondervan, 1977), 105.
5. Simon J. Kistemaker, *New Testament Commentary: Exposition of the Epistle of James and the Epistles of John* (Grand Rapids: Baker, 1986), 58.
6. Mortimer J. Adler, *How to Read a Book* (New York: Simon & Schuster, 1966).
7. Robert A. Traina, *Methodical Bible Study: A New Approach to Hermeneutics* (Wilmore, KY: Robert A Traina, 1952), 97-98.

8. Hendricks and Hendricks, *Living by the Book*, 11.
9. George Sweeting, *How to Solve Conflicts* (Chicago: Moody Press, 1973), 47.
10. Zodhiates, *The Work of Faith*, 110.
11. Geoffrey Thomas, *Reading the Bible* (Edinburgh, Scotland: The Banner of Truth Trust, 1980) 22, cited by Donald S. Whitney, *Spiritual Disciplines for the Christian Life* (Colorado Springs: NavPress, 1991), 34.
12. Whitney, *Spiritual Disciplines*, 43.
13. Lorne Sanny, "Five Reasons Why I Memorize Scripture, " *Discipleship Journal* 32, (1986): 10.
14. Kistemaker, *New Testament Commentary*, 64.
15. Zodhiates, *The Work of Faith*, 144.
16. Richard Wolff, *Contemporary Commentaries—James and Jude* (Wheaton, IL: Tyndale House, 1969), 36.
17. V.C. Grounds, *The Reason for Our Hope* (Chicago: Moody Press, 1945), 88-89.

## CHAPTER 6: *TURNING TOWARD JOY*—"THE JOY OF ADVERSITY"

1. Dave Dravecky with Tim Stafford, *Comeback* (Grand Rapids: Zondervan, 1990), 16.
2. Ibid., 196-197.
3. Charles Colson, *Loving God* (Grand Rapids: Zondervan, 1983), 248.
4. Warren W. Wiersbe, *Be Joyful* (Wheaton, IL: Victor Books, 1974), 37.
5. Moyter, *The Message of Philippians*, 65.
6. Corrie ten Boom, *A Prisoner and Yet* (London: Christian Literature Crusade, 1954).
7. Clebe McClary with Diane Barker, *Living Proof* (Pawleys Island, SC: Clebe McClary, 1978), 40.
8. Paul S. Rees, *The Epistles to the Philippians, Colossians and Philemon* (Grand Rapids: Baker, 1964) 31.
9. Anthony Robbins, *Awaken the Giant Within* (New York: Summit Books, 1991), 76-77.
10. Charles Garfield, *Peak Performers* (New York: William Morrow Company, 1986), 28.
11. David Jacobsen, "Remember Them," *Guideposts*, March 1991.
12. Ibid.
13. Guy King, *Joy Way* (London: Marshall, Morgan & Scott, 1952), 33-34.
14. Paul S. Rees, *The Adequate Man* (Westwood, NJ: Revell, 1959), 30.
15. Ferguson, *The Edge*, 1:9.
16. Moyter, *The Message of Philippians*, 72.
17. H. C. G. Moule, *Philippian Studies* (London: Hodder and Stoughton, 1897), 71, 78.
18. William Hendriksen, *New Testament Commentary: Exposition of Philippians* (Grand Rapids: Baker, 1979), 78.
19. Ralph Herring, *Studies in Philippians* (Nashville: Broadman, 1952), 53-54.

## CHAPTER 7: *SLAYING THE GIANTS IN YOUR LIFE*—"GUARDING AGAINST GUILT"

1. Cornelius Plantinga, "Natural Born Sinners," *Christianity Today*, 14 November 1994, vol. 38, no 13, 26.
2. Lynnell Mickelsen, "Robert's Deadly Secret," *HIS*, April/May 1986, 24-27.

## CHAPTER 8: *WHEN YOUR WORLD FALLS APART*—"WHEN YOU ARE AT YOUR WITS' END"

1. Leonard Griffith, *God in Man's Experience* (Waco, TX: Word, 1968) 108.

## CHAPTER 9: *OVERCOMING LONELINESS*—"LONELY SAINTS"

1. Joseph Bayle, "A Psalm in a Hotel Room," *Psalms of My Life* (Wheaton, IL: Tyndale House, 1969).
2. Anonymous.
3. James Conway, *Men in Mid-Life Crisis* (Elgin, IL: David C. Cook, 1979) 57.
4. Norman Cousins, *The Anatomy of an Illness as Perceived by the Patient* (New York: W. W. Norton, 1979), 39-40.
5. Anne Frank, *Anne Frank: The Diary of a Young Girl*.

## CHAPTER 10: *LIVING WITH CONFIDENCE IN A CHAOTIC WORLD*—"STAY CONVINCED"

1. Eiten Haber, "World War III has started," *Ynet News Opinion*, Ynetnews.com, 27 May 2009, wwwynetnews.com/articles/0,7340,L-3722339,00.html (accessed 28 June 2009).
2. Con Coughlin, "N. Korea helping Iran with nuclear testing," Telegraph.co.uk, 25 January 2007, www.telegraph.co.uk/news/worldnews/154029/N-Korea-helping-Iran-with-nuclear-testing. Html (accessed 28 June 2009).
3. Sandra I. Erwin and Stew Magnuson, "7 Deadly Myths About Weapons of Terror," national Defense Magazine, June 2009, www.nationaldefensemagazine.org/ARCHIVE/2009/JUNE/Pages/7Deadly.aspx (accessed 2 June 2009).
4. "Former Russian official says 100 portable bombs missing," AP, *Lubbock Avalanche-Journal*, 5 September 1997, www.lubbockonline.com/news/090597/LA0759.htm (accessed 2 June 2009). And Richard Miniter, *Disinformation* (Washington, DC: Regency Publishing, 2005), especially "Myth #17: Suitcase Nukes are a Real Threat," 135.
5. Elizabeth Zolotukhini, "The Loose Russian Nukes," Global Security.org, Sitrep Situation, 19 May 2009, sitrep. globalsecurity.org/articles/090519345-the loose-russian-nukes.htm (accessed 29 June 2009).
6. Ibid., "7 Deadly Myths About Weapons of Terror."
7. "Live Like You Were Dying," words and music by James Timothy Nichols and Craig Michael Wiseman. ©2004 Warner-Tamerlane Publishing and Big Loud Shirt. ASCAP/BMI. All rights reserved.

8. *ABC News.go.com*, abcnews.go.com/GMA/LastLecture (accessed 29 June 2009).
9. "The Iowa Band," en.wikipedia.org/wiki/Iowa_Band (accessed 10 April 2009).
10. Charles Spurgeon, "A Bright Light in Deep Shades," *The Metropolitan Tabernacle Pulpit, Vol. XVIII* (London: Passmore & Alabaster, 1873), 270.
11. Henry Richard, *Letters and Essays on Wales* (1884) Internet Archive/Texts, www.archive.org/stream/lettersessaysonwoorichiala/lettersessasyonwoorichiala_djvu.tex (accessed 28 June 2009).
12. A. W. Tozer (1897-1963), "Causes of a Dozing Church," *Tozer Devotional: Rut, Rot or Revival*, www.cmalliance.org/devotions/tozer/tozer.jsp?id=328 (accessed 28 June 2009).
13. Vance Havner, *In Times Like These* (Old Tappan, NJ: Fleming H. revel Company, 1969), 29, as quoted in David Jeremiah, *What in the World Is Going On?* (Nashville: Thomas Nelson, 2008, 232.
14. Ibid., Tozer.
15. Larry E. Swedroe, *What Wall Street Doesn't Want You to Know: How You Can build Real Wealth* (New York: Macmillan, 2004), 11.
16. Michael Brooks, "Space storm alert: 90 seconds from catastrophe," *New Scientist.com*, 23 March 2009, www.newscientist.com/articlel/mg20127001.300-space-storm-alert-90-seconds-from-catastrophe.html?full=true (accessed 28 June 2009).
17. "A Super Solar flare," NASA, Science.gov, 6 May 2008, science.nasa.gov/headlines/2008/06may_carringtonflare.htm (accessed 28 June 2009).
18. Charles Haddon Spurgeon, *The Metropolitan Tabernacle Pulpit: Sermons Preached and Revised*, "Wake Up! Wake Up!" (London: Passmore & Alabaster, 1879), 657.
19. Alexander Maclaren, *The Gospel According to St. John* (New York: A. C. Armstrong and Son, 1908), 228.
20. James Montgomery, "Forever With the Lord," *Poet's Portfolio*, 1835, Cyberhymnal.com.www.nethymnal.org/htm/f/w/fwithlor.htm (accessed 28 June 2009).
21. John Phillips, *Experiencing Romans*, (Chicago: Moody Press, 1969) 231.
22. "Most American Christians Do Not Believe that Satan or the Holy Spirit Exist," Barna Research Group Update, 13 April 2009, www.barna.org/barna-update/article/12-faithspirtuality/260-most=american-christians-do-not=believe-that-satan-or-the-holy-spirit-exist (accessed 28 June 2009).
23. A. W. Tozer, *The Pursuit of the Holy* (Rockville, MD: 2008), front matter.
24. Ray Stedman, *From Guilt to Glory, Volume 21* (Waco, TX: Word, 1978), 136.
25. David McCullough, *Truman* (New York: Simon and Schuster, 1992), 435.
26. Mona Charen, "Tis the Season for Porn" *National Review Online*, 19 December 2008, article.nationalreview.com (accessed 28 June 2009).
27. Ray Stedman, *Expository Studies in 1 Corinthians: The Deep Things of God* (Waco, TX: Word, 1981), 130-131.
28. "Memorable Quotes for Saving Private Ryan," www.imdh.com/title/tt0120815/quotes (accessed 28 June 2009.

**CHAPTER 11: *ANGELS*—"COMING TO CARRY ME HOME"**
None

**CHAPTER 12: *WHAT THE BIBLE SAYS ABOUT LOVE, MARRIAGE, & SEX*—"STAYING IN LOVE FOR LIFE"**

1 "Couple, married 83 years, share their secret," by Mike Celizic, published by TodayShow.com, 17 March 2008, http://www.msnbc.msn.com/id/23671580. (accessed 28 January 2009).
2 Katherine Anne Porter, *The Days Before* (New York: Arno Press, Inc., 1952), 181.
3 Gary Thomas, *Sacred Marriage*; 40.
4 Frederic Lawrence Knowles, "The Survivor," *Love Triumphant: A Book of Poems*, (Boston: Colonial Press, 1906), 36. http://books.google.com/books?id=bZYXAAAAYAAJ&pg=PA36&dq=%22love+shall+reign+immortal+while+the+worlds+lie+dead%22&ei=hfoRSYablovuMq-UsYYO.
5 Tommy Nelson; 188.
6 Adapted from Dr. Greg and Erin Smalley, *Before You Plan Your Wedding...Plan Your Marriage*, (West Monroe, LA: Howard Publishing, 2008), 50.
7 Paige Patterson; 116.
8 Gary Thomas; 40-41.
9 Daniel Akin; 256.
10 Tommy Nelson; 117.
11 Daniel Akin; 256-257.
12 Gillian Flaccus, "Unstoppable firefighters all but concede defeat to big, fast flames," *Oakland Tribune*, 24 October 2007, http://findarticles.com/p/articles/mi_qn4176/is_/ai_n21078645(accessed 5 November 2008).
13 David Sanford, "Learning to Love Means Staying When You Want to Leave," Marriage Support.com, http://www.marriagesupport.com/articles_advice/article.asp?articleNum=280&From=Col&ID=8&email=cthlrd@aol.com&orderid=1891(accessed 5 November 2008.
14 Frederick Buechner, *Wishful Thinking: A Seeker's ABC* (New York: HarperOne, 1993), 101.
15 Craig Glickman, *Solomon's Song of Love*; 151-152.
16 Craig Glickman, *Solomon's Song of Love*; 163.

17  Adapted from Cecil Osborn, *The Art of Understanding Yourself*, (Grand Rapids, MI: Zondervan Publishing House, 1967), 146.

**CHAPTER 13: *MY HEART'S DESIRE*—"WHERE A KING MAKES HIS HOME"**
1.  Source unknown.
2.  C. S. Lewis, *Reflections on the Psalms* (New York: Harcourt, Brace, & Jovanovich, 1958), 90, 93.

**CHAPTER 14: INTRODUCTION**
1.  *Christianity Today*, April 1, 1977, 25-26.
2.  Carl Jung, *Modern Man in Search of a Soul* (Harvest Books, 1955), 70.
3.  Victor E. Frankl, *Man's Search for Meaning* (New York: Washington Square Press, 1984), 128.
4.  Rick Warren, *The Purpose-Driven Life* (Grand Rapids: Zondervan, 2002), 19-20.
5.  Abba, Eban, *Abba Eban: An Autobiography* (New York: Random House, 1977), 609.
6.  Jon Krakauer, *Into Thin Air* (New York: Doubleday/Anchor Books, 1997) 3-Searching for Heaven on Earth – "Life Is Obedience—Express It!"
1.  "Trust and Obey," by John H. Sammis, 1887.

**CHAPTER 15: *THE HANDWRITING ON THE WALL*—"FIERY FAITH"**
None

**CHAPTER 16: *ESCAPE THE COMING NIGHT*—"WARNINGS IGNORED"**
1.  See Isaiah 7:14; Genesis 14:10; Jeremiah 23:5; Micah 5:12; Psalm 110:1
2.  See Deuteronomy 18:18; Isaiah 33:22; Psalm 2:6; Isaiah 42:1; Isaiah 6:1, 2

**CHAPTER 17: *UNTIL CHRIST RETURNS*—"DO BUSINESS UNTIL CHRIST RETURNS"**
1.  Laurence J. Peter and Raymond Hull, *The Peter Principle* (New York: Bantam, 1969), 7.

**CHAPTER 18: *I NEVER THOUGHT I'D SEE THE DAY!*—"WHEN CHANGING YOUR MIND COULD SAVE YOUR LIFE"**
1.  Quoted by Derek Tidball, *The Message of Holiness: The Bible Speaks Today* (Downers Grove, IL: InterVarsity Press, 2010), 216-17.

**CHAPTER 19: *WHAT IN THE WORLD IS GOING ON?*—"VANISHED WITHOUT A TRACE"**
1.  "Firefighters Gain Ground as Santa Ana Winds Decrease," KNBC Los Angeles, 24 October 2007, http://www.knbc.com/news/14401132/detail.html (accessed 26 October 2007).
2.  Bruce Bickel and Stan Jantz, *Bible Prophecy 101* (Eugene, OR: Harvest House Publishers, 1999), 124.
3.  *Merriam-Webster Online*, s.v. "rapture," www.merriam-webster.com/dictionary/rapture (accessed 5 June 2008).
4.  Alfred Tennyson, "Break, Break, Break" *Poems, Vol. II* (Boston: Ticknor, Reed and Fields, 1851), 144.
5.  Tim LaHaye, *The Rapture* (Eugene, OR: Harvest House Publishers, 2002), 69.
6.  "100 Nations' Leaders Attend Churchill Funeral," Churchill Centre, www.winstoncjhurchill.org/i4a/pages/index.cfm?pageid=801 (accessed 4 March 2008).
7.  Bickel and Jantz, *Bible Prophecy*, 123.
8.  Arthur T. Pierson, *The Gospel, Vol. 3* (Grand Rapids, MI: Baker Book House, 1978), 136.
9.  Wayne Grudem, *Systematic Theology* (Grand Rapids, MI: Zondervan, 1994), 1093.
10. Gig Conaughton, "County Buys Reverse 911 System," *North County Times*, 11 August 2005, http://www.nctimes.com/articles/2005/08/12/news/top_stories/21_13_388_11_05. Text (accessed 4 March 2008).

**CHAPTER 20: *THE COMING ECONOMIC ARMAGEDDON*—"KEEP YOUR HEAD IN THE GAME: AND YOUR HOPE IN GOD"**
1.  Erica Estep, "Portuguese Investor Lost Life Savings in Alleged Gatlinburg Ponzi Scheme," Wate.com, 29 April 2009, http://www.wate.com/Global/story.asp?S=10274802 (accessed 10 May 2010).
2.  Bill Hybels, *Just Walk Across the Room: Simple Steps Pointing People to Faith* (Grand Rapids: Zondervan, 2006), 186-187.
3.  Larry Bates, *The New Economic Disorder* (Lake Mary, FL: Excel Books, 2009), 20.
4.  Frank J. Hanna, *What Your Money Means and How to Use It Well* (New York: Crossroad Publishing Co. 2008), 7-8.
5.  Quoted by Ron Blue and Jeremy White, *Surviving the Financial Meltdown* (Wheaton, IL: Tyndale House Publishing, 2009), 38.
6.  Federal Reserve Statistical Release, "G.19 Report on Consumer Credit," 7 May 2010, http://www.federalreserve.gov/releases/g19/Current/ (accessed 10 May 2010).
7.  See http://www.crown.org.
8.  J. K. Gressett, "Take Courage," *Pentecostal Evangel*, 30 April 1989, 6.
9.  Martyn Lloyd-Jones, *Spiritual Depression: Its Causes and Its Cure* (Grand Rapids: Eerdmans Printing Company, 1965), 20.
10. Adapted from Luke Veronis, "The Sign of the Cross," in *Communion*, Issue 8, Pascha 1997, http://www.incommunion.org/2005/08/06/the-sign-of-the-cross (accessed 10 May 2010).
11. Thomas Giles and Timothy Jones, "A Prisoner of Hope," *Christianity Today*, 5 October 1992, 39-41.
12. Quoted by Philip Yancey, *Where Is God When It Hurts?* (Grand Rapids: Zondervan, 1977), 119-120.

# Permissions

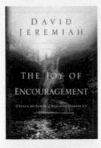

### The Joy of Encouragement

Scriptural and uplifting, *The Joy of Encouragement* is an uplift in itself. You'll find yourself basking in God's love while giving it away to those around you.

### Prayer—the Great Adventure

This award-winning classic has led tens of thousands to embark on the greatest adventure of their lives—companionship with God through prayer.

### God in You

God in you. It's no dream. It's a truth as real as this morning's sunrise. This book will show you how God's Spirit can transform a marriage, a parent, a church, a relationship at work, and attitudes toward life itself.

### Captured by Grace  *NEW YORK TIMES* **BESTSELLER**

Encountering God's grace changes lives forever. Dr. David Jeremiah explains how the transforming mercy that captured songwriter John Newton and the apostle Paul can awaken within you a fresh experience of the God who loves you fearlessly and pursues you with abandon.

### Overcoming Loneliness

Loneliness may well be the disease of our time. In this book, Dr. Jeremiah provides positive methods for healing this disease of the soul. *Overcoming Loneliness* provides reassurance that God wants to meet you in your loneliness and that, with His help, you can overcome it.

### Living With Confidence in a Chaotic World

*Living With Confidence in a Chaotic World* shows us all that with the power and love of Almighty God, we can live with confidence in this age of uncertainty and turmoil.

### Angels

In this captivating study of God's majestic messengers, you will gain fascinating insights about angels that will increase your sensitivity toward the spiritual realities of these ministering agents of God.

### What the Bible Says About Love, Marriage, & Sex

In *What the Bible Says About Love, Marriage, and Sex,* pastor and teacher David Jeremiah leads us through a verse-by-verse study of the Song of Solomon and offers a tour of the sacred domain of God-given love.

## What to Do When You Don't Know What to Do

In this study on the Book of James, Dr. Jeremiah teaches how to face life's challenges with God's strength and new resolve as you walk the rough road to Christian maturity.

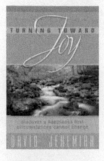

## Turning Toward Joy

In this pastoral and practical book, Dr. Jeremiah leads you through the Book of Philippians so that you, like the apostle Paul, can experience the joy of the Lord in your life even in the midst of difficulties.

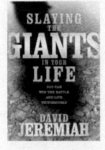

## Slaying the Giants in Your Life

Loneliness. Discouragement. Worry. Anger. Procrastination. Doubt. Fear. Guilt. Temptation. Resentment. Failure. Jealousy. Have these giants infiltrated your life? Dr. Jeremiah's book, *Slaying the Giants in Your Life* will become your very own giant-slaying manual.

## When Your World Falls Apart

When life suddenly turns upside down, there, in the midst of your trials and in the center of your pain, is God—comforting, guiding, encouraging, teaching, sustaining. Dr. Jeremiah draws from the beautiful poetry and deep truths of the Psalms—passages that gave him comfort and strength on his personal journey into the unknown and provided insights from others who faced adversity and found that God's grace truly is sufficient for every need.

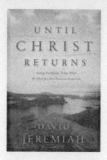

### Until Christ Returns

Drawn from the Olivet Discourse in the Book of Matthew, *Until Christ Returns* outlines priorities for believers in an era of heightened stress and confusion—teaching us how to live faithfully today while waiting for that glorious tomorrow.

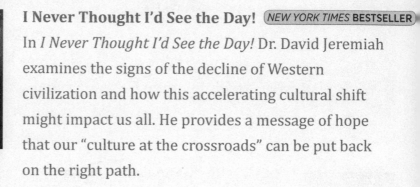

### I Never Thought I'd See the Day! `NEW YORK TIMES BESTSELLER`

In *I Never Thought I'd See the Day!* Dr. David Jeremiah examines the signs of the decline of Western civilization and how this accelerating cultural shift might impact us all. He provides a message of hope that our "culture at the crossroads" can be put back on the right path.

### What in the World Is Going On? `NEW YORK TIMES BESTSELLER`

*What in the World Is Going On?* makes Bible prophecy and the warning signs around us abundantly clear. Now you can know the meaning behind what you see in the daily news—and understand what in the world is going on!

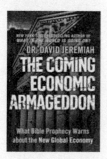

### The Coming Economic Armageddon `NEW YORK TIMES BESTSELLER`

From chaos in global financial markets to the spreading virus of public and private debt, astute teacher on Bible prophecy David Jeremiah lays out a biblical blueprint for what will happen and how to avoid the consequences. *The Coming Economic Armageddon* is a disturbing yet hopeful book calling all of us to action.

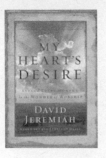

## My Heart's Desire

In *My Heart's Desire*, Dr. David Jeremiah shares how you can experience an exuberant passion for God every moment of your life.

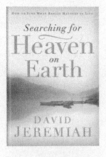

## Searching for Heaven on Earth

Tracing the writings of Solomon in the Book of Ecclesiastes, Dr. Jeremiah takes us on a journey as we review the questions Solomon asked and the answers that are to be found in the riches of God's love and mercy—the secret to finding heaven on earth.

## The Handwriting on the Wall

*The Handwriting on the Wall* shows how an understanding of prophecy opens the pathway to dynamic living today. This study of the Book of Daniel will help you learn how to live faithfully today and to anticipate the future with confidence.

## Escape the Coming Night

*Escape the Coming Night* is one of the century's clearest and most logical commentaries on the Book of Revelation. In it Dr. David Jeremiah guides the reader through an electrifying tour of world events in light of the Word of God.

Each series is also available with correlating study guide and CD audio albums. For pricing information and ordering, contact us at www.DavidJeremiah.org/SHOP or call (800) 947-1993.

# STAY CONNECTED
## TO DR. DAVID JEREMIAH

Take advantage of two great ways to let Dr. David Jeremiah give you spiritual direction every day! Both are absolutely FREE.

## *Turning Points* Magazine and Devotional

Receive Dr. David Jeremiah's monthly magazine, *Turning Points* each month:

- Monthly study focus
- 48 pages of life-changing reading
- Relevant articles
- Special features
- Humor section
- Family section
- Daily devotional readings for each day of the month
- Bible study resource offers
- Live event schedule
- Radio & television information

## Your Daily Turning Point E-Devotional

Start your day off right! Find words of inspiration and spiritual motivation waiting for you on your computer every morning! You can receive a daily e-devotional communication from David Jeremiah that will strengthen your walk with God and encourage you to live the authentic Christian life.

There are two easy ways to sign up for these free resources from Turning Point. Visit us online at www.DavidJeremiah.org and select "Subscribe to *Turning Points* Magazine" or visit the home page and find Daily Devotional to subscribe to your daily e-devotional.